Elizabeth A. I
Prof
and For
College of Mount St. Joseph

P rofessor Elizabeth A. Murray is a forensic anthropologist who is also Professor of Biology at the College of Mount St. Joseph, where she teaches doctoral-level cadaver-based human gross anatomy and undergraduate-level vertebrate anatomy and physiology, musculoskeletal anatomy, and forensic science. She received her bachelor's degree in Biology from the College of Mount St. Joseph, and she received her master's degree in Anthropology and her doctoral degree in Interdisciplinary Studies in Human Biology from the University of Cincinnati.

Dr. Murray is an award-winning teacher who has received the Sears-Roebuck Foundation Teaching Excellence and Campus Leadership Award and who has twice earned the Sister Adele Clifford Excellence in Teaching Award. She has also served as an instructor for numerous professional organizations, including the U.S. Department of Justice/National Institute of Justice's National Missing and Unidentified Persons System (NamUs) training academy, the American Academy of Forensic Sciences (AAFS) Student Academy, the Armed Forces Institute of Pathology, the Wayne State University School of Medicine's Medicolegal Investigation of Death program, and the International Association of Coroners & Medical Examiners.

Most of Dr. Murray's regular forensic casework has been in Ohio and Kentucky, where she has participated in hundreds of forensic investigations involving skeletal, decomposing, burned, buried, and dismembered human remains. A Fellow of the AAFS, she is 1 of fewer than 100 anthropologists who are certified as a Diplomate by the American Board of Forensic Anthropology. Dr. Murray is a member of the Forensic Services Team for NamUs and is the Forensic Anthropology Consultant on the National

Advisory Board for Parents of Murdered Children. She is also on the Mass Disaster Team for the Cincinnati/Northern Kentucky International Airport.

In 1994, Dr. Murray was recruited by the Armed Forces Institute of Pathology to participate in morgue operations after the crash of American Eagle Flight 4184 in Roselawn, Indiana. She also served as a visiting scientist to the U.S. Army Central Identification Laboratory, for which she led a team of military personnel in the recovery of a Vietnam War–era plane crash site in the jungle of Laos. As a consultant and on-screen personality for the National Geographic Channel's *Skeleton Crew* (aired internationally as *Buried Secrets*), Dr. Murray was dispatched to observe and participate in fieldwork with the Guatemalan Forensic Anthropology Foundation. This 4-part miniseries showcased the uses of forensic anthropology in analyzing historical mysteries and modern forensic contexts. In addition, Dr. Murray served as a regular cast member on the Discovery Fit & Health series *Skeleton Stories* and has appeared on such television shows as *America's Most Wanted*, *The New Detectives*, and *Forensic Files*.

Dr. Murray's publications include numerous entries in the *Proceedings*, published by the AAFS, as well as books and chapters covering both historical and forensic anthropological analyses. Dr. Murray's book *Death: Corpses, Cadavers, and Other Grave Matters* was named 1 of the 2011 top 10 summer reads for students by the American Association for the Advancement of Science. Her second book in this series focuses on the uses of forensic science in human identification and is scheduled for publication in 2012. ∎

Trails of Evidence:
How Forensic Science Works

Elizabeth A. Murray, Ph.D.

THE
GREAT
COURSES·

PUBLISHED BY:

THE GREAT COURSES
Corporate Headquarters
4840 Westfields Boulevard, Suite 500
Chantilly, Virginia 20151-2299
Phone: 1-800-832-2412
Fax: 703-378-3819
www.thegreatcourses.com

Table of Contents

Table of Contents

Trails of Evidence: How Forensic Science Works

Scope:

Although forensic science has become an extremely popular and pervasive subject in television programs, films, and literature, many members of the general public have only a limited understanding of the science behind forensic evidence and investigations. This course introduces the multidisciplinary field of forensic science, using real casework to illustrate basic principles.

This course begins with an overview of forensic science in the public eye and then briefly covers evidence and crime-scene investigation. Then, the course launches into a series of lectures that cover specific topics, including fingerprints, firearms, shoe prints, textile fibers, hair, plant and animal evidence, and body fluid analysis. Each lecture reviews how particular types of evidence are collected or documented at the scene and how laboratories analyze evidence and make comparisons. As the course progresses, more complex issues are introduced, such as DNA analysis, toxicology, and the various ways in which substance abuse impacts forensic science. When needed, underlying biological and chemical principles will be reviewed to help you understand the basics behind these forensic specialties.

Next, the discussion turns to the forensic analysis of questioned documents, such as forgeries, and then to increasingly more high-tech crimes, including computer forensics and other forms of digital evidence. This leads into lectures about other engineering applications, such as the forensic analyses of structural failures and building collapses, including the destruction of the World Trade Center's twin towers during the terrorist attacks of September 11, 2001. Additional lectures explore the analysis of vehicular accident reconstruction, arson, and bombing investigations. Physical science underlies the way blood is distributed at crime and accident scenes during bodily trauma, so forensic bloodstain pattern analysis will also be addressed.

Because many of the most serious forensic investigations involve the loss of human life, a lecture on the science of death leads into a discussion of death investigation in a variety of contexts. Forensic pathology and the autopsy process are introduced in addition to the ways in which investigators estimate the timing of death. Topics related to advanced decomposition explain how insects and other environmental factors destroy soft tissues and turn bodies into skeletons. Then, you will learn the basics of forensic anthropology and how bones assist in death investigations. Forensic dentistry is used to help identify unknown persons, and odontologists examine bite marks on both living and dead victims. Forensic art also involves both the living and the dead—such as when police sketch artists attempt to re-create the appearance of a suspect or when a facial reproduction is created from a skull. Real casework continues to be used to illustrate numerous principles in this part of the course.

The behavioral sciences play a major role in criminal investigations, so the next few lectures focus on the psychological aspects of forensic science. Interview, interrogation, and intelligence gathering are discussed—as well as criminal profiling and an examination of motive—using actual cases. You'll also discover how effective, or ineffective, memory is within criminal investigations through an exploration of eyewitness testimony. Forensic psychology and psychiatry play roles in the legal system—in determining issues of competency and sanity, for example—and this leads the course into a series of lectures that focus on the intersection of forensic science and the courtroom. The nature of evidence and how it is prepared for and presented at trial are discussed in regards to both civil and criminal matters. The roles of expert witnesses are examined, including rules that govern their testimony in court. In addition, career paths that lead to expertise in forensic science are briefly discussed.

Toward the end of the course, the topic of crime will be approached from a general perspective, but a few lectures will also address specific crimes in which certain pieces of forensic evidence were key. Cases deal with drunk driving, identity theft, kidnapping, arson, and murder and address both historic and modern issues involving some famous and notorious perpetrators. To showcase some interdisciplinary uses of what you have learned in the course, the final 2 lectures cover how forensic science is used in mass-disaster settings and the ways in which various forensic science disciplines intersect to identify unknown persons.

Each lecture in this course typically presents some of the basic theory behind one or more forensic techniques along with some historical background to put current methods into context. This course is intended to introduce you to the breadth of scientific disciplines used in legal contexts by taking you on a number of journeys—from the crime scene to the courtroom. Along the way, this course will help debunk some of the Hollywood hype by illustrating how forensic science is really used in the detection and resolution of criminal activity. ■

Using Science—Crime Scene to Courtroom
Lecture 1

I n the past 10 to 15 years, the popularity of forensic science—especially as portrayed in books, television shows, and movies—has exploded. This course examines real forensic casework and the technology, science, and sleuthing that is used to unravel it. During your journey through this course, you will learn that forensic science is interdisciplinary, and a single problem is often approached from multiple directions. You will also learn about the many ways that science is used in the pursuit of justice so that you can bust the myths that Hollywood has created.

What Is Forensic Science?
- The most common misconception about forensic science is that it is mostly about criminal activity that leads to death. In fact, the word "forensic" comes from the Latin word for "public," which is "forum." Therefore, something that is forensic is open to public debate or for public interpretation.

- Because the legal system is founded on debate and argument, forensic science involves using science to inform legal matters—including both criminal and civil issues. However, while legal systems may differ in what is or is not considered criminal activity throughout the world, what constitutes good science does not vary.

- Good science is universal because it is a process. Science is a search for information that helps us learn about and explain our world; it isn't just a bunch of facts that are static.

The Scientific Method
- The first step in the scientific method is to make an observation about something—such as a plant growing well in a certain part of your garden.

- The next step is to generate a hypothesis, which is your initial attempt to explain your observation.

- Then, to test your hypothesis, you have to do experiments and collect data. This step in the scientific method might be simple, or it could become complex, depending on the nature of the issue.

- Finally, you have to analyze the results of your experiments and compare them to your original hypothesis.

- If the conclusions from your experiment matches up to your hypothesis, then you might have discovered the best explanation for the issue you were trying to understand. On the other hand, if your experiments don't support your hypothesis, you need to throw out your original hypothesis and come up with another explanation for your issue.

The Human Element of Forensic Science
- In general, human beings are curious, and we're also pretty good problem solvers. Every day—in restaurants, airports, and grocery stores—we make observations and invent explanations for them. Some of these hypotheses are testable while others are not much more than sheer speculation.

- In order to become a forensic scientist, you have to first be a scientist. Forensic scientists make observations, but those observations are related to things that are possibly of legal importance. Those initial observations may end up being parts of a crime scene or criminal investigation.

- Forensic scientists, investigators, and analysts have to come up with logical and reasonable explanations for what they observe, and if they hold true to science, those hypotheses should be neutral statements—not accusatory ones.

- In order to show whether their hypotheses are sound, forensic scientists—like all other scientists—have to ask questions and collect data. If the results of their tests disagree with their original hunches, then regardless of what they would like to believe, honest and competent forensic scientists have to abandon their initial direction and come up with another plausible explanation for what happened. Then, that secondary hunch has to be tested and analyzed.

Evidence technicians are trained in how to pick up a loaded gun versus how to collect a spilled liquid.

- If we are to trust in any form of science, we have to believe that the people who are observing, testing, analyzing results, and interpreting data are as objective as possible. Human beings have biases, but good investigators and scientists need to do everything they can to leave those biases behind when they enter the crime scene, laboratory, or courtroom.

- However, there's a big difference between hypotheses and theories that are based on training and prior experience and those that are based on unfounded, preconceived, or ill-conceived notions.

Forensic Science and the Law
- Forensic science is not the same as criminology, which is a sociological study of crime, criminals, and victims. A person might enter criminology through the behavioral sciences to study the sociology and psychology behind criminal behavior.

- Forensic science is also not same as criminal justice. Graduates from criminal justice programs typically work in law enforcement—not in forensic labs.

- The best preparation for forensic science is a broad-based background that combines biology, chemistry, and physics. Law enforcement officers are heavily involved in crime-scene investigations because they assemble the pieces of crimes, but the bulk of the analysis of physical crime-scene evidence falls on scientists. As technology has advanced the field, a strong foundation in lab sciences is the basis for today's forensic careers.

- Science as a mechanism for understanding the world around us is not only international, but it is also universal. However, what's viewed as legal or illegal behavior is linked to a person's culture. Legal systems and laws vary around the world, and they change over time as cultures evolve and exchange ideas.

- The focus of this course is not to study crime, criminals, or legal systems. Instead, this course focuses on how science is applied in legal settings and addresses how evidence is gathered, tested, and considered—regardless of what a given culture considers right or wrong.

The Start of the Forensic Craze
- The infamous trial of the American football star O. J. Simpson was a highly publicized and televised 9-month ordeal, and it was the beginning of the forensic science explosion that began in the United States. During the many months of testimony, several forensic scientists took the stand and spoke not only to the judge, jury, and packed courtroom, but also to a riveted public, who suddenly were fascinated with science and how it could be used—and possibly abused—in order to demonstrate guilt or innocence.

- Regardless of how you feel about the outcome of the trial, nobody can question the impact it had upon the public perception and general awareness of the field of forensic science. From the evidence presented—including hair analysis, autopsy results, bloody socks, carpet fibers, prior offenses, and DNA profiling—the public learned that there are many different specialties and experts involved in forensics and that the legal system has rules that govern the presentation of both facts and opinions at trial.

From Professor Murray's Forensic Files

One morning, in a nature preserve just outside of a town in southwestern Ohio, a man was walking his dog and discovered a human skull almost hidden by some tall grass. The skull was taken to the Montgomery County Court's office in Dayton, Ohio, and I was called in.

After examining the skull and taking measurements, I guessed that the skull was most likely from a white female who was young to middle aged. The skull didn't have any flesh on it, but I knew it was recent because there was still a decomposition odor. Police searched the area, but they didn't find anything else. At the morgue, they took a tooth from the skull for DNA analysis.

In the meantime, based on the physical description that I had given, the police began to go through local missing persons reports and discovered that several months earlier, a woman reported her daughter Shannon missing in that same general area. When the DNA results from the skull came back from the lab, they were compared to a reference sample the mother provided, and the skull was identified as Shannon's.

Several months later, a park ranger was driving his rounds one night in a nature area in southwestern Ohio. As he turned a bend in the road, a naked woman came running out of the woods screaming, "He's trying to kill me!" The police surrounded the area and closed in on a man who was trying to make his way through the woods.

The terrified woman told police that she had willingly gone with this man to provide sex for money and that he had attempted to strangle her. Somehow, she managed to get free, and then she was discovered by the park ranger.

After the police captured the man, they searched his car and found what appeared to be blood in the trunk. Investigators developed a DNA profile from that dried blood, and it matched Shannon's profile. As a result, not only was he charged with the attempted murder of the lady in the park, he was also charged with Shannon's murder.

When the news of this attempted murder was released to the public, a handful of other women started to come forward to tell their own horrendous stories of their encounters with this man.

When it came time for the trial, one of the problems was that many of these women were drug addicts—and they were all known prostitutes—and every time they were called into the police station for a pretrial conference, they would either be high or agitated. Because these women would probably not make very good witnesses, the county prosecutor decided to offer the murderer a plea bargain if he would lead us to the rest of Shannon's remains—over 18 months after her skull was found.

The man led police to the location of the rest of her body: the backyard of his rural house, where he lived with his wife and 2 children. When asked where he buried Shannon, the man pointed to a long stretch of fencing that encompassed the cornfields behind his house. He wasn't sure of the exact location.

Then, it was my job to locate and exhume the unmarked grave where allegedly we would find the rest of Shannon's remains. I got down on my hands and knees and started to crawl slowly along the fence. I knew that the soil above Shannon's body could not have been put back exactly the way it was before he buried her.

Suddenly, I hit about a 6-foot stretch along the fence that was bumpy. This observation led to the hypothesis that Shannon was buried here, so we pulled up the grass with our hands and started to dig with shovels. Eventually, we hit something: an exposed edge of bone that was about the size of my pinkie finger that turned out to be Shannon's left iliac crest, which is the front edge of the hipbone.

Within the following few hours, I removed Shannon's remains from the man's backyard, and after almost 2 years, we were able to reunite Shannon's skull with the rest of her bones so that her family could give her a proper burial.

Questions to Consider

1. What does the term "forensic" mean?

2. How do you know what you know about forensic science?

3. What are some of the events responsible for the current public interest in forensic science?

4. What do you hope to gain from this course?

Using Science—Crime Scene to Courtroom
Lecture 1—Transcript

You've probably noticed that in the past 10 or 15 years, the popularity of forensic science—especially as portrayed in books, television shows, and movies—has exploded. If you're one of the millions who watch these investigations on screen, have you ever wondered how accurate the portrayals of forensic science really are?

Popular media has always featured things that we would now call forensic science, from Shakespeare's poisonings, the great Sherlock Holmes, Silence of the Lambs, and the many iterations of CSI. But in this course we will examine some real forensic casework, and the technology, science, and sleuthing used to unravel it. We'll see that Hollywood sometimes gets it dead wrong (pun intentional), especially in some things, like timing and looks. I'm here to tell you that young starlets in high heels are not your typical death investigators, and we definitely don't get our DNA results back after the commercial break.

I'm Dr. Beth Murray, and I've been a practicing forensic scientist since 1986, and a college professor since 1989. Because of that, I like to say, "I was forensic before forensic was cool!" My main involvement in the field of forensics is as an anthropologist, and most of what I do involves bones, but during my many years of experience, I've interacted with and learned from lots of fellow forensic experts. I also teach a survey course about forensic science that covers something about all of the specialties you'll learn about in this series.

One of the things I've learned over the years, through my many, many different interactions with others in the field and from working lots of types of cases—some suspicious and some clearly criminal—is that forensic science is very interdisciplinary. I got my Ph.D. through the Department of Interdisciplinary Studies, and I've always been intrigued by how a single problem is approached from multiple directions.

If you asked most of the general public what the term "forensic" means, you'd get lots of different answers. But I imagine the most common misconception is that many people think forensic science is mostly about criminal activity leading to death. In fact, because of the emphasis on death in today's big and small screen Hollywood interpretations, plenty of people probably believe that forensic equals death.

But those of you who are my age or older might remember that when we were in high school, the "forensic team" was not a hip group of criminal investigators, but rather the kids in the debate club! That's because the word "forensic" actually comes from the Latin word for "public," which is "forum." So, to use the term forensic actually means that something is open to public debate or up for public interpretation.

Because the legal system is founded on debate and argument, what forensic science really means is to use science to inform legal matters—and that includes both criminal and civil issues. But it's important to remember, when talking about forensic science, that while legal systems may differ in what is or is not considered criminal activity throughout the world, what constitutes good science does not.

Good science is universal. That's because science isn't really a thing; science is a process. I like to tell my students: Science is not truth. If you want truth, go down the hall to the philosophy department. Science is a really a search—a search for information that helps us explain our world. Science isn't a bunch of facts that are static; it's really a way of learning about our universe.

Those of you who had horrible science classes in school probably remember something like this: The teacher comes into the room, and writes a list of 20 words on the board, and your job in science class that day is to write the definitions of those words on your paper. Hello! That is not studying science; that's studying vocabulary! Sure, we need to have common terminology so that we can understand each other, but come on, that's not the heart and soul of science.

Those of you who had incredible experiences in science classes—like I did (and maybe that makes all the difference in the world)—well, those of you who had a great time probably remember doing some awesome lab experiments. And I have to say that understanding the inner workings behind stuff you see every day is something that still amazes me. If you were like me, you ordered the sea monkeys out of the back of the comic book, you took your radio apart, and you poked around in the woods every chance you got. Because that, my friends, is how a scientist grows up.

For those of you who forgot, let's do a quick review of how you "do" science: We call it "the scientific method," right? Now, come on, wait; don't turn the video off just yet, I promise this will be as quick and painless as I can possibly make it!

Basically, the first step in the scientific method is to make some type of observation about something, like a plant growing really well in a certain part of your garden. Then, the next step is to generate what's known as a hypothesis; that's your initial attempt to explain your observation. "Hey, maybe this plant is growing really well because it's getting plenty of sun." Or in my case, "Maybe it's growing really well because that's the spot where I buried my cat!"

Next, if you want to test your hypothesis, you're going to have to do some experiments and collect some data. That might be simple or it could get pretty complex—depends on the nature of your issue at hand. Then, you have to analyze the results of your experiments and compare them to your original hypothesis.

If the conclusions from your experiment match up to your hypothesis, then you might have a handle on the best explanation for the thing you were trying to understand. But, on the other hand, if your experiments don't support your hypothesis, you need to throw out your original hypothesis and come up with another explanation for the thing you're trying to understand.

Now this might sound pretty sophisticated, but think about how often you really do use the scientific method in your daily life, whether you realize it or not. You walk into your house, you flip a light switch, and the light doesn't come on. There's your observation. Now, you create a hypothesis as to why the light didn't come on, and then you test it. The bulb might be burned out, the lamp might be unplugged, or there may be a blown fuse. All those are testable hypotheses that we automatically come up with because, in general, we're all curious beings, and when it comes down to it we're all pretty good problem solvers.

You can probably think of a dozen more examples of how we're all natural-born scientists. You try to start your car, and it doesn't work; you follow a recipe by the book, and it doesn't turn out right; your dog refuses to use his front paw; or your grandchild is unhappy. These are all typical observations that we generate possible explanations about—and those explanations could be called hypotheses, though we don't usually use that word. Every day, at home or at work, in restaurants, airports, and grocery stores, we make observations and invent explanations for them. Some of these hypotheses are testable, while others are really not much more than sheer speculation.

So what does all of this have to do with forensic science? Well, as I often tell students who think they are going to be crime-scene analysts, but who don't want to take chemistry or physics: In order to be a forensic scientist, you have to first be a scientist. I like to say that forensic is the adjective, but science is the noun.

Forensic scientists make observations, but those observations are related to things that are possibly of legal importance. Those initial observations may end up being parts of a crime scene or a criminal investigation. Forensic scientists, investigators, and analysts have to come up with logical and reasonable explanations for the things they observe; and if they hold true to science, those hypotheses should be neutral statements— not accusatory ones.

In order to show whether their hypotheses are good or not, forensic scientists—like all other scientists—have to ask questions and collect data. And, if the results of their tests disagree with their original hunches, then regardless of what they would like to believe, honest and competent forensic scientists have to abandon their initial direction and come up with another plausible explanation for what happened. But that secondary hunch also has to be tested and analyzed.

If we're to trust in any form of science, we have to believe that the people doing the observation, the testing, the analysis of results, and the interpretations of data are as objective as humanly possible. I mean, we all know that human beings have our biases, but good investigators and scientists need to do everything they can to leave those biases behind when they cross the threshold of the crime scene, the lab door, or when they walk into the courtroom.

That doesn't mean we can't use our heads and consider the most likely possibilities based on our experience. But experience isn't the same thing as bias. It also doesn't mean that crime-scene investigators can't act on a hunch or listen to their gut. There's a big difference between theories and expectations based on training and prior experience, as compared to developing hypotheses that are based on unfounded, preconceived, or ill-conceived notions.

I'll get off my soapbox now and try to get us back more specifically to forensic science—which, by the way, is not the same thing as criminology. Criminology is more of a sociological study of crime, criminals, and victims. A person might enter criminology through the behavioral sciences to study the sociology and psychology behind criminal behavior. Forensic science is also not the same thing as criminal justice. Graduates from criminal justice programs typically work in law enforcement, including in police work and corrections, not in forensic labs.

In fact, I sometimes have a difficult time convincing students that the best preparation for forensic science is a broad-based background that combines biology, chemistry, and physics. Law enforcement officers are still heavily involved in crime-scene investigations and, in my opinion, they are the real heroes in terms of solving crimes, because they put the parts and pieces together; but today, the bulk of the analysis of physical crime-scene evidence falls to scientists. As technology has advanced the field, a strong foundation in lab sciences is really the basis for today's forensic careers.

And the really cool thing about science, as a process, is that it's truly universal. Once, in Guatemala, I got to work side-by-side with Guatemalan archaeologists who were exhuming mass graves from political conflicts that led to Mayan genocide. And even though we didn't speak the same language, we carried out the process in the exact same way. There's a real beauty to the standard ways of doing things that are recognized by everybody involved, and the scientific method is just that.

Even little kids are scientists, in the sense that they use their version of the scientific method to explain what they see. They examine things, and test things, and they test people. "How does it work?" Put it in your mouth. Even better—poke it with a stick. You all know that "poke it with a stick" is the original scientific experiment, right? Kids constantly ask, "Why? Why? Why?" That is, until parents or the educational system drums that out of them, right?

But, keep in mind, the explanations people come up with for the things they observe do vary, depending not only on their age, but also on things like their cultural and educational background. People once thought the earth was flat because the horizon looks like a straight line, right? And people used to think that evil spirits caused disease. While that may not seem very sophisticated to us, it is still an attempt to explain an observation. So, science as a mechanism for understanding the world around us, and it's not only international, it is universal, and as old as human history itself.

So, to put this all together: A forensic scientist is supposed to use the scientific method, in an objective attempt to explain what's gone on in some kind of issue that's open to legal interpretation. And while science is science around the world, what's seen as legal or illegal behavior is linked to a person's culture. What one group considers the norm, another group might consider terrible. Legal systems and laws vary around the world; that's because laws are political and cultural constructs. Laws and legal systems change over time as cultures evolve and exchange ideas.

The purpose of this series is not to debate legal issues or try to explain how or why cultures vary in what they consider moral or legal. Our focus won't be to study crime, criminals, or legal systems. We're here to talk about how science is applied in legal settings, and to try to address how evidence is gathered, tested, and considered, regardless of what a given culture considers right or wrong. So, let's stop and have you think for a minute about the first time you remember really hearing about forensic science.

If you're reasonably young, you've probably grown up with that term as part of your standard vocabulary. But if you're over the age of about, say, 35 years old, you probably did not grow up with the term "forensic science" as part of your vocabulary. The forensic craze in the United States is really not that old.

In my opinion, and I'm not alone in this idea, one pivotal event in United States legal history almost single-handedly catapulted—I mean rocketed—forensic science into the eyes, ears, and minds of the general public. Think you know what that is? Have any guesses? Think about it for a minute.

I'll give you a hint: The event occurred in 1995.

Still don't know? How about this: Although it was a single event, it lasted from late January through early October of that year. Come on—still don't know what it is? I'll give you a couple more clues—since forensic science is all about clues: The event surrounded a couple of high profile murders, and the accused was a very well known American figure. Got it yet?

Now, if I mentioned a low-speed chase in a white Ford Bronco along a California freeway, you will most likely know the answer if you haven't guessed it already. The event I'm talking about is the infamous trial of the infamous American football star, and sometime Hollywood actor, O. J. Simpson. That highly publicized and televised 9-month ordeal was the beginning of the forensic science explosion that began in the United States and has spread like wildfire throughout the popular media ever since. During the many months of testimony, a bunch of forensic scientists took the stand and spoke not only to the judge, the jury, and a packed courtroom, but also to a riveted public who all of a sudden were fascinated with science and how it could be used—and some say abused—in order to demonstrate guilt or innocence.

An entire lecture series could be devoted to the Simpson trial alone, and as of today, nearly 200 books and probably hundreds of thousands of articles have been written about it. It's often been referred to as the trial of the century. This case had all manner of forensics brought up as evidence: There was the bloody glove that created the famous line, "If it doesn't fit, you must acquit." There were bloody footprints said to be made with extremely rare and expensive Bruno Magli shoes.

The evidence included hair analysis, autopsy results, bloody socks, carpet fibers, prior offenses, and DNA profiling. The trial was a showcase for some really dramatic testimony and a handful of savvy and flamboyant attorneys. There were accusations of racial bias on the part of a key detective in the case. And of course, the allegations of evidence tampering that probably ultimately led to Simpson's acquittal—I mean this case had it all!

Regardless of how you feel about the outcome of that trial, no one can question the impact it had upon the public perception and general awareness of the field of forensic science. And one thing that the public learned from the evidence presented, was that there are many different specialties and many different experts involved in forensics, and that the legal system has rules that govern the presentation of both facts and opinions at trial.

Now, let's set the stage for this course with one of my own cases from back in the '90s. Now this case happened a long time ago, and I may not have 100% accuracy on all the specifics, but this is essentially the story.

One morning, in a nature preserve just outside of a town in southwest Ohio, a man was walking his dog and discovered a human skull almost hidden in some tall grass. The skull was taken to the Montgomery County Court's office in Dayton, Ohio, and I was called in.

After examining the skull and taking my measurements, I said I thought the skull was most likely from a white female who was roughly, what I'd call, young to middle-aged. The skull didn't have any flesh on it, but I knew it was recent, because there was still a lot of odor of decomposition to it. Police searched the area, but they didn't find anything else. At the morgue they took a tooth from the skull for DNA analysis.

In the meantime, based on the physical description that I had given, they began to go through local missing persons reports and found out that several months earlier a woman had reported her daughter Shannon missing in that same general area. A little while later, when the DNA results came back from the skull, they were compared to a reference sample the mother provided, and the skull was identified as Shannon.

Now, we have to fast-forward several months. One night a park ranger was driving his rounds in a nature area in southwest Ohio. As he turned a bend in the road, a completely naked woman came running out of the woods screaming, "He's trying to kill me, he's trying to kill me." The police surrounded the area, brought in the dogs, and closed in on a guy who was trying to make his way through the woods.

The terrified woman told police that she had willingly gone with this guy to provide sex for money. She said he took her into the park and said that he wanted to play "Tarzan and Jane" with her, if you can believe that. So, she took her clothes off, and folded them neatly at the foot of a tree. She said after that, he blindfolded her and told her that he wanted to run through the jungle with her in his arms. So he picked her up and started to carry her, and suddenly she felt a noose around her neck. And as the noose was tightening around her neck, and she was struggling to get free, somehow the rope came down from the tree, and she got away. That's when she ran out into the roadway and was discovered by the park ranger.

So, after the police captured the guy, they searched his car and found what appeared to be blood in the trunk. Investigators developed a DNA profile from that dried blood, and lo and behold, it matched Shannon's profile. At that point, it was apparent that the nude woman from the park wasn't the only girl this guy had attacked.

So not only was he charged with the attempted murder of the lady in the park, he was also charged with Shannon's murder. And if all of this wasn't already strange enough, when news of this attempted murder came out in public, a handful of other women started to come forward to tell their own horrendous stories. Several ladies came to the police and told investigators that this guy offered them money to go with him, and then he would attempt to strangle them until they lost consciousness and—get this—then he would try to revive them. He would literally use CPR to try to bring them back to life! They said this guy said things like, "What did it feel like to have your life in my hands?" And "What did it feel like to be dead?" Well apparently, Shannon didn't survive his sick little game.

But when it came time for the trial, one of the problems was that many of these women were drug-addicted—they were all known prostitutes—and every time they would come in for some kind of a pretrial conference, they would either be high or agitated. Pretty soon, the prosecutors' office began to realize that these ladies would probably not make very good witnesses. So, the County Prosecutor decided to offer the bad guy a plea bargain if he would lead us to the rest of Shannon's remains—and by this time it's over 18 months after Shannon's skull was found.

In my opinion allowing him to plead for the rest of Shannon's remains really didn't advance the case at all; we knew Shannon was dead and we knew he probably killed her, but this was an election year, and I won't even go into the politics here. But they decided to bring this guy out of jail to lead us to the location where the rest of her body was, which, unbelievably, was in the backyard of the house where he lived with his wife and 2 children! How sick is that?

So, we assemble at his house—mercifully they had his wife and children leave for the day—and there I was, slumped down in the back of a police cruiser peeking out, because I know he likes to do evil things to women, and I see him in his orange jumpsuit with his ankles and wrists shackled, being walked into his yard with couple of high-powered rifles pointed at his head. Now this is a rural area, and the guy lives in a house that literally has cornfields in the back, so they asked him where he buried Shannon, and he said, "I'm not exactly sure, but it's somewhere in this stretch of fencing, between those 2 tree stumps." The area he indicated was probably around 75 feet of fencerow; he wasn't confident of the exact spot.

After they took him away, I got out of the police cruiser, because it was now my job to locate and exhume the unmarked grave where allegedly we'd find the rest of Shannon's remains. This was in early March in Southwest Ohio, and there had been a little bit of snow coming down all day long, so it's cold. So the first thing that the guys from the prosecutor's office wanted to do was have the police bring in a backhoe, so we could all go home.

But I said, "Let me try to figure out a way to narrow down the area where she might be buried; I think I have an idea." And I got down on my hands and knees right next to the first tree stump the bad guy had pointed out, and I started to crawl slowly along the fencerow. I'm pretty sure the other investigators and the guys from the prosecutor's office thought I was nuts. But I had a hypothesis, and I was going to test it.

I knew that when the corn was planted, the plow couldn't come within a couple of feet of the fence. I also knew that if Shannon's body had been buried there, there was no way that guy could have put the soil above her back the way it was before he started digging the hole. That's Locard's principle, and we'll talk about that in the next lecture. Anyway, as I crawled along the ground, it was as smooth as glass for a while, and all of a sudden I hit about a 6-foot stretch along the fence that was all bumpy. And I said, "Let's start here." So we pulled up the grass with our hands and then started to take down the top dirt with shovels, and all of a sudden we hit something, and I said, "Stop and let me get a better look."

What we had hit was this little exposed edge of bone that was about the size of my baby finger, and I said, "It's her." And the prosecutor said, "That's not her, that's just a root or a stick or something." I said, "No, it's her; this is human bone." He tried to keep arguing with me, and I turned to him and said, "Actually, if you want to get specific, it's her left iliac crest," which is the front edge of what we call the hipbone. And within a couple of minutes he watched me expose her entire pelvis. I went from being some crazy woman crawling around on the ground to "Dr. Murray" real fast! In the next hour or 2 I took Shannon's remains out of this man's backyard. And after almost 2 years we were able to reunite Shannon's skull with the rest of her bones and her family was able to give her a proper burial.

Now, that case, that story, as bizarre and unique as it is, has all the makings of a typical forensic case—though no 2 of them are the same. There are different types of evidence. There are witnesses, there's the requisite "bad guy," there are representatives of the legal system, and a whole bunch of different forensic scientists.

In any forensic case, to get us back to the scientific method, an observation begins the investigation. Whether it's the discovery of human bones, a burglary, or a hit and run accident, the identification of some piece of evidence or some event, signals a possible crime, and that starts a chain of analysis. That initial observation causes investigators to develop hypotheses to explain what they see. Lots of different types of evidence and expertise come into play as forensic investigations unfold in a real interdisciplinary effort. And when enough scientific evidence points to a particular suspect, that allegation can lead to a trial.

So, how will this course unfold? Well, first we'll take a look at different types of physical evidence that might be indicative of criminal activity—things like fingerprints, firearms, hair, body fluids, DNA, drugs, and questioned documents. Then we'll see how complicated events unfold through analyzing things like bloodstains, vehicular accidents, and explosions. Then, we'll our attention to the science of death and decomposition, and see how experts conduct death investigations and look at bodily evidence. Then, we'll change gears a little bit and talk about investigation processes, criminal profiling, and using behavioral science to get at motive. And we'll take all of this evidence to the courtroom and see how forensic science is used at trial.

Although my focus will be on the science behind forensics, as time allows we'll look at specific cases. In fact, we'll wrap things up with a couple of segments that showcase the ways in which forensic science has been used to solve specific crimes, and to assist in mass disaster investigations, and to identify unknown persons. Along the way, I hope you'll learn a lot about the many ways that science is used in the pursuit of justice, so you can bust the Hollywood myths yourself, when you see them on TV. So, let's do another introductory lecture, now—one on crime-scene analysis—as we make our way toward a better understanding of forensic science.

Crime Scenes and Forensic Evidence
Lecture 2

A lthough there are rules of conduct and punishments for inappropriate behavior in many other groups of social animals, human beings are unique in terms of formalizing codes of conduct into laws and attempting to use logic and the scientific method to identify the unknown elements of crimes. Forensic science involves much more than forming logical conclusions. It involves analyzing specific pieces of evidence and systematically asking probative questions of the people involved—including victims, witnesses, and even potential criminals.

Crime-scene Investigation

- One of the most famous guiding scientific theorems of criminal investigation is known as Locard's exchange principle. Edmond Locard was a French forensic scientist who, about a century ago, set forth the idea that nobody can commit a crime without leaving something behind or altering the surroundings—even if the changes are imperceptible.

- As we interact with our environment and move through space and time, we always leave a trail. That trail might be made up of minute amounts of material known as trace evidence, or someone can generate a mountain of evidence. How much time 2 things spend in contact with one another is one of the main factors behind how much evidence is exchanged.

- In any crime-scene investigation, there are issues regarding the treatment of injured victims and the safety of first responders. These are critical factors in the initial response of law enforcement and emergency workers, who will always attend to lifesaving measures first—if they can.

- Sometimes, unfortunately, the initial assessment of the crime scene can damage or even destroy important evidence. However, if lives can be saved in a situation, any damage to evidence is considered an acceptable loss.

- Law enforcement officers also have to quickly figure out whether the person who committed the crime might still be on the scene—not only for their own safety, but also because there's the possibility of a quick capture.

- There can also be dangerous chemicals or disease-causing microorganisms left behind at certain crime scenes. Clandestine methamphetamine labs are notorious for the amount of toxic and combustible chemicals they generate and sometimes store.

- Some crime scenes are called hot zones when major biohazards are present—such as anthrax, nerve gas, or any other biological, chemical, radiological, or nuclear threat. These scenes can be accidental, can come from natural disasters, or can relate to crimes, such as bioterrorism.

- First responders and law enforcement investigators have to be trained in how to approach and search these types of dangerous scenes, and they need the right personal protective gear to recover victims, gather evidence, and analyze what might have happened.

- Another immediate consideration has to be containing and securing the scene and limiting access to only people with a good reason to be there. Somebody has to maintain a careful log of everyone who enters and exits a crime scene—and at precisely what time.

- Anyone at the scene becomes a potential witness at a future trial. Therefore, news reporters, curious bystanders, distraught family members, and even potential looters have to be controlled. Any of those people can jeopardize the crime scene—not only by their physical presence, but also through the information they could gather that might thwart the investigation. Unnecessary people at a crime scene can introduce additional fingerprints, footprints, tire tracks, hair, and DNA.

- Public access also has to be controlled. Media reports with specific information have the potential to tip off a suspect or reveal details that might be better kept for use by law enforcement during the questioning of any victims, witnesses, or suspects.

- Even the investigators can jeopardize evidence, so they need to have a specific search strategy for a given crime scene that will minimize their impact while maximizing the evidence they gather. Additionally, before any active search is undertaken, the appropriate legal standards for search and seizure must be met.

Identifying and Documenting Evidence

- The minute they step onto the scene of a crime, investigators have to consider everything they see around them as potential evidence. Using the context between and among objects—and the normal and abnormal relationships between things—they have to figure out what might be evidence and how it may be linked to other things they see.

- At a crime scene, there are going to be some assumptions made before any formal scientific testing. There are some tests, known as field tests, that can allow for some initial screening in the field, such as on blood or illegal drugs.

- Things of potential value to an investigation vary not only in their ability to immediately spot them, but also in their ability to preserve them for possible collection and analysis. Documentation is extremely important at the scene.

- Blood spatter, for example, is an example of pattern evidence. In order to reconstruct the history of what happened at a bloody scene, it's the pattern the blood makes on surfaces it hits that is the key to a full understanding of the scene. Photography and a careful map of the scene are crucial.

- Years can pass between when a crime occurs and when it may come before a judge and jury, and while bullets, hairs, and fibers can be picked up and preserved fairly indefinitely, some types of pattern evidence are transient and can basically only be preserved with images.

- As an alternative to photography, hand-drawn sketches and maps can be used to preserve a scene. These sketches don't have to be drawn to scale, but the idea is to map and measure the relationships between important objects at a scene. If possible, all the points on the sketch should be measured from a single fixed and permanent point called a datum, which can be anything reasonably permanent—such as the corner of a building.

- Today's state-of-the-art methods for documenting scenes include digital photography, video photography, and even portable electronic computerized mapping systems known as total station survey systems. This documentation might occur long before suspected evidence is confidently known to be a particular substance or especially long before that substance can be attributed to a particular individual.

- A potential crime scene has to be thoroughly documented not only photographically, but also by carefully written notes. Initially, you might not know the evidentiary value of a specific item. That's the reason crime-scene investigation requires keen observational skills, a methodical approach, good logic, and the willingness to being fairly compulsive about documentation.

Searching and Analyzing Crime Scenes
- Because each situation and scene is unique, different strategies have to be considered before collecting any potential evidence at a crime scene. Crime-scene analysts should do some careful planning before launching into a crime scene because evidence could be lost if they don't.

- There are a few standard patterns that are used to search scenes: Grid patterns, circular patterns, and line patterns are probably the most common.

- Searching and analyzing a crime scene is a complicated and destructive process, and any damage that is done can derail an investigation and can even make evidence unacceptable in a court of law.

- Crime-scene analysts are also subject to Locard's exchange principle. As they move through a scene to document and collect evidence, they only get one chance to view the area in the exact way in which they found it. Every item they move or pick up changes the scene forever.

- Television shows make searching a room look so easy: Actors just blunder in and start picking stuff up. Most likely, there are crime scenes where investigators have done that, but a good scene investigator puts a lot of effort into solving a crime and making sure that the proper legal conditions are maintained.

- Good communication between people who are—or may need to be—involved in the scene search is critical in the initial stages of

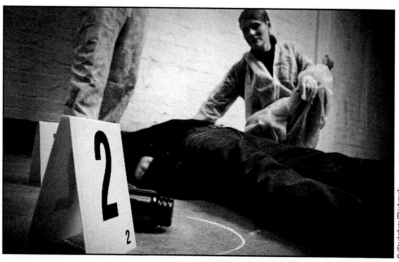

Interactions between people and things change the environment and leave clues to follow at a crime scene.

an investigation. This ranges from bringing in the medical examiner or coroner if a death is involved to making sure there is permission to search from the legal authorities. Additionally, someone has to do the mundane task of making sure that plenty of the right kind of supplies are available to gather evidence.

- Even the everyday language among the officers and investigators at the scene is important. Any type of inconsistency has the potential to complicate things in the future—especially when it comes to presenting evidence at trial.

- Another critical issue in crime-scene analysis is known as chain of custody. As soon as something is collected as evidence, the chain of custody for that item has to be maintained as a physical log of who handled the evidence, for how long they had it, and where they kept it while it was in their possession. Without a good chain of custody, critical evidence might not make it to trial.

- A good evidence custodian is critical to a forensic investigation. This person takes charge of evidence, logs it in, and makes sure that everything is properly labeled and sealed with evidence tape before it leaves the scene.

- When it comes to the physical collection of evidence—picking it up, handling it, and preserving it correctly—each type of evidence has its own specific needs, so evidence technicians have to be trained on how to collect many different types of items and substances. They also have to be sure to take known standards from the scene that might be used in future comparisons. Many forensic lab analyses involve comparing known evidence to questioned-evidence.

General Guidelines for Evidence
- Physical evidence varies in permanence, so a quick decision might need to be made when an investigator enters a scene. Crime-scene personnel have to quickly assess the situation and prioritize their actions.

- Evidence can be a direct transfer from one source to another, or it can have one or more intermediary transfers between its initial source and where it is eventually found—called an indirect transfer.

- Evidence can be classified in various ways. Recognizing that something belongs to a particular group is general and obvious, such as identifying something as hair, but further defining an item as part of a group of similar items with similar features—such as identifying the hair as cat hair—is called class identification. The most distinctive type of evidence identification puts an item into a group by itself, called individualizing identification.

- Not all evidence can be sampled, and not all of it can be tested. Crime-scene technicians need protocols for how much evidence to collect, and labs need protocols for how much to test to ensure that representative sampling and testing take place.

- Evidence typically consists of both physical objects and intangible evidence such as testimony. Technological advances have added other types of evidence that don't have a physical presence.

Questions to Consider

1. By whom and how are crime scenes discovered?

2. What are the initial responsibilities of law enforcement at a crime scene?

3. What is Locard's exchange principle?

4. What is the difference between known and unknown types of evidence?

5. What is the difference between class evidence and individuating evidence?

6. Can all evidence be collected at a crime scene?

Crime Scenes and Forensic Evidence
Lecture 2—Transcript

Although there are rules of conduct and punishments for inappropriate behavior in lots of other groups of social animals, human beings are unique in terms of formalizing those codes of conduct into what we now call laws. We're probably also rare animals in that we attempt to use logic and the scientific method, in order to identify whodunit—if we don't actually see the crime in the making.

Crime-scene analysis probably goes back to our earliest human ancestors. Picture a Gary Larson comic where Thag is standing outside of a cave with a bloody club in his hand, while Glug lies inside the cave with a smashed skull. As the other cavemen approach, it probably doesn't take much in the way of investigation to figure out who the culprit probably is. But forensic science involves a lot more than forming logical conclusions. We also need to analyze specific pieces of evidence, and systematically ask probative questions of the people involved—either victims, witnesses, or the potential criminals themselves.

In any society then, throughout human history, public order has been maintained by defining rules of behavior, identifying rule breakers, and singling them out for punishment. This is not only to provide what we might call justice, but also as a way of demonstrating to the rest of the group what will not be tolerated. Because of these punishments—and maybe due to some type of inherent knowledge of right and wrong—bad guys don't tend to commit their crimes out in the open view of the public. Instead, they try to hide them, or at a minimum they don't stick around. This means some crimes have to be pretty thoroughly analyzed in order to figure out the doer of the dirty deed.

One of the most famous guiding scientific theorems of criminal investigation is known as "Locard's exchange principle." Edmond Locard was a French forensic scientist who, about a century ago, set forth the idea that no one can commit a crime without leaving something behind or altering the surroundings, if even imperceptibly. In other words, we can't be somewhere or do something without somehow leaving our mark or without taking some evidence of the contact away with us.

As we interact with our environment, and move through space and time, we always leave a trail. That trail might be made up of minute amounts of material known as "trace evidence," or somebody can generate a mountain of evidence, like a bull in a china shop. No one truly disappears without a trace. But whether signs of a person's presence can be located and documented or not is another matter.

One book I use in my forensic course says the popular concept known as the "5-second rule"—you know, the myth that alleges if you drop food on the floor, and it's there for less than 5 seconds, it's OK to eat it—well, that's a clear application of Locard's principle. How much time 2 things spend in contact with one another is one of the big factors behind how much evidence is exchanged. (By the way, studies have shown the "5-second rule" is not accurate—not for wet or dry food; so don't go eating that pretzel you just dropped on the floor!)

I guess Locard's principle has, at times, been a huge source of frustration to crime-scene investigators; I mean, we know there's evidence present, but sometimes—especially when a perpetrator has been extremely careful—the physical evidence can escape us. Locard's exchange principle has also been the driving force for many innovations in technology in forensic science, as researchers in the field continue to try to improve our ability to find and analyze evidence, and in doing that, solve crimes.

Let's go back to my own forensic case that I talked about in the previous lecture: What types of evidence exchanges did we have? The skull that was found by the man walking his dog was a major piece of evidence. But we had no way to know, at the time, that one of the most important links we would have in that case was the exchange that happened between that victim and the trunk of a car. If I hadn't realized that the soil over the shallow grave the killer dug in his own backyard, could never have been restored to its original condition—because of his exchange with it—well, it might have been a lot more difficult to locate the rest of Shannon's remains on that cold day in early March. Those are just 2 examples of how interactions between things and people change the environment and leave clues to follow at a crime scene.

And how many crime scenes did we have in that case? There was the attempted murder of one woman in the woods, and that not only brought Shannon's death to the surface, but also caused a few other women to allege even more assaults by this predator. And we still don't actually know where Shannon was killed; we only know where her dismembered head was apparently thrown out of the creep's car, and where he ultimately buried the rest of her body.

In fact, there's an interesting side note that I didn't even mention the first time around: This guy confessed that he first buried Shannon's entire body in the, quote, "middle of the cornfield behind his house," but a couple of days later—when he realized the plow might unearth her in the spring—he went out one night, dug her up, then, quote, "chunked off her head with a flat-edged shovel." He then re-buried her headless body near the fencerow where we finally found it. And then he drove her head—apparently in the trunk of his car where Shannon's blood was ultimately found—out to where her skull was recovered.

So, just considering Shannon's death alone—her first burial, her dismemberment, her second burial, and the discard of her head—well, you can see how complicated and ill-defined crime scenes (or in this case, a trail of crime scenes) can be. Not to mention the other cases allegedly linked to this single, serial predator.

One of the books that I use in my forensic science teaching refers to the crime scene as a "piece of history with a story to tell." As an anthropologist who has worked as an archaeologist, I know a lot about trying to reconstruct the past through the artifacts and patterns people leave behind. That's exactly what goes on during the analysis of a crime scene, and I'm sure my training as an archaeologist has made me a better forensic investigator.

There are lots of issues that play a role in crime-scene investigation: First and foremost, in any scene investigation, are issues regarding the treatment of injured victims and the safety of first responders. These are really critical factors in the initial response of law enforcement and emergency workers. Fortunately for the victims, first responders will always attend to life-saving measures first, if they can.

But sometimes, unfortunately, the initial assessment of the crime scene can damage or even destroy important evidence. For example, pulling injured victims out of a mass disaster situation can do additional damage to the bodies of the people who died in the incident. Blasting a fire hose to put out or contain a fire can destroy small debris that may be critical to establishing how the fire started. But, if lives can be saved in either of those situations, any damage to evidence has to be considered an acceptable loss. Law enforcement officers, as first responders or first officers, also have to quickly figure out whether the bad guy might still be on the scene—not only for their own safety, but also because there's the possibility then of a quick capture.

There can also be dangerous chemicals, or disease-causing microorganisms left behind at certain crime scenes. Clandestine methamphetamine labs are really notorious for the amount of toxic and combustible chemicals they generate, and sometimes warehouse. Some crime scenes are considered "hot zones" when major biohazards are present, like anthrax, nerve gas, or any other biological, chemical, radiological, or nuclear threat. These scenes can be accidental, they can come from natural disasters—like the 2011 earthquake in Japan—or they can relate to crimes like bioterrorism. So, first responders and law enforcement investigators have to be trained in how to approach and search these types of dangerous situations, and they have the right personal protective gear needed to recover victims, gather evidence, and analyze what might have happened.

Another immediate consideration has to be containing and securing the scene, and limiting access to only people with a good reason to be there. Somebody has to maintain a careful log of everybody who enters and exits a crime scene, and at precisely what time. That's one of the non-glamorous crime-scene jobs you don't see on TV.

Anybody at the scene becomes a potential witness at a future trial. So news reporters, curious bystanders, distraught family members— sometimes even potential looters—have to be controlled. Any of those people can jeopardize the crime scene not only by their physical presence, but also through the information they could gather that might thwart the investigation. Unnecessary people at a crime scene can introduce additional fingerprints, footprints, tire tracks, hair, even DNA. If that happens, the work of investigators is increased because they'll have to try to sort out all the extraneous data, if they even can.

Public access also has to be controlled so that any nitwit with a cell phone isn't releasing information or photographs to the public. And we all realize that media reports with specific information have the potential to tip off a suspect, or reveal details that might be better kept "close to the vest" for use by law enforcement during questioning of any victims, witnesses, or suspects.

Even the investigators themselves can jeopardize evidence, so they have to figure out a specific search strategy for a given crime scene that will minimize their impact while maximizing the evidence they gather. And, before any active search is undertaken, the appropriate legal standards for search and seizure must be met. For example, in the United States, the fourth amendment of the U.S. Constitution requires consent to search from the property owner a legal stand-in from the justice system, except in emergencies.

So, since evidence can be material found in tiny quantities, like grains of sand in the carpet—and we call that trace evidence—or patently obvious clues like tire tracks, the minute they step onto the scene, investigators have to consider everything they see around them as potential evidence. Using the context between and among objects, and normal and abnormal relationships between things—maybe even before setting foot in a room—they have to figure out what might be evidence and how it may be linked to other things they see.

If crime-scene investigators see what looks like blood, they have to try to figure out the likely source of that blood, which might be immediately obvious or not. They also have to consider, though, that a substance that looks like blood may not actually be blood—but blood is pretty obvious. Or something that looks like cocaine might really be powdered sugar or something. So, at a crime scene, there are going to be some assumptions made before any formal scientific testing. There are some tests, though, known as field tests, that can allow for some initial screening in the field, like on blood or illegal drugs, and we'll talk about them in other lectures.

Things of potential value to an investigation not only vary in our ability to immediately spot them, but also in our ability to preserve them for possible collection and analysis. This is where documentation becomes so important at the scene. Blood spatter, for example, is an example of what we call pattern evidence. It's not enough to merely establish a substance is blood. In order to reconstruct the history of what happened at a bloody scene, it's the pattern the blood makes on surfaces it hits that's the key to a full understanding of the scene. If there's blood from ceiling to floor, and everything in between—and I've seen some pretty gruesome cases like that—photography and a careful map of the scene are crucial. A scene can't be maintained indefinitely.

If a homicide happens in an apartment hallway, that property probably won't be boarded up and protected between when the crime happened and when a suspect might be located—let alone when the case might go to trial. Years can pass between when something occurs and when it may come before a judge and jury. And while bullets, hairs, and fibers can be picked up and preserved fairly indefinitely, some types of pattern evidence are transient and can pretty much only be preserved with images.

In the old days—and I've been around long enough to remember them—Polaroid instant cameras were the primary ways we documented crime scenes. This was typically done in conjunction with regular film photography, usually in both black-and-white and color.

In the really old days—and I have not been around long enough to remember them—a crime-scene sketch was usually the best, maybe the only, way of preserving a scene. Hand drawn sketches and maps are still used today—in fact I've used them myself to document relationships between bones at a crime scene. These sketches don't have to be drawn to scale, but the idea is to map and measure the relationships between important objects at a scene. And, like we use in archaeology, if possible, all the points on the sketch have to be measured from a single, fixed and permanent point called a datum. This datum can be anything reasonably permanent—something like the corner of a building, or, if we're out in the woods, a mature tree might be the best we can do.

But today's state-of-the-art methods for documenting scenes include digital photography, video photography, and even portable electronic computerized mapping systems known as "total station survey systems." This documentation might occur long before suspected evidence is confidently known to be a particular substance—like blood or cocaine—or especially long before that substance can be attributed to a particular individual, say, in the case of a DNA profile obtained from semen. Whether evidence is in trace amounts or readily visible, documentation can't be emphasized enough.

In TV shows and movies, what needs to be collected as evidence is nearly always obvious, because the camera usually focuses our attention right on those items. But imagine yourself as an investigator, at your initial approach to a potential crime scene, and I'll bet, like me, you might have no idea where to start. Are there stray hairs in the carpeting? Are there fingerprints on that desk? Were the papers scattered on the coffee table like that before the break-in? Who drank from that glass? How many pills were in that bottle? Is this actually what we think it is, or has the scene been staged to throw us off? That list could go on and on.

So, a potential scene has to be thoroughly documented not only photographically, but also by carefully written notes. You might never know, initially, the evidentiary value of a specific item. That's the reason crime-scene investigation requires keen observational skills, a methodical approach, good logic, and the willingness to be pretty much compulsive about documentation.

I asked a cop friend once how he can tell if a place has just been ransacked or it's just a super messy house, and he had an immediate answer: He said you look at the kitchen sink to see if dirty dishes are piled up or how nasty the toilet is. Makes sense to me.

Because each situation and each scene is unique, different strategies have to be considered before actually collecting any potential evidence. Obviously, there's a big difference between trying to secure and search a small liquor store when compared to a mall parking lot, a high-rise building, or an interstate highway. Crime-scene analysts owe it to themselves, public safety, and the investigation to do some really careful planning before launching into a crime scene. They can't just move through the area at random; they need to develop a systematic strategy or all could be lost.

There are a few standard patterns we use to search to scenes: Grid patterns, circular patterns, and what are called lane or line patterns are probably the most common—and I've used all of them in my work. When I helped look for remains scattered in a soybean field from a plane crash, we used a line search. But, if I see a clear concentration of bones that suggest the site where a victim probably decomposed, and carnivores have scattered bones around the area, I might pick the central location as my core starting place, and then move out from there in a circular, spiral pattern. That's because it's more likely that bones will be found closer to the site of decomposition than further away.

I've also had to climb trees to see if there could be a clump of hair in a bird's nest above a pile of bones—because hair color and length can be important in an identification. And it sure helps to have a background in biology and to have grown up as a tomboy of sorts in an area surrounded by woods, because a knowledge of critters and how and where they travel has helped me know how and where to search.

Searching and analyzing a crime scene is a complicated and destructive process. And, I admit I've found things by actually stepping on them. But any damage done can derail an investigation and even make evidence unacceptable in a court of law. I mean, crime-scene analysts are also subject to "Locard's exchange principle." As we move through a scene to document and collect evidence, we really only get a single shot at the area in the exact way in which we found it. Every item we move or pick up changes the scene forever.

You can try this yourself: Have someone hide a mock piece of evidence in one of the rooms of your house. And, unlike an Easter egg hunt, have them choose something, without even telling you what you're looking for. Then, walk to the door of that room, stand there, and think about how you could search that room, systematically, to find that object, using the least intrusive method possible. Then, consider how familiar that room in your house is to you, as compared to being asked to search the home of a complete stranger, to try to figure out what's normal from what's not.

TV shows make searching a scene look so easy—actors just blunder in and start picking stuff up. And I'm sure there are crime scenes where investigators have done that, too. In some ways, and some crimes, it's a wonder any evidence is found and recovered at all. A good scene investigator goes a long way toward solving a crime and making sure that the proper legal conditions are maintained.

Good communication between people who are—or may need to be—involved in the scene search is critical in the initial stages of an investigation. This ranges from bringing in the medical examiner or coroner if a death is involved, to making sure permission to search comes from the legal authorities. Somebody has to do the mundane task of making sure that plenty of the right kinds of supplies are on hand to gather the evidence.

Even the everyday language among the officers and investigators at the scene is important. Something as simple as whether a piece of furniture is going to be called a "couch" or a "sofa" or a "loveseat" during documentation can be important. That's because any type of inconsistency has the potential to complicate things in the future. Remember, one of the goals in a crime-scene investigation is to preserve the evidence in the event of a future legal trial, and, well, the adversarial system that is set up in the courtroom is poised and ready to take advantage of any confusing terminology as potential ammunition.

Another critical issue in crime-scene analysis is known as chain of custody. As soon as something is collected as evidence, the chain of custody for that item has to be maintained as a physical log of who handled the evidence, for how long they had it, and where they kept it while it was their responsibility. Without a good chain of custody, critical evidence might not make it to trial. We'll talk more about that in our discussion of courtroom issues near the end of this series, but a good evidence custodian is critical to a forensic investigation; this person takes charge of evidence, logs it in, and makes sure that everything is properly labeled and sealed with evidence tape before it leaves the scene. That's another one of those non-glamorous roles you don't see on TV shows.

When it comes to the actual physical collection of evidence, meaning, picking it up, handling it, and preserving it right, each type of evidence has its own specific needs. And we'll talk about those with each type of evidence we cover. Evidence techs have to be trained on how to collect a lot of different types of items and substances. Consider how they might pick up a loaded gun versus how they might collect a spilled liquid.

Not only that, but they also have to be sure to take known standards from the scene that might be used in future comparisons. By that I mean something like taking a fiber sample from the carpeting in the room, in case a suspect is later found with unknown fibers on his shoes. As we'll see, many forensic lab analyses involve comparing known evidence to questioned evidence.

Let's review some general guidelines about evidence as we wrap this up: First, even physical evidence varies in its permanence, as we'll see, so a quick decision might need to be made if an investigator enters a scene, say, and there's blood in the sink and the water is still running. He may rush to immediately shut off the water, without even considering there may be important fingerprints on the faucet knobs. Crime-scene personnel have to quickly assess and prioritize to best fit any situation.

Secondly, evidence can be a direct transfer from one source to another, or it can have one or more intermediary transfers between its initial source and where it's ultimately found. That type of exchange is called an indirect transfer. If a lady pets her cat goodbye before leaving for work and has cat hair on her hand, that's a direct transfer. If she wipes her hand on her skirt, the skirt becomes an indirect source of the cat hair. Then, if she sits down on the subway and the cat hair clings to the seat she's on, there's another indirect transfer from the cat, and if you sit down on that seat, and the cat hair gets on your pants, well, you never saw the cat, but there you are with its fur on your pants. You get the idea. Indirect evidence transfers can really complicate things and have to be carefully considered because they have the potential to put the wrong person at a scene.

Third: Evidence can be classified in a couple of different ways. Recognizing that something belongs to a particular group is pretty general and obvious—like saying it's hair, it's a fiber, it's a piece of broken glass, or it's a paint chip. But further defining that hair as cat hair, that fiber as polyester, that piece of glass as being from a light bulb, or that chip as coming from automotive paint—and even better—from a Mercedes-Benz product, well, that lumps the item into a group of like items with similar features, and we call that class identification.

The most distinctive type of evidence identification puts an item into a group all by itself—meaning a group with only one member, and we call this individualizing identification. Not all pieces of evidence can rise to that level, as we'll see, but it's the highest form of identification. For instance, if that chip of automotive paint can be completely matched to an identically shaped void on a specific car that involved in a hit-and-run accident, well, that might rise to the level of individualizing evidence. But that's only possible if the car that it came from can be located and a direct comparison can be made. I'm sure these categories will become clearer as we use these concepts in future lectures about physical evidence.

Fourth: Not all evidence can be sampled and not all of it can be tested. If there's blood all over a room, it can't all be collected, and it can't all be analyzed. The same applies to a truckload of a number of large bags of what's thought to be cocaine. Crime-scene technicians need protocols for how much evidence to collect, and labs need to have protocols for how much to test to ensure that representative sampling and testing take place. If there are 286 cigarette butts outside the door of a 7-Eleven after a burglary, the lab is not going to test them all for DNA.

On the other hand, if only a small amount of a substance is present as evidence, analysts have to decide what tests are possible, and which are the best bet for the small amount of evidence, and in what order the tests should be done. So, if a there's bloody handprint on a weapon, detailed photos would be taken first, then a small amount of the substance would be analyzed to make sure it's blood, without messing up any more of the handprint than necessary. There may also be legal ramifications of using up a whole sample, because it might prevent the opposing side from conducting their own independent testing. We'll come back to these with more specific examples in later discussions, but I wanted to introduce those ideas here because they relate to evidence and its collection.

Remember, evidence is information that can support or refute a fact, and evidence typically consists of both physical objects and testimony—we'll talk about testimony much later in the series, but it is just one example of intangible evidence. Technological advances have added other new types of evidence that have little in the way of a physical presence.

So far, we've been thinking about a crime scene as the physical location where a murder, rape, burglary, or arson took place. But when you think about it today's technology has expanded the definition of a crime scene— like cyber crimes where funds can be shifted from one account to another through signals being bounced off of satellites without any physical money ever actually changing hands. But, there is still a perpetrator on one end of a crime like that and a victim on the other. So, there will still be a trail of evidence—it will just take different forms than what we've been talking about here.

The good news is that as technology has changed the traditional notion of the crime scene, it's also changed the ways in which crimes can be detected and analyzed. So, let's move into our first specific type of evidence, fingerprints, as an example of what's old and what's new in forensic evidence and its analysis.

Fingerprint Science—Hands-Down ID
Lecture 3

Fingerprints are one of the oldest and still most commonly used types of forensic evidence. Fingerprints are evidence of our presence that we leave on objects within our environment. Some of those fingerprints are nearly immediately erased or smeared over by the next person that comes in contact with the same object, but other prints might linger indefinitely. Even though it has been around for a long time, fingerprint science still holds new potential in solving crimes—sometimes even after a long time has elapsed.

The History of Fingerprinting

- Fingerprints have provided major evidence in countless criminal investigations, and their validity has long been widely accepted as proof of a person's identity.

- In the 1860s, William Hershel, who was a British official in colonial India, was using handprints of the Indian people he dealt with as a form of signature on contracts. Out of interest, Hershel tracked his own fingerprints for over 50 years, establishing that the patterns of fingerprints do not change over a lifetime.

- Henry Faulds is sometimes credited with the first true forensic application of fingerprints when he helped Tokyo police investigate a burglary in the 1880s. Faulds also tried to chemically alter his own prints and noticed that they grew back.

- Expanding on the work of Faulds, Sir Francis Galton—Charles Darwin's cousin—recognized that fingerprint patterns don't change as we age and that all prints can be essentially grouped into 3 main classifications: arches, loops, and whorls. Galton also did some statistical work on the probability of 2 people having the same prints, which basically established that fingerprints are unique. In fact, no 2 people have the same prints—not even identical twins.

Skin and Fingerprints

- The skin on vertebrate animals—including fish, amphibians, reptiles, birds, and mammals—has 2 main layers: an outer layer called the epidermis and a deeper layer known as the dermis. The epidermis is made of tightly packed cells that form a barrier to the outside world, and the dermis underneath has blood vessels, different kinds of glands, and other structures—such as scales, feathers, hairs, or nails—anchored in it.

- All surfaces of the skin of humans and their fellow primates have the same epidermis-over-dermis pattern. But when you consider the whole body, primate skin can be broken into 2 types: thin skin and thick skin. Thin skin has 4 main layers of epidermal cells and is found on body surfaces that bear hair follicles and oil glands. Thick skin has 5 main layers to its epidermis and is found only on the palms of the hands and soles of the feet, which are scientifically called palmar skin and plantar skin, respectively. Thick skin has many sweat glands but no hair follicles or oil glands.

- On palmar and plantar skin, the interface between the epidermis and dermis has hills and valleys called dermal papillae. The dermal papillae, in turn, project through to the epidermis, creating corresponding surface ridges on palmar and plantar skin called dermatoglyphs. All primates have these friction ridges on the pads of their hands and feet; evolutionarily, they are assumed to help in gripping by increasing surface area for contact.

- Palmar and plantar skin are rich in sweat glands compared to all other body skin, but the sweat is really watery and doesn't directly contribute much to the print. The water in sweat, though, becomes a vehicle to pick up other materials that get deposited in the print. In other words, a fingerprint is really made by the junk that winds up in sweat and clings to the ridges on the skin. Shed skin cells, body oils, and dirt and dust are picked up by sweat when we touch things—including other parts of our body.

- Chemical and thermal burns can destroy prints, but they will leave scars behind. Deep cuts into the dermis, whether intentional or not, will also leave scars. However, the scars that form can be even more distinctive than the original prints were.

The Language of Fingerprints

- To compare and discuss fingerprints, scientists developed a common language to describe and classify the patterns of fingertips. The 3 major fingerprint classifications first used by Galton—arches, loops, and whorls—are still part of modern dactyloscopy, which is the examination and comparison of fingerprints.

- The part of a fingerprint that's categorized runs from the last joint on the palm side of each finger to its tip and then all the way to either side of the nail bed. In other words, there are sides to fingerprints—which is why fingertips are rolled from side to side when someone is fingerprinted.

- There are major and minor features to any fingerprint pattern, and arch, loop, and whorl are considered major features. These describe the overall pattern of the main ridges in a print, especially how they change direction.

© iStockphoto/Thinkstock.

After about 30 minutes of wearing latex gloves, fingerprints can even be laid down through the gloves.

- Some of the 3 main categories are further broken down to give a total of 8 patterns. Smaller features within the major patterns are called minutiae, which add detail to the main pattern of a fingerprint and are behind the comparison science of dactyloscopy.

  o There are plain and tented arches, which are differentiated because a tented arch has almost a vertical core.

  o Loops are subclassified by the direction that they open in. If a loop opens in the direction of the pinkie finger, it's called an ulnar loop because the forearm bone on the little finger side is the ulna. If a loop opens in the direction of the thumb, it's called a radial loop because the forearm bone on the thumb side is the radius.

  o Whorls are more complex and subdivide into 4 types: plain, central pocket, double loop, and accidental.

- Patent prints are prints that can be seen with the unaided eye. They might be made through the friction of skin touching blood, paint, ink, grease, mud, or any semiliquid substance followed by the transfer of that material to a dry surface.

- Latent prints cannot be visualized with the unaided eye and, therefore, have to be developed or enhanced with physical or chemical means.

- Plastic prints are fingerprint impressions that are found on some types of soft materials like chewed gum and wet paint.

- Partial prints could be any type—patent, latent, or plastic—but don't reflect a full fingertip. Most crime-scene prints are partial prints.

- Patent prints can be brought to the lab if they are seen on an object that is easily transported—such as a coffee mug, photo frame, or vehicle—but many crime scenes include prints on surfaces that are difficult or impossible to move—such as a plaster wall or 25-foot-long bank countertop. Most of the time, this type of evidence is collected using only photography.

- Latent prints have to be treated in some way in order to make them visible. One way to find latent prints is by projecting ultraviolet light across a nonabsorbent surface where prints may be hidden. The residues in the fingerprints will reflect the UV light in a different way than the surfaces around them, so prints that can't be seen with the unaided eye might appear.

- Latent prints have to be developed—usually by dusting or through some type of chemical enhancement. Regardless of how prints are developed, they still have to be captured in some way as evidence.

Recording and Comparing Fingerprints
- In order for fingerprints to be useful in forensic investigations, they have to be compared to other prints, so repositories of reference fingerprint records have been collected over time.

- There are many reasons that a person might have a fingerprint record on file—or at least had one made at some point. Fingerprint records are made at the time of arrests, but people who work with large sums of money or other valuables have their prints recorded, too. Prints are also taken for background checks.

- Fingerprints are often taken by simple inking methods on a 10-print card. This standard presentation method collects a rolled print from each finger and both thumbs and a tapped print from the 4 fingers on each hand placed adjacently and then each thumb.

- Since around the early 1990s, digital technologies have been developed. Computerized fingerprint scanners now allow a digit to be put on a digital pad that records the fingerprint. Along with this movement from ink to scanning there have been changes in how prints are stored and compared.

- When comparing prints, either a known or unknown person is compared to the records of known people. However, sometimes unknown prints from a crime scene are matched to other unknown prints from other crime scenes. In these cases, even though the identity of the perpetrator isn't known, the crimes are linked by the prints found at 2 or more scenes.

- Another important use of fingerprint comparisons is to help identify the unknown dead—but only if the body is in good enough shape to allow fingerprinting.

- Fingerprints are also used for security and access purposes, and some high-tech security measures involve scanning a person's prints like a key in a lock to open a door or log on to a computer system.

Fingerprint Coding Systems

- Fingerprint coding systems turn the arch, loop, and whorl patterns on a set of 10 digits into alphabetical and/or numerical codes that can be more quickly and easily compared. This coding allows law enforcement to eliminate huge batches of data without even having to look at the prints the codes represent.

- Codes can also be communicated across distances, and if they don't correlate, then there is no relationship between the prints. If the codes do match, then the actual prints can be compared by hand, side-by-side, to look for minutiae and confirm whether the prints are a true match.

- The Henry system was developed by Sir Edward Henry, head of the Metropolitan Police of London during the early 1900s. The Henry system boils down an entire set of 10 prints into a single fraction that represents the even digits of both hands over the odd digits of both hands. Some version of the original Henry system is still used in most European countries and by the U.S. Federal Bureau of Investigation.

- As computer technologies like scanning have improved, computerized matching of prints have become possible. In 1999, the U.S. FBI developed its Integrated Automated Fingerprint Identification System (IAFIS).

- As powerful as IAFIS is, it has its limitations. Fingerprint quality—particularly from scene prints—is often lacking, and IAFIS really only searches on ridge patterns, not all minutiae. A law enforcement officer or forensic scientist still has to view any IAFIS system-suggested matches and critically examine them.

- It's not only fingers that leave prints; people's palms also have unique prints. This is also true with the soles of the feet. Even lip prints—from a coffee mug or lipstick mark, for example—have been used to link a person to a scene or object.

Questions to Consider

1. Do all primates have fingerprints?

2. Do identical twins have the same fingerprints?

3. At what point in human development do fingerprints occur?

4. What are the 3 main classes into which fingerprints are categorized?

5. Are your fingerprints on file anywhere?

Fingerprint Science—Hands-Down ID
Lecture 3—Transcript

What do the Mona Lisa, John Dillinger, and the kidnapping and murder of 12-year-old Polly Klaas all have in common? They all have some notorious connection to fingerprints, one of the oldest and still most commonly used kinds of forensic evidence.

Fingerprints are evidence of our presence that we all leave, day-in and day-out, as we move from place to place and handle all kinds of objects and materials. Without even thinking about it, from the time we wake up and reach to turn off our alarm clock each day, until the time we pull the covers up at night, we leave our mark on things in our environment. Some of those fingerprints are nearly immediately erased or smeared over by the next person that grabs the same doorknob, but other prints might hang around indefinitely—like if we straighten a picture in our office, and it's not touched again for years.

Fingerprints have provided major evidence in countless criminal investigations, and their validity has long been widely accepted as proof of a person's identity. One of the earliest fingerprint investigators, Alphonse Bertillon, solved the theft of the Mona Lisa from the Louvre Museum in Paris in 1911 using fingerprints.

When authorities gunned down the notorious American gangster, John Dillinger, in 1934, his autopsy showed evidence that at some point he had tried to destroy his own fingerprints by burning his fingertips with chemicals. And it was a palm print from a child's bunk bed that led to the conviction of Richard Allen Davis for the 1993 murder of 12-year-old Polly Klaas, who was abducted from a slumber party right in front of her girl friends in California.

There is some evidence that the Chinese used fingerprints and handprints as a form of identification or signature as long as 2000–3000 years ago. For example, an artist might sign his work with a fingerprint. By the 1860s— William Hershel—who was a British official in colonial India—was using handprints of the Indian people he dealt with as a form of signature on contracts. Out of interest, Hershel tracked his own fingerprints for about 50 years, establishing that the patterns do not change over a lifetime.

In 1880, Henry Faulds, a Scottish missionary, who was a doctor in a Japanese hospital, published a letter on the uniqueness of fingerprints in the journal "Nature." Faulds is sometimes credited with the first true forensic application of fingerprints when he helped Tokyo police investigate a burglary. Faulds also tried to chemically alter his own prints and noticed they grew back.

And here's a story worthy of its own forensic investigation: Faulds attempted to get funding for his fingerprint research by sending a letter to Charles Darwin—who, of course, is known for his theory of evolution, but you may not know also engaged in some early anthropology studies—and Darwin forwarded the information in Faulds's letter to Darwin's cousin, Sir Francis Galton, who basically took over the fingerprint project without supporting or even crediting Faulds.

Around the same time, the French police expert Alphonse Bertillon started this quasi-scientific identification method that became known as Bertillonage. This was an early form of what's called anthropometry— basically it was a systematic series of measurements of the human body. Bertillonage combined photographs and body measurements to create what amounted to identification portraits of people.

And then, in 1903, a famous case from Leavenworth Prison in Kansas showed that 2 male prisoners—a Will West and a William West—not only had essentially the same names, but also the same Bertillonage profiles. In fact, it's said these guys nearly looked like twins, but there was one key difference: They had different fingerprints. This showed that Bertillon's method didn't really discriminate among people very well, but fingerprint patterns did.

Back to Sir Francis Galton: Expanding on the work of Faulds, Galton published 3 books about fingerprints between 1892 and 1895. Galton realized that print patterns don't change as we age, and all prints can be essentially grouped into 3 main classifications: arches, loops, and whorls.

And as is required by good science, Galton also did some statistical work on the probability of 2 people having the same prints; and this basically established that fingerprints are unique.

Now, let's talk a little about skin to better understand fingerprints. The skin on vertebrate animals—that includes everything from fish and amphibians, to reptiles, birds, and mammals—has 2 main layers: An outer layer called the epidermis and a deeper layer known as the dermis. The epidermis is made of tightly packed cells that form a barrier to the outside world, and the dermis underneath has blood vessels, different kinds of glands, and other structures anchored in it—like scales, feathers, hairs, or nails—whatever you got.

As for the skin of humans and our fellow primates, all surfaces of our skin have that same epidermis over dermis pattern. But when you consider the whole body, primate skin can be broken to 2 types: thin skin and thick skin. Thin skin has 4 main layers of epidermal cells that bear hair follicles and oil glands. But thick skin has 5 main layers to its epidermis, and it's found only on the palms of the hands and soles of the feet—which are scientifically called our palmar and plantar skin. Thick skin has lots of sweat glands, but doesn't have any hair follicles or oil glands.

On this palmar and plantar skin, the interface between the epidermis and dermis has hills and valleys called dermal papillae. The dermal papillae, in turn, project through to the epidermis, creating corresponding surface ridges on our palmar and plantar skins, and these are called dermatoglyphs. All primates have these friction ridges on the pads of our hands and feet—evolutionarily, they are assumed to help us in gripping by increasing surface area for contact. And while all thick skin has these ridges, for sake of discussion, I'm going to refer mainly to fingerprints.

In humans, prints start forming about 8 weeks in utero, which in terms of timing, is right at the interface of the embryonic and fetal periods. After 17 weeks the pattern is set and the ridges only get bigger as the fetus—and then the infant and child—grows. No 2 people have the same prints—not even identical twins—so there's clearly more to the development of fingerprints than just genetics.

Did you know that squeaky-clean fingers don't leave prints? That's because there aren't any oil glands on palmar or plantar skin. And, as we all know—from TV, of course—many criminals try to wear gloves to try to prevent leaving prints. But did you know that after about a half hour of wearing them, fingerprints can even be laid down through latex gloves? Oh, there I go, making smarter criminals again!

Palmar and plantar skin is really rich in sweat glands, compared to all other body skin—but the sweat itself is really watery and doesn't directly contribute much to the print. The water in sweat, though, becomes a vehicle to pick up other materials that get deposited in the print. In other words, a fingerprint is really made by the junk that winds up in sweat and then clings to the ridges on the skin. That includes stuff like shed skin cells, body oils, dirt, and dust. Those are all picked up by sweat when we touch things—including other parts of our own body.

Try this sometime: Get a clean drinking glass out of your cabinet and then wash your hands really well. Dry your hands, and then try to make fingerprints on the glass. You won't be able to see them with your eye at all—well, unless you never learned good hand washing or you have some pretty grimy glasses in your cabinet!

Now, assuming you didn't just step out of the shower, take your fingertip and wipe it around on your forehead or on the sides of your nose where most of us typically have at least some minor amount of body oil. Now, press your fingerprint on the glass and you'll probably be able to see the print.

My students often ask whether chemical and thermal burns will destroy prints, and yes, they can, but they will leave scars behind. Deep cuts into the dermis, whether intentional or not, will also leave scars. But the thing is, the scars that form can be even more distinctive than the original prints were. So John Dillinger may have ended up with more unique fingertip patterns than the ones he was born with.

Like any other kind of pattern, scientists quickly figured out that to compare and discuss fingerprints, they would have to develop a common language to describe and classify the patterns they saw. The 3 major fingerprint classifications—arches, loops, and whorls, first set out by Galton—are still part of dactyloscopy today. Yes, I said dactyloscopy! Dactyloscopy is your million-dollar word for the examination and comparison of fingerprints. I admit, it's a fun word to say, but because it's a mouthful, I'm probably not going to use it much.

The part of a fingerprint that's categorized runs from the last joint on the palm side of each finger to its tip, and then all the way to either side of the nail bed. In other words, there are sides to our fingerprints—that's why you see fingertips being rolled from side to side when you watch shows where somebody is being fingerprinted. It's also the reason that intentionally taken fingerprint records show each fingertip as more of a square than the type of oval that would naturally lay down if you just touched the pad of your finger to something.

There are major and minor features to any fingerprint pattern—an arch, loop, and whorl are considered major features. These describe the overall pattern of the main ridges in a print, especially how they change direction. A major change in direction is known as a delta: An arch lacks a delta, a loop has a single delta, and a whorl has a pair of deltas. You can also see that some print patterns, like in a loop, exhibit a central region known as the core. Generally, about 65% of all prints show loop patterns, about 30% are whorls, and only about 5% of fingerprints are arches.

Some of the 3 main categories are further broken down to give a total of 8 patterns. So, for instance, there are plain and tented arches. These are differentiated because a tented arch has almost a vertical core. Loops are sub-classified by the direction that they open in; if a loop opens in the direction of the little finger, it's called an ulnar loop because the forearm bone on the little finger side is the ulna; and if a loop opens in the direction of the thumb, it's called a radial loop because the forearm bone on the thumb side is the radius. Whorls are more complex and subdivide into 4 types: plain, central pocket, double loop, and accidental.

But there's a lot more to fingerprint analysis than just the 8 major classification groups. Smaller features within the major patterns are called minutiae. These include things like ridge bifurcations and trifurcations, ending ridges, islands which are sometimes called enclosures, and tiny dots. Under a microscope, even the pores of sweat glands can be seen. All these and other minutiae add detail to the main pattern of a fingerprint and are behind of the comparison science of dactyloscopy. There, I said it again.

If you've never taken a good look at your own prints, you might want to try it now. The easiest way to do this is to get an inkpad, some fast-drying paint, or something like that, and then try to tap or roll your prints onto paper. My students and I have found it's not as easy as you might think—and it's certainly not as easy as they make it look on television! Just keep playing with the process until you get some clear images. For your analysis, a magnifying glass might help—especially if you're over 40 like I am. See if you can figure out the major classification designation for each of your fingers and then look for minutiae.

Let's get back to forensic investigations. Fingerprints are deposited in a couple of different ways. Patent prints are prints that can be seen with the naked eye. They might be made by friction skin touching blood, paint, ink, grease, mud, or any semi-liquid substance, and then transferring that material to a dry surface. Latent prints can't be visualized with the naked eye and, so, they have to be developed or enhanced with physical or chemical means. Plastic prints are the third type. They're fingerprint impressions on some type of soft material like chewed gum, uncured latex caulk, wet paint, or something like that.

Partial prints could be any type—patent, latent, or plastic—but don't reflect a full fingertip. As you might imagine, most crime-scene prints are partial prints—since fingertips are curved surfaces and most things we touch aren't flat, either.

Besides being deposited in different ways, fingerprints also need to be documented in different ways during crime-scene analysis. Patent prints can be brought back to the lab if they're seen on something that's easily transported, like a coffee mug, a photo frame, or even a vehicle. But when you think about it, many crime scenes would include prints on surfaces that are difficult or impossible to move—such as a plaster wall or a 25-foot-long bank countertop. There have been cases where an entire doorframe has been removed or a piece of drywall cut out if patent prints are visible on them. Most of the time, though, this type of evidence will be collected using only photography. In that sense, as we'll see with some other types of evidence, fingerprint evidence can be temporary and investigators may only get one shot at recovering it.

On the other hand, latent prints have to be treated in some way in order to make them visible. One way to find latent prints is by projecting an ultraviolet light source across a nonabsorbent surface where prints might be hidden. The residues in the fingerprints will reflect the UV light in a different way than the surfaces around them, so prints that can't be seen with the naked eye might appear.

Latent prints have to be developed—usually by dusting or through some type of chemical enhancement. Dusting uses a fine brush and a type of powder that will stick to the unseen fingerprint—making it visible and available to be photographed. Dusted prints are then captured by what's known as lifting— where an adhesive pad can be applied to the dusted print like cellophane tape, to lift it off the surface, making it able to be transported for analysis.

There are types of chemical enhancement can also be used to develop a latent print. There are lots of different methods, but one that most people have heard of is "superglue fuming." Superglue and related adhesives are made of volatile cyanoacrylate compounds. In the early '80s, some Japanese manufacturers who were trying to improve this type of glue accidentally discovered that its fumes would stick to latent prints on smooth surfaces, leaving a permanent, white residue of the print.

The thing is, this method is really only useful on objects that will physically fit into a chamber where the fumes can circulate—the chemical involved is toxic and the fumes have to be contained not only for safety, but also so they can condense on the latent print. There are cyanoacrylate "bombs" that can fume a closed car or any other kind of small space like that. Certain additions, like fluorescent dyes, can be applied over the fumed prints and then lasers or alternate light sources can be used to enhance the photography of those fumed prints.

Other chemical development methods have been discovered and used on latent prints—and each has its advantages and disadvantages. One of these is iodine fuming—but the prints developed by iodine are temporary, and so they have to be photographed immediately. Spraying a chemical called ninhydrin is a useful way to develop latent prints on paper and other kinds of porous surfaces. Regardless of how prints are developed, though, they still have to be captured in some way as evidence.

In order for fingerprints to be useful in forensic investigations, they have to be compared to other prints. So repositories of reference fingerprint records have been collected over time.

There are lots of reasons any one of us might have a fingerprint record on file—or at least have had one made at some point. I'm sure many of you have been fingerprinted, and you don't have to tell me the reason why! Fingerprint records are made at the time of arrests, of course, but people who work with large sums of money or other valuables—like at a bank—will have their prints recorded, too. Often these prints are held for what's known as exclusionary purposes, since if the bank was robbed, investigators would want to be able to figure out the fingerprints of people who have good reason to be there and exclude them.

Other times prints are taken for background checks. For instance, people who work with children will periodically have prints taken and compared to police records to help ensure the safety of vulnerable groups like kids.

Fingerprints can be and are still taken by simple inking methods on what's called a 10-print card. This standard presentation method collects a rolled print from each finger and both thumbs, and then a tapped print from the 4 fingers on each hand placed next to each other, and then each thumb.

But more recently, since about the early '90s, digital technologies have been developed. Computerized fingerprint scanners now allow a digit to be put on a digital pad that records the fingerprint. Along with this movement from ink to scanning there have been changes in how prints are stored and compared.

There are a couple reasons and ways prints can be compared: If a suspect is arrested, her prints can be run against prints in storage to see if she's linked to any other crimes. Or unknown prints from a crime scene can be compared to fingerprint records on file to try to identify whodunit.

In each of those cases, either a known or an unknown person is being compared to the records of known people. But sometimes, unknown prints from a crime scene are matched to other unknown prints from other crime scenes. In these cases, even though the identity of the perp isn't known, the crimes are linked by the prints found at 2 or more scenes. So, a series of breakings and enterings may be linked as being the handiwork of a single person—even if the police don't know yet who that criminal is.

Another important use of fingerprint comparisons is to help identify the unknown dead—but only if the body is in good enough shape to allow for fingerprinting. We'll talk more about that in a future presentation. Fingerprints are also used for security and access purposes, like when banks use fingerprints to verify identities. And some high-tech security measures involve scanning a person's prints like a key in a lock to open a door or log on to a computer system.

So, when comparing fingerprints, how do investigators come up with a match? For over a century, searching one print against others was done by hand. Considering 10 fingerprints per person, and the volume of stored reference prints, you can imagine how tough comparing prints used to be in the past. Particularly, once the value of fingerprints was known—after Bertillon and Galton's time—print records from criminals began to accumulate in police offices all over the world.

Because of how complex searching and comparing records became, a couple of fingerprint coding systems developed over time. All of these systems basically turn the arch, loop, and whorl patterns on a set of 10 digits into alphabetical and/or numerical codes that can be more quickly and easily compared. This coding has the capability to quickly let law enforcement eliminate huge batches of data without even having to look at the prints the codes represent. These codes can also be communicated across distances, and if they don't correlate, that's the end of the story. But if the codes do match, then the actual prints can be compared by hand, side-by-side, to look for minutiae and confirm whether the prints are a true match.

One coding system that evolved is the Henry system was developed by Sir Edward Henry, head of the Metropolitan Police of London during the early 1900s. The Henry system boils down an entire set of 10 prints into a single fraction that represents the even digits of both hands over the odd digits of both hands. A Henry code might look like 6 over 3, or 12 over 5, something like that. The overall possible universe of the entire Henry scheme is 1024 possible fractions—and while that's not an infinite number, it's still quite a lot. Some version of the original Henry system is still used in most European countries, and by the U.S. Federal Bureau of Investigation. Recent modifications to the Henry system used by the FBI create even more code classes that can narrow down a search even faster.

As computer technologies, like scanning, improved, then computerized matching of prints became possible. And in 1999, the U.S. FBI developed its Integrated Automated Fingerprint Identification System, known as IAFIS. There are amazing advantages to computerization: First, comparisons can be done against millions of prints in minutes. Second, a single print can be compared against all stored data—you don't need a full set or its Henry system fraction. And, local, state, and national databases are now linked for simultaneous searching—which is really crucial today because of transportation networks that literally allow a criminal to be here today and gone—sometimes across the world—by tomorrow.

I can't vouch for the complete accuracy of this story, since I wasn't there—but one of our local fingerprint guys told me about a group of high school students who visited the county sheriff's office on a field trip. The detective asked for a volunteer who would have his fingerprints scanned into the IAFIS system as a demo. One kid in the back of the group raised his hand, came up front, and put his finger on the data pad while the whole class watched. Within a couple of minutes, IAFIS was linking that fingerprint to a series of car burglaries in the local area. My cop-friend claims he simply looked at the kid and said, "Son, you're staying after school today!"

But, as powerful as it is, even IAFIS has its limitations. Fingerprint quality—particularly from scene prints—is often lacking, and IAFIS really only searches on ridge patterns, not minutiae. A law enforcement officer or forensic scientist still has to put an eye on any IAFIS system-suggested matches and give them a real critical examination.

So what constitutes an accurate match? Historically, there have been debates on the number of points of comparison required to confidently and legally declare a fingerprint match. Typically, individual jurisdictions set a minimum number of correlations that had to be there to justify a match—but that number varied from state to state and among different countries. It was usually somewhere between 10 and 16 points of agreement between prints. But, in 1990 the IAI—which is the International Association for Identification—decided there shouldn't be a mandatory minimum, but instead, each investigator should rely on his or her own expertise. Whether or not the comparison ultimately held up in court would be up to the judge and/or jury.

To wrap things up, let me add a few tidbits and close with a case. It's not only our fingers that leave prints; remember people's palms also have unique prints. And if a suspect is discovered for a given crime and palm prints are involved, that person can be made to produce palm prints for comparison. This is also true with the soles of the feet. So, if a crime scene maybe involved barefoot footprints in blood across a bathroom floor, a suspect could be forced to give footprints for comparison. Even the footprints taken of newborns in the hospital have occasionally been used in identification—especially in mass disaster settings like a plane crash—if someone has a footprint, rather than fingerprints, on file. Even lip prints—like from a coffee mug or a lipstick mark—have been used to link a person to a scene or object.

Can fingerprints from one person be recovered off the skin of another? Well, at least since the 1970s, attempts have been made to try to lift or image prints off human skin using different chemicals or alternate light sources or lasers. Fingerprints from an offender can sometimes be lifted from the skin surface of his or her victim—whether that victim is dead or alive—provided investigators act quickly enough.

A 2010 article in the Journal of Forensic Sciences summarized studies from police agencies in Europe over a 10-year period. Using 1000 corpses, researchers tested whether latent prints could be recovered on skin. Investigators were able to get ridge patterns 16% of the time using standard black powder dusting, and in a third of those cases, they could also get a DNA profile from the donor's fingerprint. So, even though it's been around a long time fingerprint science is not old news—and still holds new potential in solving crimes, sometimes even after a long time has elapsed.

Here's an example. In 1994, a 48-year-old man started dating a lady who was recently separated from her husband. One night when the new couple was eating dinner, the doorbell rang and the man got up to answer it. Now, his girlfriend couldn't see the doorway from where she was sitting, but she could see and hear her boyfriend. As he answered the door, she heard him muttering something, and then—he turned and looked right at her—at about the same time she heard 4 gunshots and then saw him collapse. Lots of people in the apartment complex heard the shots, but nobody saw the shooter.

During their search, police found 4 shell casings in the hallway outside the dead man's door. They examined the casings for prints, but even after superglue fuming and fluorescent powder, they couldn't get any latent prints off the shell casings to try to figure out who had loaded the gun—and, then by assumption, who likely shot it. So, in 2009—which was 14 years later— the investigators decided to take a second look at the case. They had just read about a study that said if you heat brass to 700 degrees Fahrenheit over an open flame it might cause the natural body salts in a fingerprint to develop into a surface corrosion image.

So, in 2009, they heated the shell casings from the 1994 homicide and when the superglue residue disintegrated they could see some faint ridges on one of the casings. From that, they developed a strong lead to a guy who not only owned a 9-millimeter handgun at the time, but was even known to wipe the bullets on his shirt before loading them. That might explain why they couldn't find prints back in 1994 and why only a few remnants of a print pattern were found even using this new technique.

We'll talk more about fingerprints in other lectures, but I hope this overview has given you a grip (fingerprints ... grip ... get it?) on an old, but really essential crime fighting tool.

Telltale Marks—Tools, Guns, and Ammunition
Lecture 4

In forensic science, a toolmark is some type of evidence—a cut, gouge, abrasion, or impression—that is left by a tool on something it contacts. Much of the science of firearms identification is actually a subcategory of toolmark analysis because a gun is really a tool that leaves its marks on the bullet and the bullet's cartridge case every time it fires a round. Forensic toolmark examination relies mainly on the overall shape of a tool and the combination of manufacturing and use defects on it.

Toolmark Basics

- Toolmarks usually take the form of impression and striated marks on a softer surface that the tool was used on. Locard's principle states that tools can also cause a physical exchange of materials between the 2 surfaces that come in contact. Toolmarks and any transferred trace evidence involved can be obvious or microscopic—depending on the tool, substrate, and actions involved during the exchange between the tool and its target.

- When a toolmark is large enough to be seen with the unaided eye, it usually offers some class characteristics, such as the general shape or size of the tool, but a microscopic examination of a toolmark gives much more detail and might even allow a suspected match to be developed between a specific tool and the object it was used on.

- No 2 tools are completely identical—not even those made by the same manufacturer in the same batch. Likewise, no 2 toolmarks are completely identical—not even those from the same tool used repeatedly during a single crime. The repeated use of a single tool involves different angles, and different amounts of force are applied each time.

- The tool changes the surface of what it's used against and leaves marks behind, but the tool itself can also be altered during the course of the crime in both obvious and microscopic ways.

Tools and Crime Scenes
- The tools that are found by investigators at crime scenes are usually easy to transport to the crime lab, but the surfaces the toolmarks are on may or may not be easily transported. Toolmark scene documentation, as with all crime scenes, involves careful photography with a measuring scale in place.

- If the situation warrants—as in the case of evidence that isn't easily transported—investigators can attempt to make a highly detailed cast of the toolmark using a casting material, such as liquid silicone or dental plaster, at the scene. Having only a cast to work from, however, can dilute the evidence and reduce the ability to make a definitive association with a suspect tool, if it is found.

- The packaging and transportation of evidence is critical, too. The tool and whatever it was used on have to be packaged separately to prevent any further interaction—and because a tool can hold important trace evidence such as microscopic chips of paint, fiber evidence, or even blood and other body tissues.

- The crime scene investigator should never try to fit the suspected tool back into the toolmark—not at the scene or in the lab—because doing so could alter the mark and compromise the investigation. Instead, at the lab, toolmark experts can use a suspected tool to make test markings for comparison, which allows the direct comparison between known and unknown toolmarks.

- It's not easy for toolmark examiners in a laboratory to exactly duplicate a toolmark left at a crime scene, but the use of a soft material, such as lead, allows an impression to be made of the edge of a recovered tool without damaging it or creating additional use or wear.

- Investigators can also use a piece of the original substrate to try to create a duplicate of the toolmark. In other words, they might try to replicate the toolmark by not only using the suspected tool, but also by using a piece of the same surface from the crime scene.

- Just as in fingerprint analysis, when investigators find a sufficient number of similarities between the test markings and the evidentiary marks from the crime scene, an association can be made. Careful documentation of the lab-created toolmarks and the ones taken from the crime scene are necessary—in case they are needed in court.

Firearms Examination

- When a projectile travels through the barrel of a gun, microscopic marks called striae are created on the bullet and on its cartridge casing; therefore, each bullet is changed and etched as it is fired—much like the way the machining of a tool creates unique microscopic properties during manufacturing.

- Firearms examination and the science of ballistics are not the same. Ballistics is a subdivision of physics that explains the way an object travels—whether it's a baseball or a bullet.

- In general, there are 5 main groups of firearms and countless different types of ammunition.

    o Pistols, which are sometimes called handguns, are subclassified as either revolvers or self-loading pistols.

    o Rifles are similar to pistols but have a longer barrel and are meant to be used with 2 hands.

    o Machine guns are automatic weapons that are fed ammunition from either a magazine (clip) or a belt.

    o Submachine guns are also fully automatic but can be handheld.

- o Shotguns are very different because they don't fire bullets; instead, they fire pellets, buckshot, or slugs.

- Firearms investigators may need to document the general condition of a recovered weapon, including checking to see if it is even capable of being fired, if it has been made illegal by modifications, or if something was wrong with a firearm that might have caused it to discharge accidentally.

The cartridge casings of self-loading pistols are ejected from the chamber automatically as each bullet is fired from the barrel.

- Firearms examiners may also try to restore the serial number of a weapon—or any object that might have a serial number stamped into its metal—because criminals often try to file the serial number off of a stolen gun. However, even if the serial number seems obliterated, the process that created the serial number leaves traces in the form of permanent stress marks in the metal that can be restored.

- A large focus of firearms examination is whether a particular weapon fired a certain round of ammunition that was recovered. This is when investigators try to match bullets recovered from a crime scene or victim—or casings that were fired—to figure out whether they came from a weapon in question.

The Makings and Workings of Firearms
- Surface irregularities produced during the manufacturing process can make it possible for a forensic investigator to tie a bullet to a particular gun—to the exclusion of all others.

- The barrel of a gun is initially produced by hollowing out a solid metal bar, which is done by a drill that leaves individual random marks on the inside of the barrel. In addition, the inner surface of a gun barrel is imprinted with a series of spiral grooves through a manufacturing process called rifling.

- Inside the barrel of a gun, the raised regions resulting from the rifling process are known as lands, and the valleys are known as grooves.

- When used as a verb, the term "rifling" means the spin that's put on a flying object—whether on a football or a bullet—by encouraging the twist with a series of raised objects. In the case of a gun, the rifling ridges inside the barrel produce the spin on a bullet, which helps the bullet stay on a true trajectory and maintain its velocity.

- The internal diameter of a firearm barrel is known as the gun's caliber—as measured between the lands. Caliber is usually expressed in either hundredths of an inch or in millimeters.

- Shotguns are not measured in the same way. Their barrel diameter is called gauge, which is the measure of the number of lead pellets of the diameter of the barrel that together would weigh 1 pound.

- When a bullet is fired, the barrel's lands and grooves make corresponding marks on the surface of the bullet as it is spiraled down the length of the barrel. The raised lands in the gun barrel etch matching grooves on the bullet, and the depressed grooves in the barrel create raised lands on the bullet.

- Firearms manufacturers choose specific rifling processes to meet their weapons' specifications, so by knowing the specifics of different gun manufacturers, a firearms examiner might be easily able to tell the class characteristics on a bullet as having been fired from a certain brand of gun—but class characteristics aren't unique to a specific weapon.

- Despite large-scale manufacturing operations, random minute markings produced mostly by drilling make the inside of one gun barrel different from another. These microscopic manufacturing imperfections result in individual characteristics that can tie a specific bullet to a specific gun.

- In order to match a bullet or cartridge case from a crime scene to a given gun, a firearms expert has to test fire the gun, using the same type of ammo, and then compare the bullet fired at the crime lab to the bullet from the scene. The expert has to fire the gun into something that will trap the bullet without damaging it.

Guns, Ammunition, Propellants, and Primers

- Bullets and shotgun pellets can be found at crime scenes—perhaps lodged in a victim, a wall, or a piece of furniture. Just as with toolmarks, if the bullet is lodged in something or someone that can be transported to the forensic lab or morgue, that's always the approach taken.

- Bullets, cartridge cases, cartridges, and guns must all be handled and documented very carefully to preserve any trace evidence that might be present. This could include fingerprints of the victim or shooter as well as blood or tissue that might be on the gun or in its barrel.

- The propellants and primers that are used in firearms are important in forensics because they constitute gunshot residue (GSR), which exits the barrel as a mixture of the partially burned and unburned powder, soot, lead, and lead vapors from the ammunition.

- Because the residue disperses in a geometric pattern as it leaves the barrel, it can help identify the distance between a weapon and its target. The primer can also leave lead, barium, and antimony residue on things or people that are within close proximity and can aid in forensic investigations.

- In the early 1990s, the Bureau of Alcohol, Tobacco, Firearms, and Explosives in the United States developed the Integrated Ballistics Identification System, which allows microscopic images of bullet land and groove rifling impressions to be compared across the Internet.

- By the late 1990s, this system was linked with one developed by the U.S. Federal Bureau of Investigation to examine firing pin and primer impressions on spent cartridge casings. These 2 tools have revolutionized the work of firearms examiners and have allowed the national networking of investigations—in much the same way that IAFIS revolutionized the fingerprinting process.

Suggested Reading

Heard, *Handbook of Firearms and Ballistics*.

Questions to Consider

1. Are toolmarks an example of class or individuating evidence?

2. How is toolmark evidence preserved, especially if it's on something that is not easily transported?

3. About how many gun-related crimes occur in the United States each year?

4. What are some specific reasons that a firearms expert might need to examine a gun?

Telltale Marks—Tools, Guns, and Ammunition
Lecture 4—Transcript

In forensic science, a toolmark is just what it sounds like: It's some type of evidence—maybe a cut, gouge, abrasion, or any impression that's left by a tool on something it contacts. You might not realize it at first, but much of the science of firearms identification is really a subcategory of tool-mark analysis; because a gun is really a tool and a gun leaves its mark on the bullet and the bullet's cartridge case every time it fires a round.

One of my friends, who is actually a former student of mine, is now the toolmark and firearms examiner at our local crime lab. He told me that firearm cartridge case examinations and comparisons make up about 70% of his regular workload. So we'll start with a general discussion of tool-mark basics, but then talk a lot more about guns and ammunition.

I'll bet you all have tools somewhere in your house—some are probably new and hardly ever used, and others might be old and used often. I actually have some that are very old but seldom used, since I have a lot of my dad's old tools, but I'm usually too busy or not skilled enough fix a lot of things around my house. And we all have things that we might use as tools that aren't official tools, like when you use a butter knife as a screwdriver. Necessity is the mother of invention, and sometimes that's the case at a crime scene, too.

What we can't see with the naked eye about our tools, and even household objects we could use as tools, is that the original surface of any manufactured tool contains random microscopic irregularities and imperfections that are created by slight variations in the manufacturing process. What we can sometimes see is that wear patterns develop over time on a tool's surface when it's used—like that old Phillip's head screwdriver that hardly has any grab left to it.

So, forensic tool-mark examination relies mainly on the overall shape of a tool, and the combination of manufacturing and use defects that are on it. These features can allow a tool to be identified as to its class by the marks it leaves. And remember class is a general category—in this case like screwdriver, pliers, wire cutter, hammer, all those are examples of classes. But toolmarks can also sometimes reveal pretty unique characteristics about a specific tool as well.

The nature of the tool—what it's made of, how it was made, and its shape—determines the type of evidence it will or it won't leave. And any mark left by a tool is also affected by the nature of the surface that the tool struck or rubbed against. So, these toolmarks usually take the form of impression and striation marks on a softer surface that the tool was used on.

And using Locard's principle, we know that tools can also cause a physical exchange of materials between the 2 surfaces that come in contact. For example, paint could chip off of a locker and be transferred to the end of a screwdriver that was used to pry it open. Or, if a softer material is used as a tool, like piece of wood, it might leave fragments on the thing it was used against. These toolmarks and any transferred trace evidence involved can be obvious or microscopic, depending on the tool, the substrate, and the actions involved during the exchange between the tool and its target.

When a toolmark is big enough to see with the naked eye, it usually gives some class characteristics, like the general shape or size of the tool. So, a round impression mark might lead an investigator to think a hammer was involved, or a squared-off "bite" out of some material might suggest the tip of needle-nose pliers; but unless the tool has some obvious defect that's easily seen, knowing a hammer or needle-nose pliers were involved might be as far is the assumptions can go without more testing.

A microscopic examination of a toolmark, though, gives way more detail and might even allow a suspected match between a specific tool and the thing it was used on. Minute random irregularities on a screwdriver, a wire cutter, a scraper, a crowbar, a shovel, or any other tool with what we can call a "use edge" can often be matched by investigators to evidence left at the scene of a crime.

So we've learned that no 2 tools are completely identical, not even those made by the same manufacturer in the same batch; but likewise, no 2 toolmarks are completely identical—even those from the same tool used repeatedly during a single crime. One reason is that the repeated use of a single tool involves different angles, and different amounts of force are applied each time. We know that from our own practical experience—if you can't pry the lid off an old paint can, you're keep going at it from different angles and using different techniques and different pressures until you open it.

And if the tool being used has a complicated shape or multi-purpose surfaces, the patterns get even more complicated. I've seen this first-hand in toolmarks on a skull in a horrendous case where a woman was bludgeoned to death with a claw hammer. You can imagine how different the marks from the head of the hammer looked from those from that its claw end made, since both were used interchangeably in the struggle.

So the tool changes the surface of what it's used against and leaves marks behind. But the tool itself can also be altered during the course of the crime. For example, if a pry bar is used to break into a convenience store, the interaction between the metal of the tool and the doorway itself can change the surface of the pry bar in both obvious and microscopic ways—especially if both are made out of hard surfaces. And if the first try is not successful, the second and third attempts to jimmy the door might continue to alter the surface of the pry bar, making not only each toolmark different, but also changing the surface of the tool in a very short period of time.

So, the surface of a single tool changes over its lifetime. Now, for investigators, this is both a blessing and a curse: Use/wear creates individualizing characteristics on a tool, but unless that tool is found immediately after the crime, or is kept in storage and not used again, or is much harder than the thing it was used on, its surface could be different when it is ultimately discovered than when it was used to commit a crime.

So, who finds and recovers these toolmarks at a scene, and how are they analyzed? Well, let's say investigators find tools and toolmarks at a burglary scene—and break-ins are a big part of tool-mark analysis—anything from trying to break into a safe, to prying open a window frame, or jimmying a doorway. Well, the tools themselves are usually easy to get back to the crime lab, if the perpetrators are stupid enough to leave them behind—and sometimes you just get lucky and they are—but the surfaces the toolmarks are on may or may not be easily transported.

If wire cutters are used to disable a security system, the cut section of wire can simply be cut again—making sure investigators know which end was their cut—and then take back to the lab for a microscopic examination of any toolmarks on it—OK, that's an easy one. Now here's a hard one: If criminals use a crowbar to break into the 16' × 30' door of a large drive-in storage locker, investigators are either going to have to completely document the door while at the storage facility, or somehow or another remove the evidence and get it back to the lab.

The toolmark scene documentation, as with all crime scenes, involves a lot of careful photography with a measuring scale in place. And if the situation warrants—like in the case of evidence that can't be easily transported—the investigators will attempt to make a really detailed cast of the toolmark using a casting material like liquid silicone or dental plaster right there at the scene.

Having only a cast to work from, though, can dilute the evidence and reduce the ability to make a definitive association with a suspect tool, if it's found. Sometimes just the affected portion of a window frame or doorjamb can be cut away and then taken to the crime lab for examination.

The packaging of evidence is critical, too; the tool and whatever it was used on have to be packaged separately to prevent them from banging into each other and causing further interactions between the 2. And because a tool can hold important trace evidence like microscopic chips of paint, fiber evidence, or even blood and other body tissues; only careful packaging and transport of that kind of evidence will preserve it for lab analysis.

Another thing: The crime-scene investigator should never try to fit the suspected tool back into the toolmark—not at the scene and not in the lab. To do that could alter the mark and compromise the investigation. So how do they figure out if there's a match between a toolmark and a tool that might have been used to make it? At the lab, tool-mark experts can use a suspected tool to make test markings for comparison, which allows the direct comparison between known and unknown toolmarks.

When you consider all the possible angles and pressures possible when a tool is used, it's not easy for tool-mark examiners to exactly duplicate a toolmark left at a crime scene in their lab. The use of a soft material in the lab, like lead, will allow an impression to be made of the edge of a recovered tool without damaging it or creating any additional use wear.

After doing microscopic exams, casting, and testing the suspected tool on lead in the lab, investigators can also use a piece of the original substrate to try to duplicate the toolmark. In other words, they might try to replicate the toolmark by not only using the suspect tool, but using a piece of the same exact surface from the crime scene.

Just like in fingerprint analysis, when investigators find a sufficient number of similarities between the test markings and the evidentiary marks from the crime scene, an association can be made. Careful documentation of the lab-created toolmarks and the ones taken from the crime scene are necessary in case they will be needed in court. They use comparison microscopes that are capable of taking side-by-side photographs during their examinations to compare known and unknown markings.

Now let's turn our attention to firearms—which like I said before, are also a form of tools. We're covering firearms with toolmarks for a couple of reasons: First off, when a projectile travels through the barrel of a gun, microscopic marks called striae are created on the bullet and its cartridge casing; so, each bullet is changed and etched as it gets fired, much like the way the machining of a tool creates unique microscopic properties during manufacturing. Also, toolmarks, firearms, bullets, and cartridge cases are analyzed in similar ways and usually by the same experts in a crime lab.

Before we really dive into this topic, though, I need to mention that firearms examination and the science known as ballistics are not the same thing. Ballistics is really a subdivision of physics that explains the way any object travels, whether it's a baseball or a glider. In forensics, the projectiles in motion we're interested in are usually shotgun pellets or bullets.

But first, let take a look at how firearms are classified. Now, some of you may know a lot more about this than others, but there are generally 5 main groups of firearms and almost countless different types of ammunition. So let's take at a look at the types of guns one at a time.

Pistols, which are sometimes called handguns, are sub-classified as either revolvers or self-loading pistols. Even if you've never seen these types of guns in person, you'd recognize them just from Hollywood movies and the television shows that you've seen. Revolvers are the types of handguns that hold individual live rounds in a revolving cylinder; each live round is a single bullet to be fired, plus the cartridge case that holds that bullet. As the revolving cylinder turns, individual rounds are hit with a firing pin and sent down the barrel. Once a bullet is fired, its cartridge case is left behind in the cylinder and has to be removed by hand. Self-loading pistols are those handguns that have a magazine or clip that gets inserted into the pistol and contains a number of cartridges that are spring-loaded from a magazine into the firing chamber. Self-loading pistols are also self-emptying in the sense that their cartridge casings are ejected from the chamber automatically as each bullet gets fired from the barrel.

Rifles are the second major class of firearms; these are like pistols but they have a longer barrel and are meant to be used with 2 hands. There are all kinds of rifles, like single shot and double shot, which refers to whether they have one or 2 barrels. Or semiautomatic and automatic rifles, which has to do with the way the ammo is fed into them and how the cartridges get ejected.

Machine guns are the third classification—and we've all seen them on TV or in movies. They are automatic weapons that are fed ammunition from either a magazine or a belt. Because they have such powerful recoil and get super hot, real machine guns have to be mounted on some type of stand.

Submachine guns are the next major group of firearms; they're also fully automatic but they can be handheld.

Shotguns are the last of the 5 major classes of firearms. Shotguns are significantly different because they don't fire bullets—instead they fire pellets, buckshot, or slugs. A shotgun shell is typically designed as a plastic cartridge that contains a group of small pellets, or larger buckshot, and those all get fired at once. A slug is a single projectile usually made of a soft metal like lead that gets loaded into a shot shell.

My friend, the firearms examiner, says the guns he most frequently sees in the lab are Derringers (which are the smallest pocket-type pistols, easy to hide), revolvers, semi-automatic pistols, submachine guns, single-shot and semi-automatic shotguns, and single-shot semi-automatic rifles, and machine guns too.

So what do firearms investigators look for in guns? Well, they may need to document a gun's general condition. They may have to check to see if a recovered weapon is even capable of being fired, or if a gun's been made illegal by modifications, or if something was wrong with a firearm that might have caused it to discharge accidentally.

Firearms examiners may also have to try to restore the serial number of a weapon—or, really, any object that might have a serial number stamped into its metal—since criminals are known to try to file the serial number off of a stolen gun. What the bad guys don't realize, though, is even after the serial number might be obliterated to the eye—by filing it flat—the process that created the serial number leaves traces. That's because the original stamping in the manufacturing process leaves permanent stress marks in the metal below where the serial number was placed.

To recover a serial number, a firearms and tool-mark expert can sand the surface metal in the area where the serial number has been filed away, and they'll sand that until it's very smooth. Then they treat the area with a caustic solution, which will differentially begin to dissolve the underlying metal that was strained and softened by the stamping process. As the metal that was directly under each digit of the serial number dissolves, the digits will briefly appear in the metal beneath where it was once clearly stamped. A forensic scientist only gets one shot at this, though, because as the chemical continues to work, all of the surrounding metal will also start to degrade; so they have to take a photograph really quickly before that restored serial number disappears again forever.

A big focus of firearms examination is whether a particular weapon fired a certain round of ammunition that was recovered. This is when investigators try to match bullets recovered from a crime scene or from a victim's body, or casings that have been fired, to figure out whether they came from a weapon in question. And to understand this, we first need to focus a little bit on how firearms are made and how they work.

Surface irregularities produced during manufacturing processes can make it possible for a forensic investigator to tie a bullet to a particular gun, to the exclusion of all others. The barrel of a gun is initially produced by hollowing out a solid metal bar; this is done by a drill that leaves random, individual toolmarks on the inside of the barrel. But in addition to that, the inner surface of a gun barrel is imprinted with a series of spiral grooves in a manufacturing process they call "rifling." Inside the barrel of a gun the raised regions resulting from the rifling process are known as lands, and the valleys are known as grooves.

When used as a verb, the term "rifling" means the spin that's put on a flying object, whether on a football or a bullet, by encouraging the twist with a series of raised objects. When a quarterback throws a football, his arm, wrist, and fingers become the rifling mechanism that puts spin to the ball as it leaves his hand. In the case of a gun, the rifling ridges inside the barrel produce the spin on a bullet. Just like a rapidly thrown football, a spinning bullet won't tumble end-over-end as it flies. So rifling helps the bullet stay on a true trajectory and helps maintain its velocity.

The internal diameter of a firearm barrel is known as the gun's caliber. That's measured between the lands—which, remember, are the raised regions inside the barrel. Caliber is usually expressed in either hundredths of an inch or in millimeters. When you hear a caliber like 22 or 38, that's actually 0.22 and 0.38 because that's in tenths of an inch. Obviously a 9 mm is measured in millimeters, duh. Actually, in practice, caliber is only an approximation of the barrel's diameter, because the exact measurement depends on how the lands and grooves oppose each other, so guns of the same caliber can vary slightly in the actual bore diameter inside the barrel.

Shotguns are not measured in the same way; their barrel diameter is called gauge. Gauge is kind of weird to me: It's the measure of the number of lead pellets of the diameter of the barrel that together would weigh a pound. So, twenty 20-gauge pellet balls would weigh a pound, and the diameter of a 20-guage shotgun would be the same diameter as one of those 20-gauge lead balls. Since there'd be twelve 12-gauge balls in a pound, as the number gets lower, the diameter of the barrel of a shotgun actually gets larger.

Back to rifling. Historically, before commercial mass production of weapons, which occurred around 1940, barrels were rifled manually using a big hook made of steel that cut maybe one or 2 grooves at a time, but today's modern manufacturing uses machining methods that cut all of a barrel's grooves and leaves behind all of its lands at the same time.

And lands and grooves aren't just found in a gun barrel. When a bullet is fired, the barrel's lands and grooves make corresponding marks on the surface of the bullet as it spirals down the length of the barrel. The raised lands in the gun barrel etch matching grooves on the bullet, and the depressed grooves in the barrel create raised lands on the bullet. So the barrel and bullet become like negatives of each other.

The beauty of this is that firearms manufacturers choose specific rifling processes to meet their weapon's specifications. So, for instance, all 32 caliber Smith & Wesson revolvers have 5 lands and 5 grooves that twist to the right, while another 32 caliber handgun from a different manufacturer might have a different number of lands and grooves and maybe a left-sided twist.

By knowing the specifics of different gun manufacturers, a firearms examiner might be easily able to tell the class characteristics on a bullet as having been fired from a certain brand of gun. But, by definition, class characteristics aren't unique to one specific weapon. So what lets investigators match a bullet to a gun then?

Well, despite large-scale manufacturing operations, minute random markings produced mostly by drilling will make the inside of one gun barrel different from another. So, when a bullet travels down the barrel of a gun, in addition to the major features of lands and grooves made by each other, the microscopic manufacturing imperfections also get transferred to the bullet. These are the money, because they result in individual characteristics that can tie a specific bullet to a specific gun.

In order to match a bullet or a cartridge case from a crime scene to a given gun, a firearms expert has to test fire the gun, using the same type of ammo. Then, compare the bullet fired at the crime lab to the bullet from the scene. They have to fire the gun into something that will trap the bullet, without damaging it; our lab has this big tank of water that's specifically designed for test-firing weapons.

Now I've been dancing around the topic of ammunition, so let's add a little detail there. Bullets used to be made of pure lead, but advances in firearms technology meant that ammunition had to change, too. One thing that happened over time was a change in propellants that made the journey down the barrel of a gun a lot hotter. Because lead is such a soft material, the extreme heat would cause it to build up inside the barrel, so eventually the elements antimony and tin were added to lead in bullets.

Shotgun shells still often hold lots of small pellets of lead, but today's modern bullet is typically a lump of lead that has a collar around its base known as a jacket. Jacketed bullets have coverings like copper, brass, or steel that keep the lead from fouling the barrel and keep the bullet less prone to deforming. Because the jacket is much harder and covers the surface of the bullet, fully jacketed bullets typically pick up more consistent striated detail as they travel over the lands and grooves inside the length of a gun barrel. There are also lots of types of cartridge cases, and some have markings that designate the gun caliber and/or the manufacturer. Cartridge cases can carry additional evidence, like impressions from a gun's firing pin, which are tiny toolmarks in themselves.

Bullets and shotgun pellets can be found at crime scenes—maybe lodged in a victim, a wall, or a piece of furniture. Just like with toolmarks, if the bullet is lodged in something or someone that can be moved back to the forensic lab or the morgue, that's always the approach they take; even if this means taking out the section of the ceiling that contains a spent round. If the bullet is removed at the scene, investigators have to take great care to prevent any surface damage that might damage the microscopic barrel markings on the bullet.

Bullets, cartridge cases, cartridges, and guns have to be handled and documented really carefully to preserve any trace evidence that might be present. This could include fingerprints of the victim or the shooter, as we saw in the last lecture, as well as blood or tissue that might be on the gun or in its barrel. Trace evidence could even include lint picked up from the gun being tucked in the waistband of a pair of pants.

Lastly, we should also talk about the types of propellants that are used in guns or ammunition: Saltpeter, which is the common name for potassium nitrate, is the basic ingredient for the type of gunpowder known as black powder, which was invented around the 9th or 10th century by the Chinese. But black powder fell out of use because it's really corrosive to a firearm and can also easily give away the shooter's location. So, in the late 19th century, smokeless powder was invented using combinations of nitrocellulose and nitroglycerin.

By the middle of the 1800s, live rounds were being made with a chemical called mercury fulminate in the cartridge head; this small amount of explosive will detonate when struck, shocked, or sparked. Today's modern cartridges contain a small container of what's called primer in the middle of the cartridge; a firing pin on the gun's hammer strikes the primer, detonates it, and ignites the propellant.

The propellants and primers used in firearms are important in forensics because they constitute what's called gunshot residue, often just called GSR. GSR exits the barrel as a mix of the partially burned and unburned powder, soot, lead, and lead vapors, all from the ammunition.

Because the residue disperses in a geometric pattern as it leaves the barrel, it can help identify the distance between a weapon and its target; but this is only reliable for distances of less than around 36 inches. The primer can also leave lead, barium, and antimony residue on things or people that are within close proximity or downwind, and that can aid in forensic investigations.

In the early '90s, the Bureau of Alcohol, Tobacco, Firearms, and Explosives in the United States developed something called the Integrated Ballistics Identification System that allows microscopic images of bullet land and groove rifling impressions to be compared across the Internet. By the late '90s, this system was linked with one developed by the U.S. Federal Bureau of Investigation to examine firing pin and primer impressions on spent cartridge casings. These 2 tools have revolutionized the work of firearms examiners and allowed the national networking of investigations, in much the same way as IAFIS did for fingerprints.

These databases led to a suggested change in the firearms industry that's known as ballistic fingerprinting. In this program, all new weapons would be test fired after manufacturing and a cartridge case recovered in order to document surface markings like firing pin impressions. This information would be stored in a database for future comparisons, using automated comparison systems.

Unfortunately, what sounded like a perfect plan has not yielded the best results. That's partly because guns purchased legally too often wind up stolen and/or sold illegally. And those are the guns most often used to commit crimes. The U.S. Bureau of Alcohol, Tobacco, Firearms, and Explosives estimated that over 80,000 firearms were sold illegally in the United States in 2002 alone. So, ballistic fingerprinting has never really taken off. Not only because it's really difficult to reconstruct the chain of hands that handle a gun after it leaves the factory, but also because many criminals discard the firearm after they commit a crime. In addition, cheaply made guns can change over time as they are fired. And guns can become fouled by gunshot residue and can rust over time.

These things can combine to change or mask the original individual characteristics documented at the factory. For these and other reasons, toolmark and firearms comparisons can't simply be automated. They will always require the eye for detail and the critical thinking capabilities of skilled forensic scientists.

Good Impressions—Shoes, Tires, and Skin
Lecture 5

In addition to fingerprints, toolmarks, and bullets, shoe prints, tire marks, and fabric impressions also constitute impression evidence and can be used in forensic investigations. Impression evidence found at crime scenes can be any kind of pattern made by—or found in—soil, dust, snow, blood, wet paint, and many other media. Just as with other kinds of evidence, impressions made by shoe prints and tire treads show general features that give class information, including the manufacturer, size, and brand. Furthermore, as with tools and firearms, shoes and tires also gain individuating characteristics as they're used and worn over time.

Impression Evidence

- Like many other types of analyses, looking at impression evidence—such as shoe prints, tire marks, and fabric impressions—typically involves comparing an unknown pattern from a crime scene with a known exemplar shoe print or tire track that is intentionally taken off a suspect's person, footwear, or vehicle.

- This kind of impression work can also involve getting exclusionary shoe prints or tire tracks from people or cars that are not related to the criminal act but were at the scene for a legitimate reason.

- Not only might shoe prints or tire tracks be easier to locate than fingerprints or microscopic striae that may be left on tools or bullets at a crime scene, but there are probably many more footprints left behind at a crime scene than fingerprints, toolmarks, or bullets because feet often make more contact with surfaces in an environment than hands do.

- However, shoes can be thrown away after a crime is committed whereas fingerprints don't change, and it's generally easier to wipe off your fingerprints than to get rid of shoe prints—but a backtracking burglar could do either.

General Forensic Photography Techniques

- One of the greatest problems that investigators might run into with impression evidence is preserving and documenting the scene. Typically, shoe prints and tire tracks have to be carefully photographed by a competent crime-scene photographer because if the material the print or track is on can't be moved—or if the substrate is temporary, such as snow—then the photographs might be the only source for future comparisons or at trial.

- Over the past decade, crime-scene photography has moved from black-and-white Polaroid instant cameras to state-of-the-art digital technology.

- There are a handful of basic principles of forensic photography that are common to most scenes.

    - A forensic photographer has to keep a careful log that tracks the pictures taken at a crime scene—including when, where, and by whom.

    - Usually, images start with broad overviews to give perspective and show relationships between things at the scene. Then, they progress to medium shots that are taken from about 6 feet away. Close-up shots—from about 1 foot or less away—are taken where detailed views are needed.

    - Photographs have to include a measuring scale so that the exact size of things can be shown. It's fairly common to take a duplicate picture without the scale just to show things as they were before the scale was there. Only with an accurate scale can things in photos be compared later, with any confidence, to other images or objects.

    - Photographs should be taken from a few different angles and use both direct and side lighting to maximize detail, which is particularly important with impression evidence. In addition, side lighting can show more of the 3-dimensionality of evidence.

o   Images should be taken in a 360° pattern from a fixed point using a wide-angle lens and tripod so that pictures can be overlapped to show the entire scene in every direction.

o   Special attention needs to be given to entrance and exit routes in the beginning because it might be difficult to preserve those areas and still get full access to the site. In addition, at an indoor crime scene, any adjacent rooms or spaces should be photographed because they could be routes the perpetrator used to get to the scene.

o   Any physical evidence—including a body—needs to have full photo documentation before it's moved, and whoever discovered the crime scene or the body has to be questioned to see if he or she moved anything in his or her effort to figure out what was going on.

o   The general rule of thumb—especially now that photography has gone digital—is that you can never have too many pictures of a scene or the evidence in it, so take as many as possible.

o   Digital photography and videophotography have become standard ways of documenting crime scenes, but videotaping shouldn't replace still photography. Forensics needs the resolution that only still images can provide.

Lifting and Casting Evidence

• Sometimes, there's no way evidence can be transported to the lab from the crime scene, but there are some cases where shoe print or tire-track evidence is portable.

- When shoe prints or tire tracks can't be moved, after the photographer is finished, investigators might try lifting or casting 3-D evidence, and they often get only one chance to correctly do so.

- If an impression is made in a thin layer of dust or dirt, investigators can try an adhesive lifting material and put it over all or part of the impression—just as a fingerprint can be lifted—but electrostatic lifting technology can also be used.

It is extremely difficult to access a crime scene on foot without disturbing latent footprints.

- When a footprint or tire track is not on a flat, dusty surface, lifting it with an adhesive or by an electrostatic process doesn't work. When there's a lot of 3-dimensionality to an impression and it can't be moved back to the lab, casting is the best way to preserve the evidence.

- Dental stone—the gypsum material dentists use to make molds of people's teeth—is the preferred casting material. Dental stone gives better detail and makes more durable casts than most other options.

- For very fragile or transient prints, there are some commercially available waxy sprays that seal footprints or tire tracks when they occur in a substrate like snow, and then the sealed impression can be casted.

- Casting methods mostly involve pouring the casting material over the 3-D surface of the impression and letting it harden. After the cast is dry, investigators do a detailed examination of it. If it is a good impression, it should be as close to a copy of the original surface as possible.

- When you step in something like soft mud, you make a negative impression of the sole of your shoe in the mud—much like a mirror reversal. However, if you cast your footprint, the cast makes a negative of the original negative, forming a positive image that matches—not mirrors—your shoe.

- If impression evidence is located on a steep incline, the casting material is going to follow gravity, so some engineering might be necessary—such as building a wooden frame around the footprint and then filling the box with casting material. In addition, removing any debris from the impression without disturbing the evidence can be an obstacle that complicates the casting process.

Comparing Impression Evidence
- There are 3 comparison possibilities to consider.

  o First, evidence is recovered from a crime scene, but a plausible suspect who might have similar evidence to match it is never found.

  o Secondly, an investigation might lead to a good suspect in a case, but that person either didn't leave much recoverable evidence or the right kind of evidence at the scene.

  o The third comparison possibility is the backbone of forensic investigation: Evidence is found at a crime scene, and later, a suspected person, tool, weapon, or shoe is discovered to have the identical properties of the crime-scene evidence.

- Like other kinds of forensic comparisons, investigators like to use test impressions to make quality comparisons between an impression from an unknown shoe or tire associated with a crime and a comparable object they want to compare to it.

- One of the ways that shoe prints and tire marks are similar to guns and ammunition—but are different from fingerprints—is that shoes and tires come in standard sizes and are made by manufacturers that work toward quality control and brand identity in how they make their products.

- The style and size of a shoe or a tire can give class characteristics. Once investigators know the brand, the measurements of and between the small jagged lines on the bottom of a shoe can let investigators figure out its size. Then, investigators might be able to contact the manufacturer to tell exactly when and where that type of shoe was produced.

- However, even if the suspect has the exact same kind of shoe in his or her closet, the style and size alone aren't individuating evidence. In other words, that similarity doesn't usually put the suspect at the scene.

- Just as with tools and guns, a shoe develops unique use characteristics when it is worn over time, so investigators might get lucky—especially if the shoe is not new or is discovered right after the crime was committed. Small gouges, cuts, and other kinds of wear marks found on a well-worn shoe might be able to be matched specifically to crime-scene evidence.

- This kind of pattern evidence comparison rises to a much higher level of certainty. Just as with fingerprints or the microscopic rifling marks on a bullet, when enough points of comparison can be made between the unknown footwear evidence and a test pattern made from a known shoe, there might be enough for reasonable people to say that this shoe—and only this shoe—was used at the crime scene.

- The ability of investigators to identify the make and model of a tire from its tread could ultimately lead them to a particular kind of vehicle, and because cars are registered to owners, a tire track might actually lead to a suspect in a way that a shoe print probably couldn't. More than likely, though, even if a tire can be matched to its manufacturer and style, many vehicles would have that brand of tire.

- In comparison to the first tires that were made by Dunlop in 1888 and didn't have any tread, today's tires are much more complex in construction and can vary a lot in size. For example, the coding on the sidewall of a tire describes the type of vehicle that the tire is made for along with some of its dimensions and other design features.

- Databases of tire details have been developed to help identify vehicles in forensic work. Because of the repetition on a tire's surface, it might not take much of a pattern to figure out the kind or brand of tire—and from that, perhaps the kind of vehicle—that made the track.

- With impression evidence, it's occasionally possible that a fabric imprint gets transferred to the surface of a vehicle that strikes a pedestrian, especially if the fabric has a unique 3-D surface. Textile marks can be left on skin and might be seen during an autopsy or in the emergency room. Things like belts, ropes, jewelry, zippers, and buttons can leave impression evidence on skin.

- Sometimes, impression evidence on human skin can't be seen with the unaided eye without alternate light source photography, which involves taking pictures under ultraviolet or infrared light.

Suggested Reading

Bodziak, *Footwear Impression Evidence.*

———, *Tire Tread and Tire Track Evidence.*

1. In addition to fingerprints and toolmarks, what other kinds of impression evidence might be found at a crime scene?

2. Can you think of examples in which impression evidence would be temporary or transient? If so, how would the evidence be preserved?

3. How is forensic photography different from other types of photography?

Lecture 5: Good Impressions—Shoes, Tires, and Skin

Good Impressions—Shoes, Tires, and Skin
Lecture 5—Transcript

Now that we've covered fingerprints, toolmarks, and the types of surface evidence linked to firearms and ammunition, let's spend a little time looking at a few other forms of impression evidence. Things like shoe prints, tire marks, and fabric impressions have also all been used in forensic investigations.

Contact evidence found at crime scenes can be any kind of pattern, made by, or found in soil, dust, snow, blood, wet paint, or lots of other media. Like other kinds of evidence, impressions made by shoe prints, bicycle tires, or the tire treads of cars and trucks, show general features that give information about the manufacturer, size, and brand. Remember, this is what we call class evidence. But, like tools and firearms, shoes and tires also gain individuating characteristics as they're used and worn over time. This can actually tie a shoe print, for example, to a specific shoe at the exclusion of others.

There can be lots of issues with evidence collection and preservation where shoe prints and tire treads are concerned—just like we saw with fingerprints and toolmarks. We'll come back to some of those topics again and add a little new detail, including the ways forensic photography can be used to capture some of the more transient forms of evidence.

And, like lots of other types of analyses, looking at these kinds of impressions typically involves comparing an unknown pattern from a crime scene with a known exemplar shoe print or tire track that's been intentionally taken off a suspect person's footwear or vehicle.

This kind of impression work can also involve getting exclusionary shoe prints or tire tracks, from people or cars that are not related to the criminal act, but for one legitimate reason or another, were at the scene—like the shoe prints of an ambulance worker who walked through blood at the scene of a shooting, to try to save a life.

So, given all those similarities to contact evidence we've talked about before, how are these kinds of impressions different? I guess we could start off with the obvious size differences, duh, between shoe prints or tire tracks when compared to fingerprints or the microscopic striae that may be left on tools or bullets.

Not only might shoe prints be easier to locate at a crime scene, but when you think about it, there are probably lots more footprints left behind at a crime scene than fingerprints, toolmarks, or bullets. Our 2-legged locomotion pretty much guarantees that our feet make more contact with surfaces in our environment than our hands do. But I'm sure more criminals think of wearing gloves than shoe covers.

On the other hand, though, shoes can be thrown away after a crime is committed, whereas fingerprints, not so much. And it's generally easier to wipe off your fingerprints than to get rid of shoe prints. But, I guess a backtracking burglar could do either—at least we've all seen that done in the movies.

But before we go thinking that shoe print and tire-track evidence is simply easy to locate and handle at a crime scene due to its size, think for a minute about the many types of surfaces that shoe prints and tire tracks might be found on. I guess the best-case scenario would be wet cement or wet paint, and the worst case might be rapidly melting snow or on the beach where the tide is coming in.

Also think about how difficult it might be to access a crime scene on foot without disturbing latent footprints, or to get a crime-scene vehicle into a location without complicating any existing tire-track evidence—especially if that evidence can't be seen until you're right up on it.

So, one of the greatest problems that investigators might run into with these kinds of impression evidence is preserving and documenting the scene. Typically, shoe prints and tire tracks have to be carefully photographed by a competent crime-scene photographer. Because, if the material the print or track is on can't be moved—or if the substrate is temporary, like in snow— those photographs might be the only source for future comparisons or at trial.

Maybe this is a good time to talk about general crime-scene photography techniques. Over the past decade or so, crime-scene photography has moved from the old, black-and-white, Polaroid instant cameras to state-of-the-art digital technology. There are a handful of basic principles of forensic photography that are pretty much common to all scenes. First, a forensic photographer has to keep a careful log that tracks the pictures being taken, including when, where, and by whom. Usually, images start with broad overviews, to give perspective and show relationships between things at the scene. And then, they progress to medium shots of, say, maybe 6 feet. Then, close-up shots—of maybe a foot or less—are made where detail views are needed. These have to include a measuring scale so that the exact size of something can be shown. But, it's fairly common to first take a duplicate picture without the scale just to show things as they were before the scale was there. Only with an accurate scale can things in photos be compared, with any confidence, later on to other images or objects.

Photographs should be taken from a couple of different angles, and using both direct and side lighting to maximize detail, which is especially important in impression evidence. Side lighting can show more of the 3-dimensionality of evidence. Images should be taken in a 360-degree pattern, from some kind of fixed point, using a tripod and wide-angle lens. That way, pictures can be overlapped, to show the entire scene, in every direction. Special attention has to be given to entrance and exit routes, early, because it might be hard to preserve those areas and still get full access to the scene. At an indoor crime scene, any adjacent rooms or spaces need to be photographed, too, because the perp had to get there somehow.

Any physical evidence—including a body—needs to have full photo documentation before it's moved. And, whoever discovered the crime scene or the body has to be questioned to see if they moved anything in their effort to figure out what was going on—like, a family member might have rolled the body over to check for signs of life.

The general rule of thumb—especially now that photography has gone digital—is that you just can't have too many pictures of a scene or the evidence in it. You know, at first there was some concern when digital photography first came out, that it couldn't be trusted, since images can be altered using computer software—meaning that digital images might not fly in court—but today's technology can detect when a digital image has been tampered with, and now, digital photography has become standard. So has video-photography, now that the costs for it have come way down. Something like videotaping a path of footprints from eye level can really give a view that you can't get any other way. Sometimes one cop will do the filming, while the other narrates what they're both seeing and doing.

Videotaping doesn't replace still photography, though—forensics needs the resolution that only still images can provide. And there are lots of types of still cameras, with different types of aspect ratios—that's the ratio of the image's width to its height. Most of your common consumer cameras have aspect ratios of 4:3 or 3:2 and so they produce rectangular images, but there are specially designed cameras that do guaranteed one-to-one aspect ratio images—often called square format. These are especially good for taking pictures of fingerprints, footprints, and tire tracks at a scene because they capture the image on the negative in the exact size the evidence was in real life.

We'll talk more about special photographic techniques for specific types of evidence in other lectures—like the alternate light source stuff that I mentioned earlier in the segment on fingerprints. But let's get back to our shoe print and tire-track impression evidence.

We've talked about how important photos can be at a scene—especially when there's no way the evidence can be moved back to the lab. But, there are some cases where shoe print or tire-track evidence winds up being completely portable—when someone leaves a bloody footprint on an area rug, or a piece of paper, for example, or the victim of a hit-and-run accident winds up with a tire tread on his T-shirt.

But when shoe prints or tire tracks can't be moved, after the photographer is finished, investigators might try lifting or casting 3-D evidence. This might involve a skilled crime-scene investigator using his or her head in some quick decision-making—because you typically only get a single shot at either lifting or casting a shoe print or tire track.

If an impression (like a shoe print or a bicycle tread) is made in a thin layer of dust or dirt, investigators can try an adhesive lifting material and put it over all or part of the impression—just like a fingerprint can be lifted. But I've also seen the use of electrostatic lifting technology, which is really cool. The evidence tech takes a sheet of Mylar film and rolls it over an impression in dust or dirt, and then puts a high-voltage electrode onto the film. The electrostatic charge that's created picks up the dust or dirt from the surface where the impression was, and transfers it to the Mylar film. Then it can be picked up and moved from the crime scene and taken to the lab.

This electrostatic technique is particularly useful, say, if a suspect walked across something like a bank counter or a tabletop; which is a surface that typically holds a little dust and is not usually walked on. I've tried this with my students on visits to the sheriff's department, and it's pretty amazing— we have a student hop up and walk across a table—and you might not even be able to see the footprints, but the electrostatic lifting not only picks them up and preserves them, it makes that evidence completely portable.

The same technique can be used over bigger areas, like a floor; but the problem there is, there are probably lots of other footprints in whatever dust and dirt is on the floor. It's the same problem you wind up with in fingerprinting—too many prints, and it's hard to know whose is who and what's what.

When a footprint or tire track is not on a flat, dusty surface, lifting it with adhesive or an electrostatic process doesn't work. So where there's a lot more 3-dimensionality to an impression and it can't be moved back to the lab, casting is the best way to preserve the evidence.

There are a couple of different casting methods that are commercially available to law-enforcement and forensic scientists. Which one they use is based on what substrate material the impression is on. Good old "plaster of Paris" used to be pretty common, but today dental stone is the preferred casting material. That's the same gypsum material that dentists use to make molds of people's teeth. Dental stone gives better detail and makes more durable casts than most other options. For really fragile or transient prints, there are even some commercially available waxy sprays that will seal footprints or tire tracks when they occur in something like snow, and then the sealed impression can be casted.

Casting methods pretty much all involve pouring the casting material over the 3-D surface of the impression and letting it harden. After the cast is dry, they can do a detailed examination of it. If it's a good impression, it ought to be as close to a copy of the original surface as possible.

See, when you step in something like soft mud, you're making a "negative" impression of the sole of your shoe in the mud—like a mirror reversal. But if you cast that footprint, the cast makes a negative of the original negative, and you wind up with a positive image that matches—not mirrors—your shoe.

You can try this yourself by getting one of those large aluminum pans from the grocery store, and then filling it with dirt or, better yet, sand—and make sure it's not too wet. Then put on some shoes with a fancy sole—like running or walking shoes—and step into the pan. If the mud mess you made isn't too dry or too runny, you should wind up with a pretty decent 3-D footprint. Then, if you want, you can get some plaster of Paris and try to cast your footprint.

We've done this in my class, and we're still not really good at it—the only tip I have is to let the plaster dry for a long time, before you try to lift it out, or even before you move the pan. Or, once the cast is pretty dry, support it with your hand and then turn the whole pan upside down. Of course you'll then have to pick the mud back up off the floor—and I am not responsible for the mess this makes—so you might want to do it outside.

But if you just want to get an idea of the detail present on the sole of your shoe and you don't want a huge mess, it's easy to just put a shoe in your hand and put a piece of paper on the sole of it and do a crayon rubbing of the surface—those fat crayons for little kids work best—peel the paper, and use the side of the crayon.

Before you go thinking that casting is just a brilliantly simple way to capture this kind of 3-D evidence, there are things that can really up the ante on how difficult it can be to cast a footprint or tire track: It can literally be an uphill—or I should say a downhill—battle, if the impression is on a steep grade. In cases like this, the casting material is going to want to follow gravity, so some engineering might be called for, like building a wooden frame around the footprint first, and then filling the box with casting material.

There can also be a problem with debris winds up in the impression either at the time it was made, or maybe junk that blew in after the suspect made the footprints, or the car drove over the surface. Removing the debris, without disturbing the evidence, can be tricky and can complicate the casting process.

So what's done with photos or casts in terms of their value as evidence? As we saw with fingerprints, toolmarks, and bullets, shoe prints, tire tracks, and a whole bunch of other types of evidence we'll talk about in future discussions require comparison. But comparing unknown evidence and known evidence can only happen when both unknowns and knowns are recovered and available.

So, basically, there are 3 comparison possibilities we can consider. First, some kind of evidence is recovered from a crime scene, but a plausible suspect who might have similar evidence to match to it is never found. Unfortunately, police evidence storage rooms are full of this type of potential evidence that never gets linked to a suspect.

Secondly, an investigation might lead to a good suspect in a case, but either that person didn't leave much recoverable evidence or the right kind of evidence at the scene. Examining every shoe in a person's closet is useless if none of those shoes were used when committing the crime being investigated. Plus—and I'm guilty of this right now as I speak—all of today's focus on forensic science just keeps making smarter and smarter criminals that know ways to avoid leaving a trail. As time goes on, I think all of us in the business have seen increasingly sophisticated attempts to hide crimes—I know I certainly have in my own casework!

The third comparison possibility is really the backbone of forensic investigation: Evidence is found at a crime scene, and later, a suspect person, tool, weapon, or shoe—you name it—is discovered to have the identical properties of the crime-scene evidence.

Like other kinds of forensic comparisons, investigators like to use test impressions—like the test-firing we talked about with guns and bullets—in order to make quality comparisons between an impression from an unknown shoe or tire associated with a crime, and a like object they want to compare it with.

One of the ways that shoe prints and tire marks are like guns and ammunition, but different from fingerprints, is that shoes and tires come in standard sizes and are made by manufacturers that work toward quality control and brand identity in how they make their products.

The size and style of a shoe or a tire can give what we call class characteristics; in other words, the standard swoosh of the Nike brand would be pretty obvious in a footprint. And once they know the brand, the measurements of, and between, all those little funky lines on the bottom of the shoe can let investigators figure out its size.

So, some footwear patterns let investigators know the manufacturer and the size of a shoe that made evidence at a crime scene. And, they may even be able to contact the manufacturer, and the manufacturer will tell then exactly when and where that type of shoe was produced. There are even some automated footwear databases so law enforcement can look up the brand and size of a shoe using a scanned shoe print image. But even if the suspect has the exact same kind of shoe in his or her closet, which is compelling by itself, the style and size alone don't rise to become individuating evidence.

In other words, that similarity doesn't put the suspect at the scene; unless maybe we're talking about some high-end designer shoe that was a one-of-a-kind production with good documentation of ownership, like O. J. and his "Bruno Maglis," which is pretty unlikely. I mean, one recent survey I found, said there are over 1.5 billion shoes sold each year in the United States alone.

So what good are footprints, then? Well, just like we saw with tools and guns, a shoe develops its own unique use characteristics when it's worn over time. Investigators just might get lucky; especially if the shoe is not new or is discovered right after the crime was committed. Small gouges, cuts, and other kinds of wear marks found on a well-worn shoe might be able to be matched specifically to crime-scene evidence.

This kind of pattern evidence comparison rises to a much higher level of certainty. Like fingerprints or the microscopic rifling marks on a bullet, when enough points of comparison can be made between the unknown footwear evidence and a test pattern that's made from a known shoe, there just might be enough for reasonable people to say that this, and only this shoe, was used at the crime scene.

So what about tire tracks? Well, one estimate I found said that about 2/3 of major crimes in the U.S. involve cars. And one way that tire marks are a little bit different than shoe prints has to do with record-keeping. The ability of investigators to identify the make and model of a tire from its tread could ultimately lead them to a particular kind of vehicle. And because cars are registered to owners, a tire track might actually lead to a suspect in a way that a shoe print probably couldn't. More than likely, though, even if a tire can be identified to its manufacturer and style, a lot of vehicles would have that brand of tire—so again, we're right back to class evidence.

Let's cover a little bit of tire history, now doesn't that sound interesting? Well, the first tires were made by Dunlop, in 1888, and they didn't have any tread; they were just smooth rubber. Tread was developed as speeds increased and road surfaces got smoother. The original tread design was pretty much a gimmick by Firestone. In 1907 they started stamping their tires in 3-D with the company name, so as it turned out, the tracks made by Firestone tires were not much more than advertising.

Today's tires are a lot more complex in their construction, and they can vary a lot in size. If you take a look at your car or truck tires, the coding on the sidewall describes the type of vehicle that the tire is made for, along with some of its dimensions and other design features.

Databases of tire details have been developed to help identify vehicles in forensic work. Because of the repetition on a tire's surface, it might not take much of a pattern to figure out the kind or brand of tire that made that track—and from that, maybe the kind of vehicle. But to get the full 360 degrees of a tire's surface to look for things like details or imperfections that could lend themselves to a positive ID, you'd need a pretty long stretch of tire impression, especially for something as big as a semi-tractor-trailer's tire.

In those cases, a series of overlapping photos would help, because a cast of that size would be nearly impossible to create or transport. And, it's not just the tire details that give information—a measurement of, say, something like the distance between the right and left tires or between a front and back tire can also help narrow down the vehicle type, and that might let investigators hone in on at least a particular mode of transportation—like a truck versus a car.

Before we change gears and leave this whole group of related topics—since fingerprints, toolmarks, bullets, footprints and tire tracks are all types of impression evidence—let me mention a couple of other things about impression evidence. It's occasionally possible that a fabric imprint gets transferred to the surface of a vehicle that strikes a pedestrian, especially if the fabric has a unique 3-D surface, like a weave pattern, or some cording, or beadwork, or something like that. The same goes for textile marks left on skin that might be seen at autopsy, or in the emergency room. Things like belts, ropes, jewelry, zippers, buttons, all these things can leave impression evidence on skin.

Not too long ago I saw a case presentation at our local coroner's group meeting, where a baby died in one of those portable cribs they now call a "pack and play"—it's like a small playpen. The baby was at another woman's home day care, where a couple of other kids came each day. And because of a snow day from school, the baby's 7-year-old brother just happened to also be at the babysitter's on that particular day.

The babysitter said she was out of the room, and she heard the baby's big brother hollering something about the baby making a funny noise. When the woman got to the playpen, she said the baby was all twisted up in a hooded zip-up sweatshirt, that had somehow gotten hooked onto one of those little dangly baby toys, you know, the kind of thing that you can hang above a crib or clip on a kid's car seat. The woman freed the baby from the tangled clothing, so the body wasn't in the original position when ambulance workers arrived on the scene. And they had to rely on her story of the events. The baby was taken to the hospital, but it turned out to be too late. The little girl had died from strangulation.

Given the situation, the babysitter—and even the 7-year-old—could be prime suspects in the baby's death. I guess police thought that either one of them could have asphyxiated the baby; after all, how could a kid's hoodie be a cause of death? It didn't even have those little string ties on it—it was just a zip-up sweatshirt with a ruffle around the edges of the hood. But at her autopsy, the baby's skin showed clear impression evidence of the top part of the sweatshirt's zipper, and her little neck even showed impressions of some of the ruffles that went around the edges of the hood.

I saw the photos from the autopsy, and you could see each tiny, bruise-like impression of each tooth of the zipper, with a wavy pattern next to it from the ruffle on the edge of the hood. Man, talk about a tragic death. The best they could figure, the little girl stood up in the playpen and somehow the hood of her sweatshirt got caught on that dangling toy, and when she felt something tugging on her, I guess she turned around. Apparently she turned around a couple of times before the sweatshirt hood basically became a noose around her neck. And then, when she lost blood flow to her brain, she must have passed out, and her own body weight—small as it was—just suffocated her.

The loss of that baby was one of those things we all call a terrible "freak accident." But at least the impression evidence found at autopsy saved the babysitter from wrongful allegations of child abuse. After I heard that story, I called my son right away and told him about it, because my own grandbaby was about the same age at the time. I told him not to put a hoodie on her if she was going to be by herself for even a second!

The impression left by that zipper was really obvious on the baby's neck— partly because she had very light and delicate skin, and that the tragic accident had just happened. But sometimes, impression evidence on skin can't be seen with the naked eye without what's called "alternate light source photography." Taking pictures under ultraviolet or infrared light, and that can sometimes show impression evidence on human tissues that can't be seen with the unaided eye. We'll talk more about this in our discussion of bite-mark analysis, and learn more about how special types of forensic photography work.

Sorry to leave you with an awful story like that, but it does emphasize something that we have to keep in mind when talking about the value of any kind of evidence, and that is to say that evidence is just as important—if not more so—when it exonerates somebody who is innocent. Partly based on TV, and maybe partly because of human nature, we're usually way too focused on "getting the bad guy," so much so that sometimes we forget how important it is to make sure that innocent people are not persecuted or prosecuted for things they didn't do.

Just put yourself in the place of that babysitter for even a second! In the U.S., our legal system is supposed to fully support the notion of "innocent until proven guilty beyond a reasonable doubt." The English lawyer, William Blackstone, put it best all the way back in the 1760s when he said: "Better that 10 guilty persons escape, than one innocent suffer." That's something we have to keep that in mind throughout this entire series, as we continue to explore the use of evidence in making sure that justice is served.

Forensics of Fibers, Paint, and Glass
Lecture 6

U nlike impression evidence, trace evidence—such as fibers, paint, and glass—is physical bits of material that can be left behind in minute quantities. Even tiny bits of polymer or glass evidence can usually be matched to comparable substances by common class characteristics to indicate chemical makeup, manufacturer, and location of sale. Occasionally, when larger pieces of fabric, paint, or glass are found, they can be individualized to the definitive source they came from at the exclusion of all others.

Forms of Trace Evidence

- Fibers—from natural and man-made sources—and paint are chemically similar. They're both polymers, which means that they are made of long chains of repeating subunit molecules called monomers that are linked together by chemical bonds.

- Many natural and synthetic materials are polymers, including many of the carbohydrates and all of the proteins we eat. Polymers also make up many structures in and on our bodies—such as muscle proteins, hair, DNA, plastics, rubbers, paints, varnishes, shellacs, stains, and some inks.

- Glass is not a polymer; it's a composite substance called an amorphous solid that is made mostly of sand—often with the addition of soda and lime.

- Glass and polymers, like paint and textile fibers, are common types of trace evidence that can be found on clothes, shoes, floors, and other surfaces. These bits of evidence can be directly deposited from a primary source or moved around by different modes of transfer.

Classifying and Analyzing Fiber Evidence

- After the usual documentation, including careful photography, fiber evidence can be removed from its surface at the crime scene if investigators see it—but often it's better to take surfaces that might hold fibers back to the lab.

- A brush can be used to extract anything that comes off of clothing, and cellophane tape can be used to pull off only surface material. Vacuuming picks up more than tape, but it results in many more fibers to look through under a microscope. If a stray fiber is obvious—on clothes or anywhere else—forceps can be used to directly pick it up for examination.

- Fibers can be broken down into 5 major types.

    o There are many types of plant fibers used in textiles, such as cotton, flax, hemp, jute, ramie, and papyrus.

    o Some fibers have an animal origin, such as wool and silk.

    o Synthetic fibers are completely man-made and include polyester, nylon, rayon, and many others.

    o There are also blends, such as a blend of polyester and cotton.

    o Fibers that aren't used in clothing but could still be found as evidence are man-made mineral fibers in fiberglass, which is sometimes called glass wool.

- Fibers can also be distinguished by their color and weave, which relate to the kind of processes used on the base materials during manufacturing. Individual fiber types are actually fairly rare in their frequency in the environment with one notable exception: indigo-dyed cotton denim.

- Microscopic analysis is used by forensic scientists as a nondestructive way to get a lot of information about the fibers that make up a fabric. Under a microscope, fibers—like many other compounds—react differently to different types of light.

- A microscope can establish the precise width of the fiber because measuring tools, known as micrometers, can be put inside microscopes. Microscopy also shows differences in the cross-sectional anatomy of fibers.

Fibers from clothing and other types of man-made materials are commonly found as trace evidence at crime scenes.

- Microscope examination might also document damage, making it possible to determine if a fabric has been intentionally cut or pulled apart. Microscopy might also identify any foreign material, such as soil or blood, that might not be visible to the unaided eye.

- There are many chemical tests that aid in fiber identification, but they are only done after nondestructive techniques are used. Chemical tests essentially break the fiber down to figure out what's in it. For example, chromatography involves separating the subcomponents in a mixture.

- By combining all of the various methods of testing—microscopy, optical properties, and chemistry—forensic scientists can often hone in on and identify specific fiber types. However, analysts cannot state with 100% certainty that a fiber came from a specific source because of the mass production of garments and textiles.

- When an actual fragment of clothing is recovered as evidence, investigators can get lucky with a tear match, where the evidence fits together like a puzzle—if they can find the garment the cloth fragment came from.

Classifying and Analyzing Paint Evidence

- Although paint is a polymer that begins with long chains, just like fibers do, paint has other cross-linkages that hold the strands together into a sheet.

- In forensic terms, there are 3 main categories of paint: automotive paint, structural paint—what's found on buildings, walls, furniture, and mailboxes—and artistic paint, which can be important in cases involving art forgeries.

- Chemically, paint is a collection of pigments and additives that is suspended in a binder with a consistency that's adjusted by a solvent, which allows it to change from a liquid to a solid.

- Forensic scientists deal with automotive paint most often. Manufacturers and refurbishers use specific chemicals, different sequences of layers of paint, and different thicknesses of layers. The complicated nature of automotive paint usually makes it much easier to match than other types of paint.

- There are some things about collecting paint evidence that mirror fiber evidence collection—such as taking the whole surface with the paint on it to the lab, if possible. However, if the paint is embedded in the road or on a phone pole, a scalpel can be used to carefully slice off a sliver of asphalt or phone pole because without the full layering, an analyst doesn't get the whole picture.

- One way that paint evidence collection differs from textiles is that crime-scene investigators should not use a tape lift because the chemicals and adhesives in the tape can make some paint tests difficult.

- For a car accident, samples from all involved cars should be taken from an undamaged area of the car as close as possible to the damaged area, especially if there's a chance any part of the car has been repainted. At the lab, forensic scientists can use a thin blade to cut a paint sample at an angle to better see the layers.

- As with fibers, the order of paint testing is sometimes determined by how large of a sample the lab has to work with. Microscopy is used first so that the layers can be examined and compared. Investigators compare known and unknown samples to see if they match in condition, color, wear, texture, and layering. After microscopic analysis, there are many chemical and high-tech instrumental methods that can be used.

- If there's no known sample for comparison, law enforcement agencies can use a database called the paint data query (PDQ) to potentially identify the year, make, and model of a car.

Classifying and Analyzing Glass Evidence

- There are estimated to be over 700 different types of glass, and only about 70 of those are used commonly. For investigators, it's the rare types that are most distinctive as forensic evidence.

- As an amorphous solid, glass doesn't contain crystals and doesn't have any other type of ordered structure. Glass is made from fused inorganic materials—mostly silicon oxides, which are better known as sand, and some metal oxides. These are melted together at high temperatures and then cooled without crystallization.

- Depending on the size of a piece of broken glass, some features can be discerned with the unaided eye, and other details can only be seen through microscopic analysis. To narrow glass to a source, investigators look at many different properties, including thickness, color, texture, design, curvature, and tinting.

- Microscopy can also show debris, such as gunpowder residue or soil, on glass fragments, and unless it's recently been cleaned, the amount of debris can usually help identify which side of a piece of window glass was the outside surface.

- The way glass fractures can also tell something about its makeup. Tempered safety glass is made stronger than ordinary window glass by rapid heating and cooling of surfaces so that it breaks into small squares or spheres instead of shards with sharp edges. Laminated glass is used in car windshields; it has a layer of plastic between 2 pieces of window glass, so it also breaks differently.

- Like paint, the additives in glass—including sodium, calcium, boron, and tin—give it different properties and can be useful in forensic glass identification.

- The refractive index and density of glass are the 2 most important properties that forensic examiners look at. The refractive index is the result of the way the speed of light changes when it goes through a material. Light refracts, or bends, as it passes through glass. The refractive index is also why objects look different above and below the surface of water.

- The density of glass, or any other material, can be determined with a float test, which involves floating an unknown glass fragment in a series of clear, gradient columns filled with liquids of known density. The glass fragment stops dropping in the density gradient when it reaches its own density.

- The FBI laboratory created a database of refractive index and density values that can help narrow down the type and frequency of use of the glass involved in a crime.

- If an investigator has large enough pieces of broken glass, he or she might be able to put the pieces back together like a jigsaw puzzle to re-create all or part of whatever was broken.

- Sometimes, examiners can figure out whether glass breakage was due to a high- or low-velocity impact. In high-velocity impacts, there's usually a cone, or crater, effect, in which the smaller opening—the top of the cone—is on the side of the glass that was first hit by the impact, and the larger opening—the base of the cone—is on the exit side of the glass.

- The same principles can be used when analyzing bone trauma—especially when examining the skull for high-velocity trauma like gunshot wounds. When a bullet passes through a skull, it's as if it is passing through 2 pieces of glass—with one representing the entrance wound and the other representing the exit wound.

- With gunshots through both glass and bone, the diameter of the hole can't be directly correlated with the caliber of a bullet, other than to give a maximum possible size, because you can't end up with a hole that's smaller than the bullet itself.

- Examiners can sometimes establish the order of multiple impacts, in both glass and skull fractures, using radial and concentric fractures. Radial fractures extend out like rays from the initial point of impact while concentric fractures are circular fractures around the point of impact.

Suggested Reading

Caddy, ed., *Forensic Examination of Glass and Paint.*

Questions to Consider

1. What is the physical makeup of glass?

2. Can broken glass be class evidence or individuating evidence?

3. What types of polymers constitute crime-scene evidence?

Forensics of Fibers, Paint, and Glass
Lecture 6—Transcript

From 1979 to 1981, in the Atlanta, Georgia, area, investigators started to see patterns among nearly 30 homicides of young, black males, most of whom were children. Many of the victims had been dumped in the Chattahoochee River after being bludgeoned or asphyxiated. As the investigation unfolded, 2 main kinds of fiber evidence kept turning up on the bodies and clothing of the victims—one was a purple-colored acetate fiber, and the other was a yellow-green nylon fiber that was tri-lobed or "Y-shaped" in cross-section.

Detectives decided to stake out the Chattahoochee to see if they could catch the killer disposing of his next victim. And on May 22, 1981, they heard a splash in the river and saw the vehicle of Wayne Williams drive away from a bridge. The next morning another victim was found in the water. A search of Williams's home turned up a yellow-green carpet as the possible source for the tri-lobed nylon fibers. But how common was that particular textile? Was it rare enough to implicate Williams as the serial killer in a string of incidents that became known as "The Atlanta Child Murders"?

Investigators discovered that particular fiber was made by only one manufacturer. The fiber type was then sold to several carpet makers, who in turn added their own dyes. Williams's carpet came from a Georgia company, who made their particular color and style in a fairly limited run. In fact, based on the small quantity of carpet that was produced, and average square-foot room sizes, that particular carpeting was ultimately estimated to be in fewer than 100 homes in the Atlanta area.

Based on this, Williams ended up being tried for 2 of the murders and found guilty, based mainly on the carpet fiber evidence. There was plenty of other supporting evidence, too, including hair from Williams's dog, which was also found on some of the victims' bodies.

We'll talk about hair and fur in the next lecture, but now we'll take a look at fibers and other types of man-made materials that are commonly found as trace evidence at crime scenes. Unlike fingerprints, toolmarks, or footprints, which are examples of impression evidence, trace evidence like fibers, paint, and glass are actual physical bits of material that can be left behind in minute quantities.

Fibers (whether they're from natural or man-made sources) and paint are chemically similar in that they're what scientists call polymers. That means they are made of long chains of repeating subunit molecules called monomers, all linked together by chemical bonds. Lots of natural and synthetic materials are polymers, including many of the carbohydrates and all the proteins we eat. Polymers also make up many structures in and on our bodies—like muscle proteins and hair; heck, even DNA is a polymer of repeated units. But plastics, rubbers, paints, varnishes, shellacs, stains, and some inks are also polymers.

Glass is structurally different. It's not a polymer; it's a composite substance, technically called an amorphous solid, made mostly of sand, often with the addition of soda and lime. Humans have known how to make glass for over 5000 years at least, but glass can occur naturally where sand has been heated to very high temperatures, like when volcanic glass is formed.

Glass and polymers, like paint and textile fibers, are pretty common types of trace evidence that can be found on clothes, shoes, floors, and other surfaces. These bits of evidence can be directly deposited from a primary source or moved around by different modes of transfer. We'll see in this lecture that even tiny bits of polymer or glass evidence can usually be matched to like substances by common class characteristics. Meaning these materials can be identified as to their chemical makeup, and even sometimes to their manufacturer and where they were sold. We'll also see that occasionally, when larger pieces of fabric, paint, or glass are found, they can actually be individualized to the definitive source they came from at the exclusion of all others.

Let's talk in more detail about textile fibers. Fiber evidence can come from lots of sources; it could include part of a gag, rope, or cord used to bind a victim, a blanket, a small piece of torn clothing, or carpet and upholstery fibers from homes, offices, or cars. Fiber transfer evidence might be found on clothes—so one person's clothing fibers might be found on another person's clothes, or the fibers from a knit cap a robber left behind might be found later in his hair. Stray fibers can also be found underneath the fingernails or in the hair of a perpetrator or a victim. They can be found on hit-and-run vehicles and at crime-scene entry points—especially where the criminal had a tight squeeze or went through a jagged opening like a broken window.

After the usual documentation, including careful photography, fiber evidence can be removed at the scene if investigators see it—but it's often better to take surfaces that might hold fibers back to the lab. So if fibers are seen or suspected on something, the whole item can be bagged. Most fiber evidence isn't obvious to the naked eye, so if all of the victim's or suspect's clothing, for example, can be completely taken to the lab, collection is best done there.

There are a couple of ways fiber evidence might be gathered from clothing— our local crime lab uses a brush to get what comes off. Some investigators use cellophane tape since it pulls off only the surface material. Vacuuming picks up more stuff than tape, but that just means a lot more to look through under the microscope. If a stray fiber is obvious, on clothes or anywhere, forceps can be used to directly pick it—and only it—up so that they can take a look at it.

Since fiber analysis looks at the physical properties of different materials, let's talk about how textiles are classified. You could break down fibers into 5 major types that are kind of familiar to us from when we read clothing labels. First, we could talk about different types of plant fibers used in textiles, like cotton, flax, hemp, jute, ramie, even papyrus. Secondly, some fibers have an animal origin, like wool and silk. Although plant and animal fibers are natural, they are usually processed in some way, and we'll talk about processing in a minute. The third major classification includes synthetic fibers that are completely man-made, like polyester, nylon, rayon, and lots of others. Fourth are blends, like a polyester/cotton blend. And the last class of fibers really isn't used in clothing but could still be found as evidence, and that's man-made mineral fibers in fiberglass, sometimes called glass wool.

Fibers can also be distinguished by their color and their weave. This relates to the kind of processes used on the base materials during the manufacturing process. So, for example, if the color goes all the way through the fiber, an investigator would know a soluble dye was used, but if there are small pieces of color visible in the fiber, a pigment was used, instead.

Some fibers have a twist to them—they either go clockwise or counterclockwise. Fibers will have different diameters, and some fabrics will have multiple fibers of different diameters and even different twists in them—they put one fiber in one direction, the other in another direction. We also see ropes and cords have different numbers of individual strands, and fabrics have different thread counts, like we see in sheets. Cloth can be knitted with interlocking loops; it can be woven with alternating strands that go above or below each other to interlock, or they can be non-woven, like felt where they make it out of friction.

Individual fiber types are actually each pretty rare in their frequency in the environment with one notable exception. Any idea what that exception is? Indigo-dyed cotton denim. Unless you wear a work uniform of some type, or never wear blue jeans, that may be the most reoccurring fiber in your closet.

Really, you could take 6 fabrics that all look the same color to your eye and just pull out one thread from the hem of each one, and you'd be surprised at how differently those threads may "behave" when they are subjected to different experimental treatments. We do this in my forensic science class: The students see how threads from seemingly identical fabrics react to heat and fire, by taking a fiber in a pair of forceps—not the fabric, but the fiber from it—and they push it nearer and nearer to a flame.

What we see is some fibers melt while others burn, and that happens at different distances from the flame for each fiber. If you sew or do crafts, you could try that by taking fibers from a few types of fabric and holding them—carefully!—near a candle. Make sure you use some man-made types, along with some natural fabrics like cotton.

My students also pull a thread from each of our study fabrics and put them into a couple different solvents, like we used hydrochloric acid, acetone, and sodium hypochlorite. I doubt you have any hydrochloric acid at home, but you might have acetone, since that's nail polish remover, and sodium hypochlorite is bleach. Different fiber types react pretty differently when subjected to certain chemicals.

But those tests are really far simpler than what's actually done at a forensic lab—plus, they're destructive techniques, and so would have the potential to use up a preciously small amount of trace evidence. So let's get more realistic. Microscopic analysis—which is something my students also do in their fiber lab—is a nondestructive way to get a lot of information about the fibers that make up a particular fabric.

Under the scope, fibers—like many other compounds—react differently to different types of light. This is because the speed of light gets altered as it travels through any medium, as compared to how light travels in a vacuum. Scientifically, we call that measure the material's refractive index.

A microscope can establish the precise width of the fiber since measuring tools, known as micrometers, can be put inside microscopes. You can also see the "waviness" of a fiber within a given amount of its length, and the type of "wave" it has, can be seen under the scope, too—like is it "kinky," "twisted," or "straight"? Microscopy also shows differences in the cross-sectional anatomy of fibers when you cut them. Some are round, others are triangular, and some have really funky shapes—that's especially true with carpet fibers.

Under the scope, more can be seen about the fabric's luster, if it's shiny or dull. They often add a chemical to synthetic fibers during manufacturing to cut down on how shiny they are. Some plant fibers can even be microscopically identified to their particular plant source—like cotton or bamboo.

Any of these microscopic details has the potential to match an unknown fiber to a known source—like matching a fabric fiber on a victim to a piece of clothing worn by the suspect. This kind of detailed examination can also document damage, making it possible to determine if a fabric has been intentionally cut or pulled apart. Microscopy might also identify any foreign material in the fiber, like soil or blood that might not be visible with the naked eye.

You've probably heard of these really high-tech scopes called scanning electron microscopes—or SEM's—that can be used to see a lot more 3-dimensional detail. Using SEM a forensic scientist can actually determine if a puncture in a piece of clothing is a bullet hole or something else, or get a way more detailed look at cut ends in a fabric to tell what type of sharp surface made the cut—so, in a sense, that's a form of tool-mark analysis. In combination with some high-tech X-ray methods, SEM can show something about fabric chemistry—for example, the presence of tin and bromide suggests the fabric has a fire retardant on it.

There are lots of chemical tests that aid in fiber identification, but these are only done after all the nondestructive techniques are used. These chemical tests are going to essentially break the fiber down to figure out what's in it. For instance, you might have heard of chromatography—which is chemistry that separates the subcomponents in a mixture. This can be done on either the fibers themselves or just the dyes in them. And that's just one example of the type of analytical chemical testing that goes on in forensic labs around the world every day. By putting all of the testing data together—which includes the microscopy, optical properties, and the chemistry—forensic scientists can often hone in on and identify the specific fiber types involved.

The end result from nearly all fiber evidence testing is the same, though: Analysts can't state with 100% certainty that this fiber came from a specific source, because of the mass production of garments and textiles. But they can determine similarity, and like we saw with shoes and tires, estimates can be made of how frequently that particular fiber occurs in the general population of clothing or carpeting.

Every once in a while, though, when an actual fragment of clothing is recovered as evidence, investigators can get lucky with what's called a "tear match" where the evidence fits together like pieces of a puzzle—if they can find the garment the cloth fragment came from. The same holds true for paint chips and glass pieces, so let's move on and talk about those now.

Paint is a polymer that starts with long chains like fibers do, but paint has other cross-linkages in it that hold the strands together into a sheet. Forensic investigators often examine automotive paint, like maybe from a hit-and-run or other car accident, where paint gets transferred from one car to another—or from a car to some other surface—like a phone pole, bike, curb, or even the clothes of a pedestrian who was struck. Paint evidence can also include something like microscopic flakes on a pry bar after a breaking and entering.

In forensic terms, we could break paint down into 3 main categories. There's automotive paint, structural paint—like what's on buildings, walls, furniture, or mailboxes—and then artistic paint, which could be important in cases involving art forgeries.

Chemically, paint is a collection of pigments and additives that are suspended in what is called a "binder," with a consistency that's adjusted by a solvent, so it can go from a liquid to a solid state. Pigments include both organic and inorganic chemicals, and additives are things like the bits in car paint that give it its metallic finish. The binder is often a polymer to hold the ingredients together; it helps dry paint into smooth layers as the solvent evaporates. So, for instance, if we're talking about water-based paints, water is the solvent that evaporates to leave the pigments, additives, and the binder behind as a dry surface.

Let's focus on automotive paint, then, because that's what forensic scientists deal with most often. An automotive paint job is surprisingly complicated—maybe that's why they charge you so much at the body shop when a car gets damaged.

First they use a primer and that gets applied to the bare metal of the car body, usually by dipping the whole car frame into a tank; it's a mixture of epoxy-based resins to provide rust-proofing. Next, a primer surfacer is applied over that—or sometimes mixed with it; the color of this layer is dependent on what the base color is going to be, the next coat. The base coat color is applied next, combined with any additives, like if they want a metallic finish.

The last layer is a clear coat, and that gives the paint a shiny surface—this is the stuff they put on older cars to give them that "like new" look. And it's not uncommon that if there's a flaw seen during the factory painting, any or all parts of this process can be repeated without removing the flawed paint job. So you can imagine how complex the layering might be, even in a brand new car.

The thing about all this layering that's important in forensics is that manufacturers and refurbishers use specific chemicals: They use different sequences of layers. They use different thicknesses of layers. And the repainting of older vehicles makes the layering even more unique. So, the complicated nature of automotive paint usually actually makes it much easier to match than other types of paint.

There are some things about collecting paint evidence that mirror what we talked about with fiber evidence collection—such as taking the whole surface with the paint on it to the lab, if they can. But if the paint is more or less embedded in the road or stuck onto a phone pole, they can use a scalpel to carefully slice off a sliver of asphalt or phone pole, with the paint and all, because without the full layering, an analyst doesn't get the whole picture. One way that paint evidence collection differs from textiles is that crime-scene investigators should not use a tape lift, because the chemicals and adhesives in the tape can make some paint tests more difficult.

For a car accident, they take samples from all involved cars—all the way down to the base metal—from some undamaged area of the car. But they want to get as close as possible to the area damaged, especially if there's a chance any part of the car has been repainted. Back at the lab, forensic scientists can use a thin blade to cut a paint sample at an angle, and then you'll be able to see the layers.

Same as with fibers, the order of testing is sometimes determined by how big of a sample the lab has to work with. So they'll use microscopy first, so the layers can be examined and compared. And they'll look at known and unknown samples together to see if they match in condition, color, wear, texture, as well as the layering. After microscopic analysis, there are all kinds of chemical and high-tech instrumental methods that can be used, too.

What if there's no known sample for comparison? Well, law enforcement agencies can use a database called the Paint Data Query, or PDQ, to potentially identify the year, make, and model of car. This database was started in 1975 by the Royal Canadian Mounted Police, but ultimately became a multi-national effort that included the cooperation of the FBI, the German Federal Police, the European Forensic Institute, and the Japanese National Police. With the cooperation of all these regions known for auto manufacturing, the database now contains information on over 50,000 automotive paints.

Now let's move on to glass: Did you know there are estimated to be over 700 different types of glass? Only about 70 of those are used commonly, so for investigators, it's the rare types—again like O. J.'s Bruno Magli shoes—that are the most distinctive bits as forensic evidence.

Glass, remember, is not a polymer; it's actually more interesting in its nature. As an amorphous solid, it doesn't have any crystals in it or any other type of ordered structure. Glass is made from fused inorganic materials, mostly silicon oxides, which we know better as sand, and some metal oxides. These are melted together at high temperatures and then cooled without crystallization. So glass winds up being reasonably hard, but easily broken. It can be transparent or translucent. And glass comes in all kinds of colors, shapes, and sizes.

Depending on the size of a piece of broken glass, some features can be discerned with the naked eye, and other details can only be seen through a microscope. Investigators look at a bunch of different properties to narrow glass to its source: Is it thin like a light bulb or thick like plate glass? Is it clear like a window or colored like a beer or wine bottle might be? Is it colored glass from a car's turn signal? Is the glass uniformly clear or does it have decorative bubbles or flecks of something in it? If there are bubbles are they intentional, or are they accidental during the manufacturing process? Does the glass have a design on the surface like from a car turn signal or a piece of glass block window? Is the fragment completely flat like from a window, or is it curved like it came from a vase or bottle? Does it have tinting in it so maybe it's a car window?

Microscopy can also show debris on glass fragments like gunpowder residue or soil from a rock that was thrown through a window. And, unless it's just been cleaned, the amount of debris can usually help identify which side of a piece of window glass was the outside surface that gets dirty all the time.

The way glass fractures can also tell something about its makeup. Tempered safety glass is made stronger than ordinary window glass by rapid heating and cooling of surfaces; so it ends up breaking into small squares or spheres instead of shards with sharp edges. Laminated glass is used in car windshields so it's got a layer of plastic between 2 pieces of window glass, so it breaks differently, too.

Like paints, the additives in glass are going to give it different properties, so they can be used in forensic glass identification. For example, there's a high sodium and calcium content in the soda lime glass that's used for making bottles, jars, and windows. Borosilicate glass, which we know better by its trade name Pyrex, has a high boron content that resists heat shock. Tin can diffuse into panes of glass during the manufacturing of what's called float glass, which is a method that ends up making glass really flat and more uniform in its thickness, like we want with window glass. And sparkly, decorative glass has usually in it elements with high atomic numbers that increase its refractive index. The refractive index and density of glass are 2 of the most important properties that forensic examiners look at; so let me say a little about both of those.

I mentioned refractive index before when we talked about fibers; it's the result of the way the speed of light changes when it goes through a material. But understanding the refractive index is a lot easier when talking about glass than it was when talking about fibers. That's because we've all probably seen light refracted—which means bent—as it passes through glass, like a prism. The refractive index is also why objects look different above and below the surface of water.

If you've never noticed that, try this: Put a pencil in a clear drinking glass full of water and then look at it from the side—the pencil will look like it's in 2, shifted pieces at the water's surface. That's because of the difference between the refractive indices of the 2 media that the pencil's suspended in—the water and the air.

If you want to try another refractive index experiment, get a clear marble or a small piece of glass, put it in a container of water, and then take a look at it. Then put the same marble or piece of glass in some cooking oil, and look at it again. Whichever liquid is harder to see the object in, in that substance— that has either the oil or the water in it—has a closer refractive index to the marble or the piece of glass you used.

Now, how about density? The density of glass, or anything else, can be determined with what's called a "float test." They have these fancy, clear, gradient columns filled with liquids of known density that an unknown glass fragment can be floated in. The glass fragment will stop dropping in the density gradient when it reaches its own density.

There's a mathematical way to estimate density that I use in my forensic class: You take a cup completely filled to its brim with pure water, put your glass fragment into it, and then measure how much water spills over the top of the cup when you put the glass fragment in. That gives you the volume of the fragment. Then you divide the weight of the fragment by its volume, which gives you its density.

So, what's the point of having the refractive index and density of a piece of glass? Well, the FBI lab has created a database of refractive index and density values from glass samples submitted to them for evaluation since back into the 1960s. This database can not only narrow down the type of the glass, but because of the records kept by the FBI on those samples, even help determine how frequently that type of glass occurs in the U.S. or in any given geographic area, and even look at glass samples across time.

A couple of other points about glass fragments: If an investigator has big enough pieces of broken glass, he might be able to be put the pieces back together like a jigsaw puzzle to re-create all or part of whatever was broken. And sometimes examiners can figure out whether glass breakage was due to a high- or low-velocity impact.

In high-velocity impacts, there's usually a "cone" or "crater" effect—you might have seen this on your windshield or where a BB went through a window. The smaller opening—what would be the top of the cone—is on the side of glass that was first hit by the impact. The larger opening—what would be the base of the cone—is always on the "exit" side of the glass.

To figure this out in glass that was shattered by the impact, the investigator may have to reconstruct the glass first, from all the tiny shards, and that can be really time consuming! In glass, even if examiners can't reconstruct the actual entry or exit hole, they can look at microscopic details, known as conchoidal fracture lines, that tell which side of the glass the impact came from.

I use some of these same principles in my work as a forensic anthropologist when I analyze bone trauma—especially on the skull, where I'm looking at high-velocity trauma like gunshot wounds. What happens is the entrance wound has a smaller diameter on the outside of the skull, and its cone, what I call a beveled edge, will be of a larger diameter on the inside surface of the entrance wound—just like with glass.

But if the bullet passes completely through the skull, I'll have a corresponding exit wound somewhere else. And it will have a smaller diameter on the inside of the skull, and then it will blast a larger crater on the outside surface of the same exit wound when it finally leaves the skull. Really, when the bullet passes through the skull, it's kind of like passing through 2 pieces of glass—one representing the entrance wound, and the other representing the exit wound.

And in gunshots that go through either glass and bone, the diameter of the hole can't be precisely or directly correlated with the caliber of a bullet, other than to give a "maximum possible size," since you can't wind up with a hole that's smaller than the bullet itself.

Examiners can sometimes even establish the order of multiple impacts, in both glass and skull fractures, using what are known as radial and concentric fractures. Radial fractures extend out like rays from the initial point of impact, while concentric fractures are circular fractures around the point of impact. The sequencing can be established by looking at where each crack starts and where it ends. This is because a crack will terminate when it hits an already-existing crack.

So, if a glass investigator sees a pattern in broken glass, or if I see one in a damaged skull, we can actually reconstruct past events. This not only provides key physical evidence, but can also be used to corroborate or refute a witness or suspect's statement. Forensic evidence like this—whether clothing fibers, microscopic paint chips, or tiny bits of glass—can all be small elements that help tell a much larger story.

Traces of Hair and Fur
Lecture 7

Among the many varieties of trace evidence, hair is one of the most commonly analyzed forms of trace evidence. One of the great values of hair in forensic science is that it's very stable when compared to other body tissues. However, if 2 hairs are similar, it does not automatically indicate that someone is guilty, but it will allow investigators to continue to focus on the person as a suspect and gather additional evidence, including DNA testing, to either prove the guilt or support the innocence of the suspect.

The Structure of Hair

- Hair is a unique feature of mammals that is abundant in some animals and less abundant in other species, including whales and modern humans. There's really no difference between hair and fur—except that fur typically refers to the hair of nonhuman mammals.

- Hair form differs not only among different types of mammals, but also within different regions of the same animal's body. Humans have many different types of hair on their bodies—including eyebrows, eyelashes, beard hair, and body hair—but only pubic and scalp hair are typically analyzed in a forensic lab. The other types don't have enough internal detail for meaningful comparisons.

- Hair has interesting growth patterns and functions. Some hairs on the body have a long lifespan with near continuous growth—such as beard hair and head hair—but other hairs—such as arm and leg hairs, eyebrows, and eyelashes—have a fairly consistent and relatively short length on an individual and are shed and replaced once they achieve that length.

- All hairs have a nerve ending at their root, so hairs act as a means of sensation; in other words, hair allows us to feel the approach of something before it actually comes in direct contact with our skin. This is one reason hair may be found at a crime scene.

- Human hair, like that of other mammals, is a dead extension of the skin made mostly of proteins. The main protein is keratin, which is a widespread component of the body coverings of many animals—including reptile scales, bird feathers and beaks, cat claws, primate fingernails, and rhino horns. Other proteins in hair, such as melanin, give it color.

- The root of the hair is anchored into the dermis layer of the skin, which is surrounded by epidermal cells that make up the follicle. Blood vessels at the hair root transport the raw materials for hair production and growth.

- Because the substances needed to build hair come from the bloodstream, hair becomes a lasting repository of certain chemicals in the body. This can include illicit drugs, such as THC from marijuana, and certain poisons, such as arsenic, that can be incorporated into the shaft of the hair as it grows.

- If there is a suspicion of drug use or poisoning, chemical analyses can be performed on hair during drug testing or at autopsy. Blood and urine samples can show only a relatively recent history of drug use or toxins in the body, but the chemical stability of hair makes it an excellent and long-standing record of body chemistry.

- Because hair growth rates are fairly standard, investigators are able to roughly date when a chemical substance was laid down in hair. References vary on the typical rate of scalp hair growth, but estimates range from about 1 to 1.25 centimeters a month, which is about 0.5 inches.

The Life Stages of Hair
- At any given time, most hairs are in an actively growing stage called the anagen phase, in which new cells are being added at the hair root, pushing the hair shaft further toward the body surface.

The anagen growth phase can last as long as 2 to 7 years for scalp hair, depending on the type of body hair and possibly genetics.

- If a hair is pulled forcibly during this growth phase, a follicle tag will remain on the ribbon-like end of the hair root; you may have seen this white residue if you have plucked an eyebrow. In violent crimes in which people struggle with each other, hair may be pulled out and left at the crime scene or transferred from one person to another.

- Near the end of a hair's life cycle, it enters the catagen phase, where growth begins to slow down. During the catagen phase, the hair root begins to shrivel away from the follicle and becomes elongated.

- The final phase in the life of a single hair is the telogen phase and is the time when a hair is getting ready to be shed naturally. It breaks away from the follicle, and the root takes on a more bulbous shape. A hair may remain lodged in its follicle in the telogen stage for several months before actually falling out.

- Numbers of typical hairs lost per day range from a few dozen to 100 or more, depending on age and health, and it takes about 6 months to regrow a full scalp of hair.

- Telogen hairs are typically the type found at crime scenes and analyzed in case samples. In fact, depending on the amount of body hair a person has and how often that person vacuums, there may be hundreds or even thousands of shed hairs in someone's home or vehicle at any given time.

- However, shed hairs can easily be transferred from one place to another by an object or person that the hair doesn't belong to. In that sense, hair is always circumstantial evidence.

The Microscopic Anatomy of Hair

- The 3 main regions of a hair are the cuticle, cortex, and medulla. The cuticle of a hair is made up of scales that have the microscopic appearance of a shingled roof.

- All humans have the same cuticle pattern, so looking at the cuticle of a human hair is no help in identification. However, nonhuman animals have different cuticle patterns that can be observed microscopically to differentiate among nonhuman hairs.

- Beneath the cuticle, the cortex of a hair is made up of many cells that are regularly arranged parallel to the hair's length, giving the hair most of its strength. Looking at the cortex is a critical part of hair comparison because the cortex contains the pigment granules that give hair much of its color.

Hair may be found or analyzed years after a death or crime because it is such a stable form of trace evidence.

- When hair is bleached, it loses pigmentation from its cortex. When hair is dyed, the color can either coat the surface or penetrate into the cortex, depending on the type of hair color used. Only the portion of the hair that is treated will show color change. At examination, therefore, the root end will not only show the true color, but also the line where it was dyed. Untreated regrowth also shows the original color of the hair.

- The core of a hair, known as the medulla, is a hollow region at its center. In humans, the medulla takes up only about 1/3 of the total diameter of the hair, but in most nonhuman mammals, the medullary index—the fraction of the medulla when compared to the hair shaft—is more than 1/2. In general, human scalp hairs either have no medulla or a fragmented medulla.

- Telling the difference between hairs from different parts of the human body is fairly easy—sometimes with the unaided eye—by using characteristics such as length, texture, color, and diameter, but there are underlying microscopic differences that relate to the obvious differences that can be seen.

- The ends of hair that have been cut or shaved have a blunt tip while body hairs that are not have a naturally tapered end, and scalp hairs that are long and not recently cut usually show a frayed end—often called a split end.

- Knowing the average rate of hair growth, investigators can gauge the age of a hair by its length. However, the age or sex of the person that the hair belongs to can't be judged with any confidence—except maybe for the very fine hairs found on the scalp of a baby. Even gray hair doesn't necessarily relate solely to a person's age.

Hair Comparison

- There are specific steps involved in a hair comparison. First, a questioned hair has to be identified among all the evidence at a scene, which can actually be difficult, and then the unknown hair has to be classified by type—such as head or pubic hair—and be assessed to determine which tests it's likely suitable for.

- Then, a representative group of known standards of the same type of hair—head or pubic—have to be taken from a suspect or someone who investigators need to exclude.

- If there are similar features, they should be noted before a microscopic exam. If there are not similar features, the comparison is concluded and the report is issued. However, if the questioned and known hairs warrant a complete comparison, then they have to be examined microscopically.

- Using a side-by-side comparison microscope, detailed observations can be made using all of the features of the cortex and its pigment distribution as well as the medulla and its form.

- An investigator has 3 options with regard to reporting on the comparison between any 2 hairs.

  - If there are no unexplainable differences and many commonalities between 2 hairs in question, a trace analyst may conclude that the 2 hairs could have come from the same person.

  - If there are clear differences that go beyond the typical range of variation seen in a single person, then an analyst may conclude that the 2 hairs could not have come from the same individual.

  - If there are both similarities and differences, then no conclusion can be made about a potential association between the hair in question and hairs taken from a known person.

- Investigators have attempted to classify hair in much the same way that fingerprints are categorized, but human hair can't be fit into any reasonable number of classes to allow for discrete categories the way they've been able to do with fingerprints and genetic markers.

- Furthermore, when people change their hair—or as it changes naturally when they age—the hair changes class groups. This is different from fingerprints and genetic markers, which don't change as people age.

- To come up with a good hair standard for a single person, many known hairs are needed because even on the same person's scalp, any number of hairs might vary in diameter, length, and color.

- An investigator should collect at least 50 full-length, intact hairs—which means with the root—from the scalp of a single subject to serve as that person's known reference sample. Because of regional differences, these hairs should come from a variety of locations on the person's head.

- Similarities between hairs can be noted and dissimilarities between hairs can definitely provide exclusions, but there is currently nothing short of nuclear DNA technology to positively link a hair to a specific person.

Suggested Reading

Robertson, *Forensic Examination of Hair.*

Questions to Consider

1. What do hair and fur have in common, and how are they different?

2. If someone's hair is found at a crime scene, is it conclusive evidence that the person was at that location?

3. What types of information can be gained from the examination of hair?

4. Is hair an example of class or individuating evidence?

Traces of Hair and Fur
Lecture 7—Transcript

Among the many varieties of what is known as trace evidence, hairs have a long history of being used in the attempts to solve crimes. In fact, hair is still one of the most commonly analyzed forms of trace evidence. One of the great values of hair in forensic science is that it's so stable when compared to other body tissues. Hair might be found or analyzed years after a death or a crime, and the recent reopening of "cold cases" in the United States and elsewhere has shown the stability of hair as trace evidence over long periods of time.

But let's begin by stating right up front what hair analysis can do and what it cannot: Standard hair analysis cannot conclusively match 2 hairs. So, then, what good is hair in forensics, and why is it still so useful?

Many people think that since DNA technology has come along, it has eliminated the need for other forms of testing, like forensic hair analysis. But consider a case where a woman was at a big party and claims to have been raped on her way home by a guy who was also at the party. The victim shows up at the emergency room, and the sexual assault nurse examiner takes the woman's clothing for submission to the crime lab. The victim says that the perpetrator wore a condom, and there are no obvious semen stains anywhere.

Back at the lab, the trace evidence examiners find several head hairs on the victim's clothing, and in her panties there are a couple of pubic hairs. None of these hairs seems to be a visual match to the victim's own hair in terms of length or color. So the police round up the suspect, but he says he has an alibi. He claims he left the party with somebody else and spent the whole night with her. He claims he never touched the lady who said she was raped.

Do you have any idea how long it takes to get DNA samples back from the lab? On TV they get them back after the commercial break, right? But in reality it usually takes months or even longer. Besides, it's not always possible to get DNA out of a hair sample.

So what can investigators do? If the suspect is willing—or sometimes, by a court order, even if he is not—the crime lab can get a sample of his head and pubic hair for comparison. The suspect's hairs are the known hairs, which my trace-examiner friend refers to as the "K" sample, and the hairs on the victim's clothing are the unknown hairs, called the "Q" sample— Q being for questioned.

If microscopic comparison reveals clear differences between the K and Q hairs, right then and there, that guy from the party is no longer a suspect. Without going to all the taxpayer's expense of DNA testing, and without months passing while an innocent man stands accused of something terrible, the crime lab has conveniently eliminated him from suspicion— just by looking at some hairs under a microscope. That's the power of exclusionary evidence.

But what if the hairs are similar? Does that prove the man is guilty? No, but it will certainly allow investigators to continue to focus on him as a suspect and gather additional evidence to either show his guilt or support his innocence. Microscopic hair analysis only serves as class evidence, that is, remember, evidence associated with a group rather than an individual. But if the hairs are similar, DNA testing will probably be one of the next steps taken.

Now that we understand something about the value of hair as forensic evidence, let's take a closer look at its structure. Hair is a unique feature of mammals, abundant in some animals but less so in species like whales and we modern humans. There's really no difference between hair and fur, except the term fur is typically used for the hair of nonhuman mammals.

Hair form differs, not only among different types of mammals, but also on different regions of the same animal's body. For example, we know that the whiskers on a cat or a dog are different from the long guard hairs of its coat, which are different from the rest of its fur.

Humans have lots of different types of hairs too, including eyebrows, eyelashes, beard hair, and body hair—we all know that. But did you know that none of those types of human hairs are routinely used in forensic hair examinations? Only pubic or scalp hair are typically analyzed in a forensic lab; the other types just don't have enough internal detail for meaningful comparisons.

Because hair is so familiar to us, it's something we pretty much take for granted—but hair has interesting growth patterns and functions. Some hairs on the body have a long lifespan with near continuous growth, like beard hair and head hair, but other hairs, like arm and leg hairs, eyebrows, and eyelashes, they have a fairly consistent and relatively short length on an individual, and once they achieve that length they are shed and replaced.

All hairs have a little nerve ending at their root, so hairs act as a means of sensation—in other words, hair allows us to feel the approach of something before it actually comes in direct contact with our skin. So, a predator might wind up with a mouthful of fur, instead of breaking the flesh of its prey. Now you might not think that has anything to do with forensic science, but the fact that hair is in a sense a "breakaway structure" is one reason it might be found at a crime scene.

Human hair, like that of other mammals, is a dead extension of the skin made mostly of proteins, the main one being keratin. Keratin is a widespread component of the body coverings of many animals, including reptile scales, bird feathers and beaks, cat claws, primate fingernails, and rhino horns. Other proteins in hair, like melanin, give it color. Humans typically have hair on all body skin, except the thick skin on the palms of our hands and the soles of our feet where we have the type of friction ridge skin we talked about in our discussion of fingerprints.

The structure of hair has often been compared to a standard pencil: There is a thin outer layer called the cuticle; this would be like the paint on the surface of a pencil. Beneath the cuticle is a layer called the cortex—like the wood part of a standard pencil; this is the thickest region in a human hair. At the core of some hairs is a hollow region called the medulla; in our analogy this would be like the lead or graphite in a pencil.

The root of the hair is anchored into the dermis layer of the skin, surrounded by epidermal cells that make up what's called its follicle—blood vessels at the hair root truck in the raw materials for hair production and growth. Because the substances needed to build hair come from the bloodstream, hair then becomes a lasting repository of certain chemicals in the body. This can include illicit drugs (like THC from marijuana) and certain poisons (like arsenic) that can get incorporated into the shaft of the hair as it grows.

If there is a suspicion of drug use or poisoning, chemical analyses can be performed on hair during drug testing or at autopsy. As we'll see in a future lecture, blood and urine samples can only show a relatively recent history of drug use or toxins in the body, but the chemical stability of hair makes it an excellent and long-standing record of body chemistry. Plus, since hair growth rates are fairly standard, investigators are able to put a rough date as to when a chemical substance was laid down in hair.

So what is the typical rate of hair growth? Now, I'm not admitting to anything, but if you color your hair, you have some idea of how fast your hair grows. References vary on the typical rate of scalp hair growth; and estimates range from about one to one and a fourth centimeters a month, which is about half an inch.

Although it might appear that hairs grow continuously, there are actually life stages to each and every hair on the body. Most hairs on our body at any given time are in an actively growing stage, called the anagen phase, in which new cells are being added at the hair root; this pushes the hair shaft further towards the body surface. The anagen growth phase can last as long as 2 to 7 years for scalp hair.

The growth rate varies for different types of body hair, and according to some authorities, seems to vary by genetics; the hairs of people with African ancestry tend to have a shorter life cycle than those with Caucasian heritage, and people with Asian ancestry have hair with the longest anagen phase.

If a hair is pulled forcibly during this growth phase, a follicle tag will remain on the ribbon-like end of the hair root; you may have seen this white residue yourself if you have plucked an eyebrow. A follicle tag is always indicative of a pulled hair, rather than a hair that was naturally shed. So, in violent crimes in which people struggle with each other, hair may be pulled out and left at crime scene or transferred from one person to another. The follicle tissue can also be a source of nuclear DNA, and we'll come back to that in a little bit.

Near the end of a hair's lifecycle it enters what's called the catagen phase, where growth begins to slow down. During the catagen phase, the hair root begins to shrivel away from the follicle and becomes elongated.

The final phase in the life of a single hair is called the telogen phase and is the time when a hair is getting ready to be shed naturally. During the telogen phase, the hair breaks away from the follicle and the root takes on a more bulbous shape. A hair may remain lodged in its follicle in this telogen stage for several months before actually falling out, but a hair with a bulbous root, and with no follicular material, indicates a hair that was shed naturally in the normal course of our hair replacement. I've seen different estimates, but numbers of typical hairs lost per day range from a few dozen to 100 or more, and we all know that's dependent somewhat on age and health, too.

After all hair is lost, for example from chemotherapy, which targets cells in rapid growth and division, like cancer cells, but also targets normal body cells that undergo rapid growth like those at the root of a hair. Anyway, it takes about 6 months to re-grow a full scalp of hair.

Telogen hairs are typically the type found at crime scenes and analyzed in case samples; as you can imagine, they might be found on the inside or outside of clothing, among bed sheets, on the head rest of a car seat, or in a hairbrush. In fact, when you think about it, depending on the amount of body hair a person has, and how often that person might vacuum, there may be hundreds or even thousands of shed hairs in someone's home or vehicle at any given time.

We have to keep in mind, though, that shed hairs can easily be transferred from one place to another by an object or person that that hair doesn't belong to—so in that sense hair is always circumstantial evidence. Remember what we learned earlier about evidence transfer: You might occupy a subway seat after a person who owned a cat, and unknowingly you could transfer cat hairs onto your own clothing without ever having met the cat's owner, let alone seen the cat—and if we're talking about a plane seat, that transfer can happen across the country in a matter of a few hours.

Now, let's look in more detail at the microscopic anatomy of hair. I mentioned the 3 main regions of a hair—cuticle, cortex, and medulla. Let's start on the surface with the cuticle and work our way toward the center of a hair shaft.

The cuticle of a hair is made up of scales that have the microscopic appearance of a shingled roof. All humans have the same cuticle pattern, so looking at the cuticle of a human hair is really no help in identification. But, nonhuman animals have different cuticle patterns that can be observed microscopically to differentiate among nonhuman hairs.

Details of the cuticle can be seen using a scanning electron microscope, but in my forensic science class, we just put a thin layer of clear nail polish on a microscope slide; we rest the surface of a hair on it briefly; and then gently pull the hair away from the slide. This results in an imprinted cast of the hair's surface cuticle on the microscope slide that can then put under the microscope to look at.

Beneath the cuticle, the cortex of a hair is made up of many cells that are regularly arranged parallel to the hair's length, and that gives the hair most of its strength. Looking at the cortex is a critical part of hair comparison, because the cortex contains the pigment granules that give hair much of its color. Melanin is the primary pigment found in all types of hair, and it comes in varieties ranging from yellow to red, and brown to black.

Pigment granules also differ in shape and in distribution within the cortex of a hair, giving more continuity or intensity to the color of the cortex. The complete absence of pigment causes hair to appear white as in albino hair, but the gray color changes that we usually associated with age are due to an accumulation in hydrogen peroxide production that causes a gradual decline in melanin production.

When hair is bleached, it will lose pigmentation from its cortex. When hair is dyed, the color can either coat the surface or penetrate into the cortex, depending on the kind of hair color used. And we all know that only the portion of the hair that is treated will show the color change. So, at examination, the root end will not only show the true color, but also the line where it was dyed. And we all know that untreated re-growth also will show the original color of the hair.

The core of a hair, known as the medulla, is a hollow region at its center. In humans the medulla takes up only about a third of the total diameter of the hair, but in most nonhuman mammals the medullary index—meaning the fraction of the medulla when compared to the whole hair shaft—is more than half. Scientists classify the shape of the medulla within a human hair as continuous, interrupted, or fragmented; and in some cases, there may be no medulla present within a human hair shaft. In general, human scalp hairs either have no medulla, or they have a fragmented medulla.

In the hair of nonhuman animals, the medulla is often the most unique and obvious microscopic feature. Most nonhuman mammals have a continuous medulla pattern, with a variety of interesting shapes that are classified in different ways than human hairs are. For nonhumans we use terms like ladder, lattice, and vacuolated patterns. Databases of medulla patterns for many different mammals have been developed for rapid species identification when nonhuman hair analysis is necessary in a forensic setting.

One of the main reasons nonhuman animal hair identification and comparisons will be useful is to try to link transferred hair—like from a pet—to a suspect, victim, or a crime scene. But species identification is also an important tool in what is known as wildlife forensics where issues of poaching or illegal importation of animals is suspected; we will talk about this more in our next lecture.

Now, back to humans. Telling the difference between hairs from different parts of the human body is fairly easy—sometimes even with the naked eye. You can probably tell the difference between the different types of hair you or others in your house shed on the floor of your shower, just by the length, texture, color, and diameter alone. But, there are underlying microscopic differences that relate to the obvious differences we can see. For example, pubic hairs have wide variations in shaft diameter along their length, and they often exhibit a continuous medulla, whereas male facial hair usually has a shaft that is more triangular than it is round.

Hairs also differ at their ends. Ends that have been cut or shaved will have a blunt tip, while body hairs that are not will have a naturally tapered end, and scalp hairs that are long and not recently cut usually show a frayed end—often called a split end on TV commercials. By the way, shaving hair does not make it grow back faster or thicker. That's a myth. Shaved hairs only feel more coarse because of the thickness of their blunt ends when compared to the tapered ends they would have if they hadn't been cut.

Knowing the average rate of hair growth, the age of a hair can be gauged by its length. But the age or sex of the person that that hair belongs to can't be judged with any confidence, except maybe for the very fine hairs found on the scalp of a baby. Even gray hair doesn't necessarily relate solely to a person's age.

There are some differences, though, in hair among people from 3 general racial classifications—Caucasian, African, and Asian—provided those people have a fairly strong single-race heritage. Some of these features can be observed with the naked eye, while others require looking at hairs through a microscope. Scalp hairs from Caucasians will have more continuously distributed pigment granules in the cortex, and the shaft is often round if they have straight hair or oval if they have wavy hair. Hairs from people with African ancestry have more uneven distribution of very dense pigment granules, and they are generally flat to slightly oval in cross-section, resulting in a kinky to wavy texture to the hair. Asian people have a medulla that is usually continuous, and a round hair shaft that results in straight hair.

Now that we've learned something about forensic hair analysis, let's summarize the specific steps involved in a hair comparison. First, a questioned hair has to be identified among all the evidence at a scene, and that can be difficult in itself. Then that unknown hair has to be classified as to its type—like is it head hair or pubic hair—and then be assessed to see what tests it's likely suitable for. For example, does it have a follicle that could yield nuclear DNA or not?

Next, a representative group of known standards of the same type of hair, head or pubic, have to be taken from a suspect or someone who needs to be excluded. If there are similar features, they should be noted even before a microscopic exam. If there are not similar features, the comparison is done and the report gets issued. But, if the questioned and known hairs warrant a complete comparison, then they have to be examined microscopically.

Analysts typically embed each hair to be compared on a microscope slide in what's called a mounting medium. If you just put a hair on a microscope slide and looked at it under the scope, or examined it in a water mount, you know, where you just put water on the slide, you really won't see the details of the cortex and the medulla. In order to allow light to penetrate the hair so that the details of the cortex and the medulla can be seen, investigators use a mounting medium with a refractive index similar to that of hair itself— remember we talked about refractive index when we talked about fibers and glass.

Using side-by-side comparison microscopes, detailed observations can be made, using all of the features of the cortex and its pigment distribution, as well as the medulla and its form. If there's a positive association between the 2 hairs being compared, my trace examiner friend said she always gets a second opinion from another qualified hair examiner. This is because of the subjectivity involved in drawing conclusions by comparing 2 hairs.

In fact, there have been an unfortunate number of forensic cases—including relatively recently—where investigators stretched the boundaries of what can and cannot be known from hair analysis. Most often, these cases are related to a single hair from a crime scene being linked to a suspect, allegedly at the exclusion of nearly all other individuals. In other words, more was made out of the evidence than was scientifically possible, often accompanied by unsubstantiated statistics.

Take for example the case of forensic analyst Joyce Gilchrist, who was employed by the Oklahoma City Police Department for 21 years and participated in thousands of forensic investigations. Evidence she analyzed, including numerous hair comparisons, contributed to over 23 death sentences; tragically, 11 of those people had already been executed by the time her conclusions and the methods she was using were seriously called into question. DNA testing has now exonerated some of Gilchrist's victims, and case reviews have shown that she either lost or destroyed evidence, and she made specific conclusions about hair comparisons that were completely unwarranted.

So what kind of valid conclusions can be made from hair comparisons? My trace evidence friend put it this way: She said if she could take a couple of questioned hairs (remember those are her Q hairs) and mix them up with a sample of known hairs from someone (those are her K hairs) and shake them up, dump them out, and not be able to tell them apart—even after using all of her cool tools—then the most she can say is the Q hairs are consistent with originating from the known person. But, it also has to be understood—especially in court—that those same questioned hairs could also have come from any other person whose hair exhibits all those same characteristics.

An investigator really has only 3 options with regard to reporting on the comparison between any 2 hairs, and the same goes for lots of other types of evidence comparisons. First, if there are no unexplainable differences and lots of commonalities, a trace analyst may conclude that the 2 hairs could have come from the same person. Secondly, if there are clear differences that go beyond the typical range of variation seen in a single person, then an analyst may conclude that those 2 hairs could not have come from the same individual. And third, if they see both similarities and differences between 2 hairs in question, then no conclusion can be made about a potential association between the hair in question and hairs taken from a known person.

This is because hairs exhibit features that are shared among a group of people, which again means we're talking about class evidence. And the size of these groups that share hair characteristics is not even close to being known. Investigators have attempted to classify hair in much the same way fingerprints are categorized—but human hair can't be fit into any reasonable number of classes to allow for the same discrete categories like they have been able to do with fingerprints, and as we'll see, with genetic markers in DNA. So, there is just no way to establish probabilities among individuals and say, for example, that the chances of 2 similar hairs coming from 2 different people are 500 to 1, or something like that.

The other problem is that when people change their hair—or as it changes naturally when they age—the hair then changes class groups when it changes its features. This is different, then, from fingerprints or genetic markers, which don't change as we age.

So, because of the inherent difficulties and the subjectivity involved in hair comparisons, only a highly skilled and very experienced trace evidence examiner can make a quality assessment of the similarities among human hairs. This is not only because there can be strong similarities between the hairs of 2 different individuals, but also because there can be striking differences among multiple hairs taken from the scalp of just one person.

In fact, you might remember one of the questions raised at the famous O. J. Simpson trial was how representative a single hair is with regard to a person's entire head. The answer to that seems to depend a lot on the person. To come up with a good hair standard for a single person, many known hairs are needed. That's because even on the same person's scalp, any number of hairs might vary in diameter, length, and color.

Protocols differ, but I've seen it suggested that an investigator should collect at least 50 full-length, intact hairs—that means hairs with the root—from the scalp of a single subject to serve as that person's known reference sample. And because of regional differences, the hairs should come from a variety of locations on that person's head. In rape cases, it's suggested that at least 20 intact pubic hairs be collected from a suspect before attempting a comparison with an unknown pubic hair from a crime scene. But more is better; and the FBI recommends 100 scalp hairs for a known standard, and the RCMP (that's the Royal Canadian Mounted Police) suggest pulling 150 sample hairs. Man, that's got to hurt!

So where does that leave us? Similarities between hairs can be noted, and dissimilarities between hairs can definitely provide exclusions, but there is currently nothing short of nuclear DNA technology to positively link a hair to a specific person.

We have a DNA lecture coming up shortly, but let me highlight some of the fundamentals now: There are 2 basic types of DNA found in human cells, nuclear and mitochondrial DNA, and both are relevant to hair analyses. Nuclear DNA is inherited from both parents, and it's unique to each one of us, except in the case of identical twins.

Analysts can get nuclear DNA from follicle cells surrounding the hair root, or sometimes even from the actively growing anagen root itself. But remember, follicle tissue is only found on hairs that have been forcibly removed—hairs that are on their way to being naturally shed are in the catagen and telogen stage, and they don't have actively growing root.

On the other hand, mitochondrial DNA—which is inherited only from a person's mother—can be obtained and analyzed from a hair shaft. The problem with mitochondrial DNA, though, as we'll see, is that it is not as discriminatory as nuclear DNA, since it's shared among all people in a maternal bloodline. It certainly does add additional data to a case, but it is not considered positive identification.

In 2002, the FBI published a study that used mitochondrial DNA to try to assess the validity of microscopic hair analyses that they conducted between the years 1996 and 2000. Their self-study looked at 80 so-called positive microscopic associations that qualified FBI hair analysts had made, and compared them to mitochondrial DNA analyses on those same hairs. The results showed that 11.25% of those microscopic associations made by the FBI were, in fact, not true associations. That doesn't mean the analysts were wrong—the hairs themselves did show microscopic associations—it just means those associations were not valid when compared to DNA testing, and reminds us that hair is class evidence.

That study is an example of good science and critical self-analysis. It doesn't negate the usefulness of hair analysis, since nearly 90% of those FBI associations did hold up. But it certainly suggests that all evidence comparisons—not just hair analyses, but all of the types we've covered and those yet to come—should only be undertaken by the most experienced and ethical of professionals and always backed up with additional evidence and testing.

Soil, Protist, Plant, and Animal Traces
Lecture 8

E lements such as hair and fur from various animals are useful in forensic investigations, but there are many more ways in which the natural world is involved in forensic science. Soil, wood, pollen grains, animal hairs, and single-celled organisms called protists can all be used to link a person or object to a crime scene. Animals are used directly in some investigations—particularly insects, which forensic entomologists use to estimate time of death—and, of course, larger animals are investigated as suspects if they are accused of attacking people.

Analyzing Soil

- Soil is a mixture composed of both natural inorganic and organic materials but can also include man-made materials. The inorganic stuff in soil is mostly decaying or weathered rocks and minerals. Because they tend to vary geographically, the types and percentages of rocks and minerals can indicate a possible location associated with a suspect or victim.

- Soil testing requires experience and skill in a variety of microscopic, physical, and chemical-testing methods. Forensic investigators— and sometimes geologists, soil scientists, or archaeologists—test the questioned soil to determine where it was originally found and, therefore, where known samples should be taken from for comparison.

- Depending on the type of test being done, the soil may need to be pulverized and homogenized, but this can only be done after any tests that require the soil to be untouched are finished.

- Soils can vary a lot in color; it's estimated that there are over 1000 distinguishable soil colors. The Munsell system, which was developed by Alfred Munsell and adopted by the U.S. Department of Agriculture, uses 3 main descriptors with regard to color: hue, value, and purity.

- Soils also vary in texture: Some are loamy like garden soil while others are silty like soil from a creek or river. In addition, particle size differs in soils, and this can be measured using a graduated set of mesh soil sieves.

- Furthermore, the specific rocks and minerals in soil can be examined. Fracture patterns are the ways pieces of rock and minerals break off, leaving jagged or smooth edges. The optical properties, such as refractive index, can also be examined; some grains appear to be different colors at different angles.

Analyzing Pollen, Spores, and Protists

Soil that is found on the tires of a vehicle can be analyzed to possibly link a car to the scene of a crime.

- Palynology is the study of pollen and spores, but it can also include the study of other microscopic organisms in soil and water. Pollen grains are the male gametes of seed-bearing plants, which include all flowering plants and cone-bearing plants. Spores are the reproductive units of lower plants like fungi, ferns, and mosses. Some protists also reproduce using spores.

- Pollen and spores make good forensic evidence because they both have durable coverings that resist being degraded in the environment, and localities have distinctive plant and fungus distributions, so they have distinctive pollen and spores. Different populations of protists in a sample of soil or water may even point to a specific season because plants and fungi reproduce at specific times of the year.

- Soil or water samples that include pollen grains, fungal spores, and protists need to be examined microscopically using a typical light microscope for general structure and a scanning electron microscope (SEM) for 3-D detail. Distinctive features usually include the size and complexity of these biological bits of evidence.

- If a body is found in the bushes, but the pollen on the clothing doesn't match the type of bushes it's found in, the body might have been moved from somewhere else to its current location.

- Furthermore, if the clothing can be assessed for the specific types and amounts of pollen and spores, analysts may be able to come up with a general profile of the type of area and the plants in it that investigators should be looking for.

- Characterizing the microscopic life forms, including pollen, spores, and protists, in the clothing or the airway of a body that was in water might lead investigators to a possible location—or at least tell them more about how or where the person died or where the body has been.

Analyzing Wood
- Some forensic specialists can identify species of trees and other woody plants by the microscopic patterns seen in

In addition to pollen, wood is another type of plant evidence that has forensic value.

wood. Different woody plants have characteristic cell structures and grain that can lead to identification down to the genus level—such as spruce, oak, pine, or maple—even with small samples.

- This type of identification can't usually go down to the species level, though, the way it can with pollen, flowers, or leaves. So far, DNA testing is not possible with wood because there are only minute quantities of DNA contained in wood.

- Some wooden objects that could be involved in crimes are cultural artifacts or prized antiques that may need authentication by a wood expert, and some types of trees are protected species and are illegal to harvest, but there are also crimes against people that require forensic wood identification or the linking of pieces of wood by examining fracture patterns and other clues.

- The Lindbergh kidnapping is a famous example of a case that used wood matching as critical evidence to identify a carpenter named Bruno Hauptman as the man who abducted and murdered the infant son of Charles Lindbergh, who was the first man to fly solo across the Atlantic Ocean.

Analyzing Animal Evidence

- Some types of forensic investigators specialize in identifying animal abuse and ensuring animal safety to try to guarantee that domesticated animals are treated humanely, and when forensic evidence suggests otherwise, charges may be brought against the perpetrators.

- A relatively recent branch of forensic science called wildlife forensics has a few main focuses: Forensic wildlife investigators examine poaching violations and help protect endangered species—both animals and plants—and they look into the poisoning of wildlife to try to figure out if an event stems from malicious and intentional baiting of animals or is an accident.

- As a science, wildlife forensics emerged out of the U.S. Endangered Species Act of 1973 and the UN Convention of International Trade in Endangered Species, which is comprised of 175 member parties that have agreed to be legally bound by its guidelines in order to protect our natural world.

- In terms of criminal activity, the illegal trade of international wildlife is third only to drugs and guns and affects hundreds of millions of plant and animal species. Some of the problem is that cultural customs, understanding of ecology, and environmental awareness vary significantly around the world.

- One of the problems with investigating various poaching violations—as well as other forms of illegal collection of plant and animal products—is that the evidence rarely involves whole plants or whole animals, which can be easily identified by zoo, museum, and botanical experts.

- Some animal violations have to be detected by examining food products, such as fresh, frozen, or smoked meats. Other animal evidence comes in the form of commercial or handmade products that are made from protected species. Some animal and plant materials can be significantly altered—ground up, dried, or crushed—sometimes making them even more difficult to identify.

- Although wildlife forensics deals with many different species as compared to traditional forensics, it still involves many of the same experts. In addition, however, mammalian osteologists examine teeth, bones, and antlers to see if age requirements for hunting have been met, and they can also try to match dismembered body parts. Ornithologists examine feathers and talons as potential evidence of illegal hunting of protected bird species.

- Out of a need to enforce established laws and protect our natural world and the creatures in it, the U.S. Fish and Wildlife Service Forensics Laboratory was founded in 1988. This high-tech crime lab and its team of experts perform a large number of forensic examinations covering all parts of the United States.

- In the United States, the entity that governs the trade of animal and plant products, including their import and export, is the Department of Homeland Security. The regulations that are enforced through the Customs and Border Protection division are important not only for the preservation of endangered species, but also to protect our environment from the introduction of nonnative species that could harm U.S. ecosystems.

Analyzing Environmental Damage and Contamination

- Abnormal odors, areas called dead zones in plant growth, and dead fish in waterways can all be clues that something or someone could be poisoning the environment. Whether the toxicity is due to an intentional release of chemicals or is accidental contamination, these types of incidents need to be investigated and often culminate in criminal and/or civil litigation.

- Commonly encountered poisons include heavy metals, different types of insecticides, toxins intended to kill rodents, and even barbiturates that can leach into the environment when the carcasses of euthanized animals are dumped into landfills. Sometimes, the patterns in the dead animals can reveal the particular toxin involved.

- The forensic identification of pesticides and other toxic chemicals in the environment is critical because not only does it damage plant and animal life, but it can also harm and kill humans. Because plants and animals are lower on the food chain, they are often the first indicators of environmental damage. When wildlife investigators pick up on these clues, the work they do might ultimately protect human health.

- Even if rehabilitation groups step in to help sick or injured animals after an oil spill or other toxic event, important documentation— such as photos, carcasses, tissue samples, and even feces and vomit—has to be kept because of its eventual importance if there is ever a trial.

When Animals Attack Humans

- When people travel to or live in relatively remote places, there's an increased likelihood that they will encounter potentially dangerous wildlife. Sometimes, diseased animals—such as those with rabies—lose their fear and enter areas they normally wouldn't.

- Fatal attacks by animals to humans must be reported to the governing coroner or medical examiner—just as with any other unexpected death. Even when someone survives an animal attack, the proper authorities should be notified, and any necessary media releases should be made through the proper channels, especially if the animal is still at large.

- When animals attack, the bites they leave on a victim can be examined using the same type of bite-mark analyses that forensic odontologists use when people bite each other. Bite-mark analysis can be used to help identify the type of critter involved in an animal attack and possibly even to tie the victim to a specific animal, if it's found.

- When investigators have to search for an animal at large, they use the same types of strategies as when searching for a human predator, but they track for paws, fur, and scat (animal feces). If necessary, paw prints can be cast using the same types of methods that are used with shoe and tire impressions.

- If the suspect animal is caught, it may have to be analyzed to see if it is, in fact, the perpetrator. This is usually done by examining the animal's stomach contents.

Suggested Reading

Gunn, *Essential Forensic Biology*.

1. How can soil be used as evidence in a crime?

2. What are protists, and where might they be found?

3. What types of plant materials constitute crime-scene evidence?

4. How are animals used in forensic science?

5. Can environmental contamination be a criminal act?

Soil, Protist, Plant, and Animal Traces
Lecture 8—Transcript

As we saw in our last lecture on hair and fur, elements from our fellow creatures can be useful in forensic investigations. But there are lots of other ways in which the natural world is involved in forensic science, including but not limited to, what some people call "wildlife forensics."

For instance, soils, wood, pollen grains, animal hairs, and single-celled organisms called protists can all be used to tie a person or object to a crime scene. Animals are used directly in some investigations, particularly insects, which are used by forensic entomologists to estimate time of death. Sometimes, of course, larger animals are investigated as suspects, if they are accused of attacking people. Let's start our discussion with the smaller stuff and work our way up the food chain.

Soils, pollen, and plant or fungal spores are all examples of microscopic evidence that have the potential to link people, objects, events, and locations. For instance, soil analysis can link the shoes of a suspect to the scene of a crime, or if it's found on the tires of a vehicle, might show where a car traveled or where a victim was transported.

This type of microscopic evidence has also been used to investigate crimes against humanity. In the Bosnian war crimes trials, pollen analysis showed that the war criminals exhumed bodies from mass graves and then reburied them in smaller graves to try to make it look like the victims had been killed in smaller clashes rather than mass executions. Distinctive wheat pollen grains from one of the secondary burial sites helped to pinpoint the site of the execution as happening near a particular wheat field. And pollen from plant species found near the original mass grave was found on the remains and in the soil of the smaller, individual graves.

Soil is something we take for granted, but most of us probably really don't know what's in it. Soil is a mixture composed of both natural inorganic and organic materials, but it can also include man-made materials.

The inorganic stuff in soil is mostly decayed or weathered rocks and minerals. We all know what rocks are, and minerals are naturally occurring crystals. There are about 2200 minerals known; and about 40 common ones occur in soil, and those include quartz, feldspar, mica, and lots of others. At their most basic levels, minerals are crystalline solids with regular shapes, and some with very distinctive colors. Because they tend to vary geographically, the types and percentages of rocks and minerals can indicate a possible location associated with a suspect or victim.

The organic fraction of soil is known as humus, which is mainly a mixture of plant and fungal matter like decaying wood, grass, pine needles, pollen grains, and spores. There's also animal matter in the organic constituents of soil, like feces, parts of bugs, and the remains of other decomposing animals.

Any manufactured objects in soils are going to depend on the surroundings, and can include stuff like glass, paint chips, asphalt, gravel, concrete, brick fragments, cinders, and even insulation. If big enough particles of these man-made materials are found, they might be useful to link the soil to a particular structure or road type.

Soil testing requires experience and skill in a variety of microscopic, physical, and chemical-testing methods. It's usually done by a forensic chemist in a crime lab. But sometimes a geologist, a soil scientist, or even an archaeologist, or maybe somebody from a local university, who has particular knowledge of a specific area and knows how to use geological maps—well they might be able to help determine, or at least narrow down, the area where the questioned soil was originally picked up. That might help forensic investigators determine where known samples should be taken from for any comparison they want to do.

The U.S. Geological Survey, the American Society of Testing and Materials (known as ASTM), and the British Standards Institution have all developed standard methods of soil analysis. Depending on the type of test being done, the soil might have to be pulverized and homogenized, but this can only be done after any tests which require the soil "as is" are finished. For example, chemical testing is only done after the soil's particle size and shape have been determined.

You might think soil is boring, but there are lots of different features to soils, and I'm familiar with some of them from my days working as an archaeologist. For one thing, soils can vary a lot in their color; it's estimated there are over 1000 distinguishable soil colors. The Munsell system, which was developed by a guy named Alfred Munsell, and then adopted by the U.S. Department of Agriculture, uses 3 main descriptors with regard to color. Those are hue, which is the color itself; the value, which is how light or dark the color is; and the purity of the color, which is called chroma.

The color of soil will be darker if it's wet, so soil samples have to be dried before they're analyzed. And then they're compared to a Munsell chart—which is this big book of color chips—sort of like you'd use with paint. When it's done, each color winds up with a code that's this universal standard fraction. I know a lot about Munsell charts because the archaeologist I used to work with most often was color blind—so I always got stuck doing the Munsells for both of us.

Soils vary in texture, as well; some are loamy like garden soil, others are silty, like soil from a creek or river—and in Ohio, we have a lot of dense clay, which I can tell you is no fun for an archaeologist.

Particle size differs in soils, too, and we measure this using a graduated set of mesh soil sieves. You put the soil sample through a series of sieves, each with smaller and smaller holes. And then each fraction that comes off is weighed to determine the percentage of each particle size in the soil.

The specific rocks and minerals in soil can be examined, too. Important features include fracture patterns—you know, maybe the way pieces of rock and minerals break off, leaving jagged or smooth edges. The optical properties of these inorganic components can be examined, too, like their refractive index—which, in the case of soil, is the way light bends going through a particle or crystal in the soil. Crystalline solids like quartz can have 2 refractive indices because of their structure. And some grains appear different colors at different angles. So, soil really isn't as boring as you might think! Or maybe it really is to you, so I guess I'll move on.

Have you ever heard of palynology? If not, there's your big word of the day today. Palynology is specifically the study of pollen and spores, but it can also include the study of other microscopic organisms in soil and water. For instance, dinoflagellates and diatoms are 2 groups of really cool-looking single-celled protists that are part of the plankton and algae we find in water.

Pollen grains are the male gametes of seed-bearing plants—those include all flowering plants and cone-bearing plants—essentially, in other words, pollen is nothing more than plant sperm. Spores, on the other hand, are the reproductive units of lower plants like fungi, ferns, and mosses; some protists also reproduce using spores.

Pollen and spores make good forensic evidence for a couple of reasons: First, they both have durable coverings that resist being degraded over time in the environment. Secondly, localities have distinctive plant and fungus distributions, so they have distinctive pollen and spores, too.

The same kind of thing can be said for populations of protists, like dinoflagellates and diatoms in a pond or other water source. The types of these microscopic little bits of evidence in a sample of soil or water may even point to a specific season, since plants and fungi reproduce at specific times of the year. There is also seasonality to some protist cycles, like algae blooms that happen in water.

Soil or water samples that include pollen grains, fungal spores, and protists need to be examined microscopically, using a typical light microscope for general structure, and then a scanning electronic microscope for 3-D detail. Distinctive features usually include the size and complexity of these biological bits of evidence.

Most pollen is super small—in the neighborhood of only 10–70 micrometers; and in case you forgot—or you never learned the metric system—a single micrometer is one millionth of a meter, or one ten-thousandth of a centimeter. So, these pollen grains range in diameter from about 4 ten-thousandths of an inch to a little over 2 1/2 thousandths of an inch. That's really tiny!

Pollen and spores also vary in their unique, complex, and often really cool-looking structures. A scanning electron microscope, often called an SEM, can be used to determine what plant a pollen grain came from or the specific spore type in a water or soil sample.

So, let's get to the forensic value of pollen, spores, and protists. If a body is found in the bushes, but the pollen on the clothing doesn't match the type of bushes it's found in, that may suggest the body was moved from somewhere else to its current location.

That's a good clue, as far as it goes. But, there may be more that can be done. If the clothing can be assessed for the specific types and amounts of pollen and spores, analysts may be able to come up with a general profile of the type of area and the plants in it that investigators ought to be looking for.

The same goes for pollen, spores, and protists on—or even in—a body that's found in water or suspected to have been in water. Characterizing the microscopic life forms in the clothing or the airway of a body that was in water might lead investigators to a possible location, or it will at least tell them something more about how or where the person died or where the body's been.

In addition to pollen, wood is another type of plant evidence that has forensic value. Some forensic specialists can identify species of trees and other woody plants by the microscopic patterns they see in wood. Different woody plants have characteristic cell structures and grain that can lead to identification down to the genus level—like spruce, oak, pine, or maple—even with small a sample.

This type of ID can't usually go down to the species level, though, the way it can with pollen, flowers, or leaves. And so far, DNA testing is not possible with wood because there are only minute quantities of DNA contained in wood.

So, why would you need to identify a specific type of wood in forensics? Well, for one thing, some wooden objects that could be involved in crimes might be cultural artifacts or prized antiques that may need authentication by a wood expert. And some types of trees are protected species, and so they are illegal to harvest.

But there are also crimes against persons that require forensic wood identification or the linking of pieces of wood by examining fracture patterns and other clues. The Lindbergh kidnapping is a famous example of a case that used wood matching as critical evidence.

Lindbergh was the first man to fly solo across the Atlantic Ocean. His infant son, Charles, Jr., was abducted in 1932, apparently through the second story window of the family's New Jersey home, leaving a homemade ladder behind. After a ransom was paid, the decomposing body of the Lindbergh child was found in the woods near their home.

As events unfolded, including tracking the ransom money, much of which was being spent in the Bronx, authorities brought in a wood expert who analyzed the ladder. This analysis included toolmarks from how the ladder was made, the types of wood that composed it—there were 4 different types of wood. A section of one of the rails of the ladder seemed to be from a floorboard made out of the wood called fir, and it didn't match the rest of the ladder's construction.

Police followed a trail of clues that spanned a couple of years, and finally honed in on a guy named Bruno Hauptman as their prime suspect. He was a carpenter who had used one of the ransom bills at a gas station. When they searched Hauptman's home, which was in the Bronx, by the way, they found that a section of the fir floorboard in the attic was missing from a joist. And in that joist were 4 nail holes that exactly matched the spacing of 4 nail holes on the questioned piece of fir from the kidnapping ladder. So that wood evidence—and a lot of other clues—led to Hauptman's 1935 conviction for murder and kidnapping, and his execution that came just a few months later.

Now let's turn our attention to the types of animal evidence used in forensic science. We covered mammal fur in our last lecture, along with our discussion of human hair. But have you ever heard of snarge? Believe it or not, that's the name investigators use for the pulverized bird guts they wipe off of airplanes.

Do you remember in 2009 when U.S. Air Flight 1549 landed in the Hudson River in New York? It took a team of feather investigators at the Smithsonian—led by a scientist, ironically named Dr. Carla Dove—to figure out that the accident was caused by a bird strike. The Smithsonian Institution holds a reference collection that contains over 620 thousand feather and other body part samples from 85% of the world's bird species. They analyze about 4000 samples a year for the airline industry and the military. The team's ability to figure out the bird species involved in these types of incidents is really an important form of pest management that protects us all as air travelers.

If the Smithsonian's researchers can't define the type of bird or birds involved from the goo they pull out of the engines, they can send tissue or blood samples to a forensic wildlife DNA lab to get the species identification. There was one really interesting case where DNA in some snarge from a plane strike at 1500 feet was identified as coming from—are you ready for this?—a deer. Nobody could figure out how that happened until one of the feather fragments turned out to be from a black vulture that must've recently dined on a deer carcass. Mystery solved.

Animal evidence is also used to investigate crimes against our fellow creatures and even crimes against our Earth itself. There are laws intended to protect both animals and the natural environment, so these are forensic cases, too.

Some types of forensic investigators specialize in identifying animal abuse and ensuring animal safety. This includes looking into possible cases of hoarding and neglect, dog and cock fighting, and illegal activity at what are often called puppy mills. Specialists also examine practices and conditions in the horse and dog industries, including the showing and racing of both types of animals. The meat production industry is also monitored and inspected. All these types of investigations are intended to help make sure that domesticated animals are treated humanely, and when forensic evidence suggests otherwise, charges can be brought against the perpetrators.

There's a relatively recent branch of forensic science that's often called "wildlife forensics." It has a couple of main focuses: Forensic wildlife investigators examine poaching violations and help protect endangered species—both animals and plants. They look into the poisoning of wildlife to try to figure out if an event stems from malicious and intentional baiting of animals or if it was an accident.

As a science, wildlife forensics really emerged out of the U.S. Endangered Species Act of 1973, and the UN Convention of International Trade in Endangered Species—that organization has roots that go back to the 1960s, but wasn't formalized as an entity until 1975. This UN Convention currently protects 30,000 species of animals and plants and is comprised of 175 member parties—most of those are countries—and they have agreed to be legally bound by its guidelines in order to protect our natural world.

Did you know that illegal trade in international wildlife is worth billions of dollars a year? In fact, in terms of criminal activity it's third only to drugs and guns and affects hundreds of millions of plant and animal species. As you can imagine, some of the problem is that cultural customs, as well as an understanding of ecology and environmental awareness, all vary significantly around the world.

Let me give you a prime example: In the 1990s, 3 adult female black bears were found dead in a garbage dump in Canada. They were apparently killed for their gallbladders because that was the only thing that had been taken from their bodies. Bear gallbladders are prized in some forms of traditional Chinese medicine. To add even more to this tragedy, 5 cubs were left orphaned, and 2 other cubs were found killed—also for their gallbladders, which were really way too tiny to be of any actual value. It was specifically the killing of the 2 cubs that was the illegal event in this case.

Wildlife investigators were able to examine the bodies, and used entomology to help estimate the time since the cubs' deaths. Forensic entomology, as you might know, is the use of insects in forensic science, and we'll talk a lot more about it in a later lecture. Anyway, the insect evidence in that case showed that the cubs had been dead for only a few hours by the time they were discovered. This timing ultimately led to the arrest of 2 poachers who were known to be among the few people in the area at the time the cubs were killed.

In this case, the bodies of the cubs were easy to identify and examine, but one of the problems with investigating many other kinds of poaching violations—as well as other forms of illegal collection of plant and animal products—is that the cases rarely involve whole plants or whole animals as evidence. After all, zoo, museum, and botanical experts can easily identify whole animals and plants, even to the species level. But wildlife forensics can involve a whole range of types of animal and plant evidence.

Some animal violations have to be detected by examining food products—things like fresh, frozen, or smoked meats. And fish roe, used in caviar, may come from endangered and protected species. Sometimes, all investigators have to work with as evidence is blood or loose hairs maybe on a suspected hunter's clothing.

Other animal evidence comes in the form of commercial or handmade products that are made from protected species. Mammal pelts and furs can be used in clothing and rugs, and mammal and reptile skins can be turned into leather for purses, shoes, belts, and boots. Feathers from protected birds can be used in jewelry or their down used in pillows or insulation. And shells from protected species can be used in jewelry or other decorative objects.

Some animal and plant materials can be significantly altered, sometimes making them even more difficult to identify. For example, some animal parts can be ground up for medicines, like powdered rhino horn. Protected herbs might be dried and crushed. And ivory and wood can be carved or inlaid in small pieces, but that doesn't usually obscure their origin.

When you think about it, though, wildlife forensics work is so much more diverse in scope than traditional criminalistic studies. Wildlife experts deal with many different species as compared to the focus of traditional forensics, which is mainly on humans. But wildlife forensics still involves many of the same "experts" as in other forensic labs: They have trace evidence specialists, firearms experts, pathologists, entomologists, microbiologists, molecular biologists, chemists, and even fingerprint analysts for nonhuman primates.

Out of a need to enforce established laws, and protect our natural world and the creatures in it, the U.S. National Fish and Wildlife Forensics Lab was founded in 1988 in Ashland, Oregon. This high-tech crime lab and its team of experts perform a huge number of forensic examinations covering all parts of the U.S.

For example, like we saw in the bear case, they can use forensic entomology to determine when an animal was killed. Even legal hunting has seasonality, and insect evidence on a body can narrow down a pretty specific time frame. Pathologists can determine the cause of death in an animal and judge whether the hunting methods used were legal or not. Firearms experts can analyze bullets removed from carcasses or casings found at the site of poaching, and from that they can try to link the kill to specific weapon.

The Wildlife Forensics Lab can even do DNA testing to determine the species and sex of animals, and they can even identify individual animals. This can include figuring out the number of animals involved distinguished by how many unique genetic profiles they find—this can be important if the animals have been rendered down to only "meat." Forensic chemistry can be used to show what's in a powdered "medicine," what type of poison killed an animal, or even differentiate the male and female hormones in meat, which could be important if the sex of a species is regulated during the hunting season.

Wildlife forensic experts do include some specialists you wouldn't typically find in a standard criminalistic lab, though. For instance they have mammalian osteologists that can look at teeth, bones, and antlers to see if age requirements for hunting have been met; these experts can also try to match up dismembered body parts. Ornithologists can look at feathers and talons used in things like headdresses and dream catchers as potential evidence of illegal hunting of protected bird species.

In the U.S. the entity that governs the trade of these kinds of animal and plant products, including their import and export, is the Department of Homeland Security, through its Customs and Border Protection division. They have a pretty interesting website that lists all the prohibited and restricted imports, including wildlife, food products, plants, seeds, soil, and hunting trophies.

These regulations and their enforcement are important not only for the preservation of endangered species, but also because they protect our environment from the introduction of non-native species that could harm U.S. ecosystems.

And this brings us to another way that forensic science is involved with the natural world: the investigation of environmental damage and contamination. Things like abnormal odors, areas called "dead zones" in plant growth, and dead fish in waterways can all be clues that something or someone could be poisoning the environment. Whether the toxicity is due to an intentional release of chemicals or is some kind of accidental contamination, these types of incidents need to be investigated, and they often culminate in criminal and/or civil litigation.

Commonly encountered poisons are things like heavy metals, such as arsenic, lead, mercury, and thallium; different types of insecticides, like organophosphates; toxins intended to kill rodents, like strychnine; and even barbiturates used by humane societies can leach into environment when the carcasses of euthanized animals are put into landfills. Sometimes, even the patterns in the dead animals themselves can reveal the particular toxin involved, like the clenched talons seen in eagles after they consume the rat poison, mono-fluoro-acetate.

The forensic identification of pesticides and other toxic chemicals in the environment is critical, because not only does it damage plant and animal life, but it can hurt and kill humans, too. Since plants and animals are lower on the food chain, they are often the first indicators of environmental damage. When wildlife investigators pick up on these clues, the work they do might ultimately protect human health.

Even if rehabilitation groups step in to help sick or injured animals after an oil spill or other toxic event, important documentation, like photos, carcasses, tissue samples, and even poop or vomit, has to be kept—just like it would be in any other suspected crime-scene investigation—because of the eventual importance of stuff like this if there's ever a trial.

Really, all the same types of scene and evidence collection protocols have to be maintained, like protecting self and others, securing the scene, proper collecting and preserving techniques, maintaining a chain of custody—all in the event the case winds up in court someday.

Now in the interest of fairness, we'll wrap up this lecture by taking a look at the forensic investigation of cases where animals occasionally attack humans. We all know that when people travel or live in remote places there's an increased likelihood they'll encounter potentially dangerous wildlife. And this isn't just in just remote areas anymore; coyotes are moving more and more into suburban and even urban areas, as I've seen in my own backyard. And sometimes diseased animals—like ones with rabies—lose their fear and come into areas they normally wouldn't inhabit.

When fatal attacks by animals on humans occur, they have to be reported to the governing coroner or medical examiner, just like any other unexpected death. Even when someone survives an animal attack, the proper authorities have to be notified. This also means that any necessary media releases come out, through proper channels, especially if the animal is still at large.

In October of 2011, in Zanesville, Ohio, which is not too far from where I live, the owner of a bunch of exotic animals released them all before killing himself. This guy let loose a total of 56 creatures, including lions, tigers, and bears (now I can just hear you saying "oh my"—but this really is not funny). He also released leopards, mountain lions, wolves, and even a couple of primates.

At home, all that afternoon and into the next day, I heard media releases from all over Ohio telling people to be careful of these animals, and to report them if they were spotted anywhere. Sadly, nearly all of the animals were shot by law enforcement, including 18 endangered Bengal tigers. Of course the goal of the killings was to protect the public from these potentially dangerous animals—but I sure wish they could have found a better way to do it.

Anyway, when animals do attack, the bites they leave on a victim can be examined using the same type of bite-mark analyses that forensic dentists—known as forensic odontologists—use when people bite each other. We'll talk about bite-mark analysis in a later lecture, but in this context, it can be used to help identify the type of critter involved in an animal attack, and possibly even tie the victim to a specific animal, if it's found.

When investigators have to search for an animal at large, they also use the same types of strategies as when searching for a human predator, but they track for paws, fur, and scat (that's animal poop). If necessary, paw prints can be cast using the same types of methods we talked about with shoe and tire impressions.

If the suspected animal is caught, it may have to be analyzed to see if it is, in fact, the perpetrator. This is usually done by examining the animal's stomach contents. In fact, I have a friend and colleague in South Carolina who is a fellow forensic anthropologist. He was once involved in a case where a shark was caught off the coast of the Atlantic near where he lives, and a human leg was found in its belly—just like in the movie Jaws! The anthropology exam was able to reveal a few clues as to the man's identity, but the case has still never been resolved.

To close on a more positive note, let me mention a couple of topics that remind us how animals and plants help forensic scientists. In lectures to come, we'll not only talk more about how insects aid estimations of the time since death, but we'll see that plants can help do this, too. Plant growth can also maybe help locate a buried body, and so might a well-trained cadaver dog. We'll also talk about some of our 4-legged crime fighters, when we cover a little bit about bomb, arson, and drug-detection dogs in action.

Serology—Blood and Other Body Fluids
Lecture 9

Violent crimes are the most likely to produce body fluid evidence, consisting primarily of blood and semen from rapes or other physical attacks, but the science of body fluids—known as serology—can be applied to many other substances, such as saliva, sweat, tears, vomit, and vaginal secretions. The difficulty with analyzing body fluids at crime scenes is that the perpetrator often does everything in his or her power to clean up the scene—at least on the surface.

Detecting Body Fluids at Crime Scenes

- If body fluids are suspected at a crime scene, the investigator has to consider several questions: What type of body fluids might be present? What state is the fluid in—liquid or dried? Is it fresh or degraded? These factors impact how the substance can be collected and analyzed. The next major consideration is whether the fluid came from a human or some other animal.

- The science of serology can be used to answer all of those questions, and some can even be answered at the crime scene. Serology can even automatically exclude a person as a suspect—just as with hair. However, just as with hair evidence, serology cannot tie a body fluid to a specific and unique source, which requires DNA testing.

- At some crime scenes, the presence of blood or other body fluids might be obvious, but in other cases, investigators might not see clear signs that blood is present. In order to determine whether or not blood is present, there are a few types of presumptive tests that can be done at the crime scene.

- A presumptive test is a quick way to figure out the likelihood of whether something is what you think it is in the field. With regard to serology, presumptive testing helps investigators figure out where blood and other body fluids might be, which will help them determine what might have happened and what to collect.

- Some presumptive tests occasionally produce a false positive result, so these types of tests always have to be followed up in a forensic lab with confirmatory tests, which are much more reliable and discriminatory—but also take more time and cost much more money.

- Luminol is the presumptive test that is most often used in cases where the perpetrator has tried to clean up the scene because luminol can detect blood in minute quantities by spraying it and turning off the lights. Unfortunately, it doesn't work if chlorine bleach was used to clean up blood. However, you can use it in the field and it doesn't completely ruin the blood for further testing.

- On television shows, investigators spray what looks like a clean wall with a phony chemical, but when they turn out the lights, there are a bunch of spots—a blood spatter pattern—not a cleaning smear with wipe marks, which is what is seen in reality.

- There are some other presumptive tests, specifically for blood, that use chemistry to produce a color change. The most commonly used test is the Kastle-Meyer test, which detects the hemoglobin in red blood cells.

Human Blood Typing and Immunology

- Austrian physician Karl Landsteiner discovered how to type blood in 1901. In 1925, it was discovered that about 80% of the human population secretes a variety of proteins native to their blood in their tears, saliva, sweat, urine, and semen—making it possible to test some nonblood body fluids and still determine a person's blood type in the majority of cases.

- The 2 main protein systems that are typically used to determine human blood type are the ABO system and the Rh protein. These 2 proteins are both found in human red blood cells. The Rh protein isn't used in forensic science—it's mainly used in blood tests for compatibility—but the ABO system is.

- The cell membranes of red blood cells have proteins known as antigens on them, and they come in 2 forms: A and B. If someone has type-A blood, their red blood cells have the A form of the protein antigen; if they have type-B blood, their red blood cells have the B-protein antigen. If a person has type-AB blood, they express both the A and B forms of the proteins, and if they have type-O blood, they express no proteins for this particular blood system.

- Immunology is the study of the interactions between the 2 major groups of genetically determined biological proteins known as antigens and antibodies. An antigen is anything that the body reacts to by producing an antibody. Antibodies are proteins that our immune system can make to fight a specific intruder.

- Normally, we develop antibodies through vaccines or by encounters we have with foreign substances in the environment—such as when we get sick—but in the strange case of the ABO blood system, we are born with genetically determined antibodies in the liquid part of our blood known as plasma. We have antibodies to the opposing types of red blood cells that we might encounter.

- Our antibodies attack and attach to foreign antigens in order to deactivate them, and the antibodies we make are specific to the antigens they encounter in a one-to-one relationship. Serologists target the original blood sample with a solution of antibodies and let the antibodies reveal what antigens are present because those antigens determine blood type.

Applications of Blood Typing
- Blood can be found at a crime scene in many different forms. It can be relatively fresh, or it can be dried up. In fact, all items of evidence that have blood on them are dried by the time they reach the forensic lab because blood is more stable when it's dry.

- Blood typing in a forensic lab is often very different from the standard blood typing done in a hospital lab because forensic scientists are typically dealing with blood and other body fluids that are degraded, old, contaminated, and sometimes commingled.

- Figuring out whether blood is from a human and not an animal requires the use of antibodies that are specific to antigens only found in human blood. Forensic labs have commercially prepared stock solutions of antibodies to the blood of many common animals that are typical pets or those we eat.

Dried blood—on a knife, for example—resists bacterial growth better and is much more stable than liquid blood.

- A person's blood type is genetically inherited, and before DNA technology, blood types were used routinely in paternity tests.

- Human red blood cell typing can only exclude or include someone as being a suspect; it cannot show that the blood in question came from a specific person. In other words, blood type is class evidence—not individuating evidence.

- There are different distributions of the ABO blood groups in different human populations. The long-standing genetic isolation of major ancestral or racial groups has led to some blood types being more common in some groups over others.

Fluids Other Than Blood
- In addition to blood, the science of serology also deals with other body fluids. Saliva, semen, and vaginal fluid may also be exchanged between perpetrators and their victims in sexual assaults. The testing for these types of fluids is similar to blood; there are presumptive tests that can be done in the field and then confirmatory tests that are done later in the lab.

- One presumptive test for semen involves looking for a chemical known as acid phosphatase, a chemical made by the male reproductive glands known as the seminal vesicles. Those glands produce the bulk of the fluid portion of semen.

- The problem with acid phosphatase is that it's fairly common in nature, including being present in the body fluids of nonhuman animals. Confirmatory tests for semen include a microscopic exam to look for sperm cells, which can still be detected even if the sperm are dead and starting to degrade.

- If the rapist had a vasectomy, looking for sperm would be useless. Fortunately, though, seminal acid phosphatase levels are not affected by a vastectomy and neither is the chemical prostate-specific antigen (PSA), which is considered a confirmatory test for the presence of semen because unlike acid phosphatase, it is unique to semen.

- Timing is important in serology cases involving sexual assault. If a woman is raped and murdered, the medical examiner may find evidence of sperm in her vagina for up to about 2 weeks, but in a living victim, live sperm will only be found for about 5 hours after a rape occurred, and after about 72 hours, there may be no remaining evidence of sperm or semen.

From Professor Murray's Forensic Files

I was once involved in a case where a man in the military was caught on duty on base cheating on his 8-month-pregnant wife with one of his female subordinate officers. He was immediately dismissed from duty and was facing a court-martial procedure.

When he didn't come home for a few days, his wife flew to her mother's house until the baby was born. A few weeks later, the man's truck was located in a wooded area, which prompted a search. Down a rocky ravine, his decomposing body was found along with a bottle of whiskey and a shotgun.

The man's skull was in about 65 pieces, and the medical examiner wanted me to try to reconstruct the skull to make sure this was, in fact, a suicide as they suspected. After I glued the skull back together, I was able to see that there was a close-contact gunshot wound to the temple—not the forehead. I also saw gunshot residue on the bone, suggesting that this man had been shot at close range from the side.

It's possible for a full-grown man to hold a shotgun out to the side of his head and shoot himself, depending on the length of his arm, but this man wasn't very large, and the typical length of a shotgun barrel is 24 to 34 inches. Furthermore, that's an awkward direction to generate the kind of force needed to pull the trigger.

The police called the man's wife and got access to search their home with her permission, but nothing seemed out of place. Then, one of the cops decided to fly out to the mother's house to speak more directly with her. Within a few minutes of questioning, the man's pregnant widow crumbled and told the officer that she had shot her husband in their bed on the night she heard about his affair.

The cops went back to the couple's house and used luminol in the bedroom, where they found evidence of blood on the headboard, the wall, and the carpeting—but not on the mattress. Even though the surfaces looked clean to the unaided eye, when luminol was sprayed and the lights were turned off, the bloodstains become immediately visible.

They later found the full-sized bloody mattress the wife had dumped in a different location. Incidentally, the wife was found not guilty after using the battered wife defense on a sympathetic jury.

Suggested Reading

Gaensslen, *Sourcebook in Forensic Serology, Immunology, and Biochemistry.*

Questions to Consider

1. What types of body fluids can be found at a crime scene?

2. What values do the analyses of body fluids have—other than the DNA evidence they contain?

3. How do investigators sample body fluids from a crime scene?

4. What is the difference between a presumptive test and a confirmatory test?

5. Do the same types of body fluids need to be compared—blood with blood, for example—to get a conclusive match between a suspect and crime-scene evidence?

Serology—Blood and Other Body Fluids
Lecture 9—Transcript

Imagine a crime scene where investigators walk into the bedroom after a bloody homicide happened. Now we all have an image in our minds and I'm sure it's a pretty gruesome one, but also consider for a minute that the perpetrator might have done everything in his or her power to clean up that scene. We've been talking about crime scenes and evidence for quite a while so far, but as we've all seen on television, sometimes the bad guys and the bad girls do a pretty good job—at least on the surface—of covering up their dirty deeds.

I was once involved in a case where a military guy was caught on duty on base in what we'll call a compromising position, literally, with one of his female subordinate officers. He was immediately dismissed from duty and was facing a court martial procedure. His wife, who was about 8 months pregnant at the time, needless to say, was pretty ticked off by this situation, and she also threw him out.

When he didn't come home for a couple of days, his wife flew out West to stay with her mother and commiserate until the baby was born. A couple of weeks later the guy's truck was located in a wooded area, which then prompted a search. Down a rocky ravine, wearing nothing but his underwear, this guy's decomposing body was found along with a bottle of Jack Daniels whiskey and a shotgun. The cops actually called it a typical Kentucky suicide. They said there was a supranasal entry—that's right above the nose—and a right temporal exit wound.

The reason I got involved in this case is because this guy's skull was in about 65 pieces, the biggest one about the size of the palm of my hand. The medical examiner wanted me to try to reconstruct the skull to make sure this was, in fact, a suicide as they suspected—talk about 3-D jigsaw puzzle! After I glued the skull back together—and yes, that's actually what I do in a case like that—I was able to see that there was a close contact gunshot wound to the temple, not the forehead.

Now it's possible for a full-grown man, I suppose, to hold a shotgun out to the side and shoot himself, depending on the length of his arm, but this guy wasn't very big—and the typical length of a shotgun barrel is about 24 to 34 inches—besides, that's a pretty awkward direction to generate the kind of force needed to pull the trigger. It's more common that people who are bent on killing themselves with a shotgun, rig up some kind of mechanism, like a string that they can pull, or prop the gun between their feet and use their toes to pull the trigger.

Anyway, I saw gunshot residue that was actually on the bone, suggesting the guy had been shot at close range from the side, and I told the medical examiner that. The police called the guy's wife and got access to search their home with her permission, but nothing seemed out of place there. Then, one of the cops decided to fly out to the mother's house and speak more directly with this man's pregnant widow. Within a few minutes after he got there, she crumbled and told the officer that she had blown her husband's head off, right there in the bed where he slept, on the very night she heard about his little tryst with his coworker.

Now as I mentioned the cops had already searched this couple's house and nothing seemed out of place. They went back there then and used a chemical spray known as luminol in the bedroom, and to quote one of the cops, the place lit up like a Christmas tree. Well, the headboard, and the wall, and the carpeting did, but not the mattress. They later found the full-sized bloody mattress the wife had dumped in a different location.

Can you imagine this woman, 8 months pregnant, and allegedly with no accomplice, dragging a bloody mattress onto the roof of her car and then dumping it out in the woods? But that's exactly what she said she did, before cleaning up the bedroom and then buying a new mattress: She dumped her husband in his underwear in one spot with the shotgun and whiskey, to make it look like a suicide, and then dumped the blood-soaked mattress in another. Unbelievable, but apparently true. I saw her at the trial, and she was quite a sturdy woman. Incidentally, at the trial, she was found not guilty after using the battered wife defense on a sympathetic jury. (We will talk about courtroom concerns in a much later lecture.)

Now, maybe you've seen luminol used on TV, where they spray a surface, turn off the lights, and bloodstains become immediately visible, even though the surface looked clean to the naked eye. So before I explain how that's done, let's talk about the variety of body fluids and how they can be detected at a crime scene.

Violent crimes are the most likely to produce body fluid evidence, consisting primarily of blood and semen from rapes or other sorts of physical attacks. But the science of body fluids—which is known as serology—can be applied to lots of other substances, like saliva, sweat, tears, vomit, and vaginal secretions. The places that this kind of evidence might be found are infinite.

Saliva might be found on a cigarette butt, a licked stamp, or a drinking glass. Sweat, tears, and semen could be found on clothing or bed sheets. Skin and other tissue might be left on a vehicle after a hit-and-run accident. And female secretions could be found on a foreign object used in a sexual assault. And any of all of those fluids might also be found on the skin or transferred to the clothing of a perpetrator or a victim.

If body fluids are suspected at a crime scene, the investigator has to consider several questions: First, what type of body fluids might be present? Also, what state is the fluid in? Is it liquid or dried? Is it fresh or is it degraded? Those factors are going to impact how the substance can be collected and analyzed.

Liquid blood has a lot more genetic markers in it than dried blood, and it can be taken up by a syringe; but dried blood resists bacterial growth better and in that sense is much more stable. The next major consideration when fluid is found at a scene is whether it came from a human or some other animal—like, could that blood be from the victim's unfortunate dog that tried to defend her?

The science of serology can be used to answer all of those questions—and some can even be answered right there at the crime scene. Serology can even automatically exclude a person as a suspect, just as we saw with hairs. But, just like with hair evidence, the thing that serology cannot do is to tie a body fluid to a specific and unique source. That takes the power of DNA testing, which we'll talk about in the next lecture.

At some crime scenes the presence of blood or other body fluids might be obvious, but in cases like the one I mentioned earlier, investigators might not see clear signs that blood is present. So in order to determine whether or not blood is present, or to make certain that some type of stain that looks like blood is actually blood, there are a couple of types of what are known as presumptive tests they can do right there at the scene.

A presumptive test is a quick and dirty way to figure out the likelihood of whether something is what you think it is in the field. Basically, with regard to serology, presumptive testing helps investigators figure out where blood and other body fluids might be—so that will help them determine what may have happened, and what to collect or not. When I say it's "quick and dirty," that's true—that's because there are presumptive tests used that occasionally produce a false positive result—but that can be sorted out later at the lab.

We'd never want to use a field test that could produce a false negative result, or investigators would walk away from real crime scenes thinking their job was done. Presumptive tests always have to be followed up in a forensic lab with what are called confirmatory tests, and those are a lot more reliable and discriminatory, but also take more time and cost a lot more money.

With regard to presumptive tests, luminol is the method of choice in cases where the perpetrator has tried to clean up the scene, because it can detect blood in minute quantities—as little as one part blood per 10 million of something else. I've seen luminol even work through fresh paint on a basement floor. This was a dismemberment case, where the perpetrator cut a woman up in his basement, thought he washed the blood down the floor drain, and painted the concrete floor, as an additional cover up. But, the little bit of blood that was mixed with the paint—that he couldn't even see himself—was still there and detectable with luminol.

One problem with luminol, though, is that it doesn't work if chlorine bleach was used to clean up blood. There I go making smarter criminals again! But a good thing about luminol is that you can use it in the field and, although it does dilute a sample to some degree, it complicates—but doesn't completely ruin—the blood for further testing.

There was a precursor to luminol that goes back to the early 1900s called fluorescein. It's still used today because it doesn't react with chlorine bleach like luminol does. And it's a thicker chemical so it's sometimes easier to use against gravity on vertical surfaces. So once again, we see that investigators in the field have to make smart decisions in real time because crime scenes and evidence collection are never one-size-fits-all.

What they tend to show on TV is not luminol. Because it's more dramatic, they usually show fluorescein being used with a UV or blue light and those orange goggles. Both luminol and fluorescein work the same way—they're both based on the fluorescence of blood—but luminol doesn't need the lights; in fact, it needs darkness. Both of those are good for finding stains that have been cleaned up, but when there is an attempt to clean blood up, you see wipe marks, not a blood spatter pattern.

Watch for that on TV shows, because that's not the way they usually show it. They usually show CSIs spraying what looks like a clean wall with their phony chemicals, but when they turn out the lights and we see the "invisible stain," it's a bunch of spots, not a cleaning smear. Now I'm making smarter TV people instead of smarter criminals!

There are some other presumptive tests, specifically for blood, that use chemistry to produce a color change. One is just like what they use on those dipstick test strips used for urinalysis in doctors' offices. If crime scene investigators think a substance is blood, they can take a moist cotton swab, and dab a tiny bit of the suspected blood, and put it on the test strip. The strip will turn blue-green if blood is present. Another field test is called leuco-malachite green. (Guess what color change it produces?) But the most commonly used presumptive field test is called the Kastle–Meyer test, and it uses phenolphthalein and hydrogen peroxide to detect the hemoglobin in red blood cells. It produces a dark pink color that some of you might remember from phenolphthalein indicator tests from high-school chemistry lab.

The thing about tests for hemoglobin, though, is that hemoglobin is a really ancient oxygen-carrying protein that's found in all of our relatives with a backbone, and I don't just mean our fellow mammals, but even fish, amphibians, reptiles, and birds. So just because field tests indicate blood, that doesn't mean it's human blood. So, let's talk for a few minutes about human blood typing, and then follow up with a little bit about how human blood can be differentiated from nonhuman blood.

Since at least the 1920s, human blood typing has been used in forensic investigations. An Austrian physician named Karl Landsteiner figured out how to type blood in 1901, and he won the Nobel Prize in Medicine for it in 1930. Another major milestone happened in 1925 when it was discovered that about 80% of the human population actually secretes a variety of proteins native to their blood in their tears, their saliva, sweat, urine, and semen—making it possible to test non-blood body fluids and still determine a person's blood type in the majority of cases. Those people are called "secretors" because they secrete aspects of their blood type. The forensic lab at Scotland Yard was a major pioneering group that studied the whole gamut of variable biological proteins found in body fluids. They ended up setting up serology protocols that ended up being used by forensic labs around the world.

As you probably know, a person's blood type is genetically inherited. There are 2 main protein systems typically talked about when discussing human blood type: One is the ABO system, and the other one is the Rh protein. These 2 proteins really don't have anything to do with each other except for the fact that they're both found in human red blood cells. Reporting them both at the same time, as in I'm A-positive or O-negative. It's kind of like reporting your eye color and your height; those 2 things are totally unrelated but are both descriptors about your physical appearance. And we don't really need to talk about Rh here, except to say that it isn't used in forensic science—it's really only used in blood tests for compatibility, like when somebody's getting a transfusion.

For the ABO system, the cell membranes of red blood cells have identity flags that are proteins on the surface called antigens on them, and they come in 2 forms: an A-form and a B-form. If someone has type-A blood, their red blood cells are sporting the A-protein antigens, and if they have type-B blood, their red cells have the B-form of the protein antigen. If a person is type-AB, they express both the A and the B form of the proteins, and if they have type-O blood, they express no proteins for this particular blood system. O is used here like zero, meaning no proteins for the ABO system on their red cells.

Now let's talk a little about immunology—that's the study of interactions between 2 major groups of genetically determined biological proteins known as antigens and antibodies. An antigen is anything that the body reacts to by producing what's called an antibody. Antibodies are proteins that our immune system can make to fight off a specific intruder. Normally we develop our antibodies through vaccines or by encounters we have with foreign substances in the environment—like when we actually get sick—but in the strange case of the ABO blood system, we are born with genetically determined antibodies in the liquid part of our blood known as plasma. We have antibodies to the opposing types of red blood cells that we might encounter in each other.

So, in other words, if you are blood-type A, you have those A-proteins on your red blood cells, but you have anti-B antibodies in your plasma. If you are type-B, you have type-B proteins waving on your red blood cells and anti-A antibodies in your plasma. If you are type-AB, you have both types of proteins on your red cells, but no antibodies in your plasma for the ABO system, since you don't recognize either A or B as being foreign to you. And if your blood type is O, you express neither protein on your red blood cells, but you have both anti-A and anti-B antibodies in your plasma.

It's important to understand how antibodies and antigens interact in order to understand how blood type testing is done. Our antibodies attack and then attach to foreign antigens in order to deactivate them, and this reaction between antibodies and antigens is called agglutination, or more simply put, just clumping. The antibodies we make are highly specific to the antigens they encounter—in a one-to-one relationship between antibody and antigen. Once it's made in the body, an antigen-antibody complex will precipitate out of the liquid part of blood and then certain white blood cells can degrade and destroy the antigen-antibody complex. Scientists have capitalized on the formation of antigen-antibody complexes and then developed tests for blood type based on that concept.

What they do is treat the blood with antibodies to the major blood types, and they see what those antibodies cling to and pick up. In other words, if there is a piece of evidence that contains blood, it can be treated with a commercially prepared solution of antibodies, and they will attach to any antigens that are present in the blood sample. Next they do a washing step to get rid of any antibodies that didn't attach because they did not find their corresponding antigen in that blood sample.

The next step is called elution, and that's a method of heating up the sample high enough to break any antigen-antibody bonds that did form. By doing that, the antibodies that were matched to the blood sample are removed and can be tested. If they turn out to be anti-A antibodies, then the A antigen was present in that blood sample on the evidence, and they found it and stuck to it. If the antibodies that come off during the elution process are anti-B antibodies, then that's because the B antigen was found in the original blood sample in the evidence. And if both anti-A and anti-B antibodies come off, the blood sample was type AB. Essentially what serologists are doing is targeting the original blood sample on the evidence with a solution of antibodies and letting the antibodies reveal what antigens are present, since those antigens determine the person's blood type.

Now I'm sure my description makes testing for blood sound pretty simple, but consider that blood can be found at a crime scene in a whole lot of different forms. It can be a congealed puddle—and that's another way Hollywood typically gets it wrong, we often see dripping blood at crime scenes when blood actually clots within about 5 minutes—but blood can be relatively fresh, or it can be dried up at a scene.

In fact, all items of evidence that have blood on them are dried by the time they reach the forensic lab, because blood is so much more stable when it's dry. Most morgues have climate-controlled cabinets that they can hang a victim's clothing in so that they can dry it out before examination.

A blood sample might come in on any type of surface—carpeting, upholstery, a piece of drywall that's cut from the wall of someone's living room, or even a ceiling tile. We'll talk about how blood behaves when it leaves the body and gets thrown around at a crime scene in another lecture about blood spatter. But, suffice it to say that blood typing in a forensic lab is often really different from the standard blood typing done in a hospital lab, because forensic scientists are typically dealing with blood and other body fluids that are degraded, old, contaminated, sometimes even commingled.

Figuring out whether blood is from a human and not a cat, a dog, or a butchered deer requires the use of antibodies that are specific to antigens only found in human blood, and not the blood of other animals. Forensic labs have these commercially prepared stock solutions of antibodies to the blood of lots of common animals. They've got dog, cat, rabbit, chicken, deer, pig, horse, and cow—basically those animals that we have as typical pets or those we eat, since those nonhuman types of blood might be found in a residence, or a business like a restaurant or a butcher shop, where a crime could occur. Wow, just imagine trying to figure out a murder that happened in a slaughterhouse. I think I feel a novel coming on. Well, either that or I'm creating smarter criminals again.

Another interesting application of human blood type that relates to the law, so in that sense I guess is forensic, is paternity testing. In the past, before DNA technology, blood types were routinely used in paternity tests. In order to understand how that works, let's take a look at how blood type is inherited.

The A form and the B form of the red blood cell proteins are said to be co-dominant because if somebody inherits the gene for blood type A from one parent and the gene for blood type B from the other parent, that person's red blood cells will have both the A and B antigens—and as we've seen, they will have blood type AB. And both the A form of the blood type gene and that B form of the blood type gene will both trump the recessive type O. So, if you are blood type A, you have at least one gene for blood type A, but you may be carrying the recessive gene for O. You might have inherited the A gene from both of your parents, or you might have inherited the A gene from one parent and the O gene from your other parent. The same goes for blood type B. But, if you have blood type O, you definitely inherited the recessive

O gene from both of your parents. And, in turn, the genes you inherited determine what you can pass to your own offspring.

So let me ask you this, can a mother who is blood type B and a father who is blood type A ever have a child who is type O? Think about that for a minute and stop the DVD if you want to work out that genetic problem with a good old Punnet square like you may have done in high school biology. The answer is yes, they could, but only if each parent is carrying the recessive O gene.

Now, here's a real case: The famous silent movie actor Charlie Chaplin was involved in a paternity suit in 1944 in which a young starlet by the name of Joan Barry accused Chaplin of being the father of her child. Now Chaplin was reportedly type O, Barry was type A, and her child was type B. So, could Charlie Chaplin have fathered Barry's child? What do you think?

Blood tests proved that Charlie Chaplin could not have been the father of that child but, interestingly, because blood tests were not admissible in court at the time, the judge ordered Chaplin to pay child support anyway. And, hey, the man did play a reoccurring role called the Little Tramp, right? But, the good news was that the notoriety of this case prompted California to re-examine the issue of allowing blood tests as evidence and the law was ultimately changed. That's just one more example of science, society, and the law moving hand-in-hand.

This example really shows how nonspecific blood typing is, doesn't it? All that human red blood cell typing can do is exclude or include somebody as being a suspect. It cannot show that the blood in question came from a specific person. In other words, blood type is class evidence; it is not individuating evidence.

There are different distributions of the ABO blood groups in different human populations. The long-standing genetic isolation that led to our major ancestral or racial groups has led to some blood types being more common in some groups others. But, considering just one of those facts, that blood type O is found in nearly half of all white people of northern European descent, well, you can see that blood type alone doesn't get you very far in forensic science.

In addition to blood, the science of serology also deals with other body fluids. In sexual assaults, saliva, semen, and vaginal fluid may also be exchanged between perpetrators and their victims. The testing for these types of fluids is pretty similar to blood in that there are presumptive tests that can be done in the field, and then confirmatory tests that are done later in the lab.

One of the presumptive tests for semen involves looking for a chemical known as acid phosphatase. That's a chemical made by the male reproductive glands known as the seminal vesicles. Those glands produce the bulk of the fluid part of semen. The problem with acid phosphatase, though, is that it's fairly common in nature, including also being present in vaginal secretions, the body fluids of nonhuman animals, and even the juices of certain kinds of plants and fungi. But, if acid phosphatase is found at a crime scene, it's considered presumptive evidence of the presence of semen. Again, we allow false positives, but not false negatives with regard to field tests.

Confirmatory tests for semen include a microscopic exam to look for sperm cells, which can still be detected even if the sperm are dead and starting to degrade. But what if the rapist had a vasectomy? In that case looking for sperm would be useless. Fortunately, though, seminal acid phosphatase levels are not affected by a vasectomy. Neither is the chemical called PSA, which stands for prostate-specific antigen. Both the seminal vesicles and the prostate gland contribute fluids to semen and both of those glands are located beyond the male ductwork that's cut during vasectomy. PSA is considered a confirmatory test for the presence of semen, because unlike acid phosphatase, it is unique to semen.

Timing is also important in serology cases involving sexual assault. If a woman is raped and murdered, the medical examiner may find evidence of sperm in her vagina for up to about 2 weeks. This is because her body is no longer actively producing and sloughing off the surface cells from her female tract. But in a living victim, live sperm will only be found for about 5 hours after a rape occurred, and within about 72 hours there may be no remaining evidence of sperm or semen.

Relevant to this, one of the more recent fields that's emerged within forensic science is called forensic nursing. An important role that forensic nurses play in emergency rooms is to understand how to properly collect this type of critical evidence in rape cases. The chain of custody that begins in the ER may ultimately get any potential evidence to a courtroom someday.

We've talked mostly about blood and semen, but the bottom line with regard to the serological and chemical testing of body fluids—including saliva and vaginal secretions—is that it's just not very discriminatory.

These types of tests, though, are still important in the field in order to make sound decisions about gathering evidence. And presumptive tests are the first strategy a forensic lab uses before they waste a lot of time and money chasing down a bum lead. But the real power in body fluids lies inside the cells they contain. The advent of DNA technology revolutionized the study of body tissues in a way like nothing since the microscope. In the next lecture we'll look at the forensic science of DNA.

The Forensic Analysis of DNA
Lecture 10

D NA evidence is similar to other kinds of evidence in the way that it relies on comparisons between samples taken from people—whether the samples are from known or unknown persons or from the crime scene. Unlike hair and serology, however, DNA is one of the rare pieces of evidence that can be statistically linked to a single person at the exclusion of all others, and because DNA can be found in all body tissues and fluids, it has even greater identification potential than fingerprints.

Using DNA Evidence to Convict and Exonerate

- In England in 1983, the body of a 15-year-old girl named Lynda Mann was found. She had been raped, strangled, and left on a path in the woods. After a semen stain was found on her clothes, investigators at the UK's Forensic Science Service performed a standard serology exam and discovered that the semen came from a man with type-A blood. They also did an enzyme analysis, which showed a protein pattern that would likely match about 10% of the male population.

- Almost 3 years later in the same county, another 15-year-old girl named Dawn Ashworth was found raped and strangled in the woods. A serology exam showed that the blood type and enzyme profile from the semen was the same as the 1983 case. Police honed in on a 17-year-old boy named Richard Buckland, who admitted to killing Dawn Ashworth but denied having anything to do with the 1983 murder of Lynda Mann.

- At nearby Leicester University, a professor named Dr. Alec Jeffreys had figured out that there were some repeated sequences in the genetic code of DNA that varied from person to person. With the semen samples from the 2 murders and the DNA from the confessed killer, Jeffreys discovered that the DNA profile from the semen on the 2 girls was identical—but it didn't match up to Buckland.

- Then, the police asked every 17- to 34-year-old man in the county to give them a blood and saliva sample. After analyzing about 5000 samples, they found no match. Eventually, a woman contacted police because she overheard a friend saying that he was paid 200 pounds to submit a sample in the name of Colin Pitchfork.

- When the cops found Pitchfork, his DNA matched the semen from both of the murder victims. Not only was this the first case of conviction through DNA evidence, but it was also the first case of exoneration because Buckland was shown not to have been the murderer—despite his false confession.

The DNA Molecule
- Deoxyribonucleic acid (DNA) is the genetic molecule that makes up our chromosomes and encodes the instructions for when and how to make proteins in a living organism. All standard cells have DNA—from bacterial cells to the cells of the most complicated creatures.

- The DNA molecule is like a twisted ladder, where the sides of the ladder are made out of phosphates and sugars and the rungs of the ladder are made out of pairs of smaller molecules called nucleotides.

- In spite of all the genetic diversity on Earth, the alphabet that makes up the genetic code of all living things has only 4 letters: A, C, G, and T.

- Living things are more similar when they share more of their genetic code in common and less similar when they don't. Humans share about 97% of our genes with our closest living relatives, chimpanzees.

- It's estimated that human beings differ from one another by less than 1% of our DNA because most of it is devoted to making basic body structures and controlling standard functions—with only a little variability related to family history.

- When DNA differs in a group like humans, the difference is known as a polymorphism, a term that means having many forms. There are 2 kinds of polymorphisms in human genes: a sequence polymorphism, in which there's a difference in the order of the nucleotide base pairs in a stretch of DNA, and length polymorphism, in which a phrase in the genetic code gets repeated a number of times.

- Scientists have figured out some of the more standard genetic repeats and call them variable number tandem repeats (VNTRs), which are used to categorize, or type, DNA.

- When scientists look at multiple stretches of DNA at the same time between 2 people, the statistical probabilities that any 2 people could have the same VNTR pattern by coincidence become strong enough to let genetic comparisons link a single person to a DNA profile—at the exclusion of anyone else, except an identical twin.

DNA and Inheritance
- We have 2 types of DNA in our cells: Nuclear DNA is located inside the nucleus of our cells, and mitochondrial DNA is located inside the small energy-producing organelles called mitochondria that are in our cells.

- Nuclear DNA is the double-stranded, twisted-ladder molecule. Within the nucleus of our cells, it's packaged into units called chromosomes. Nuclear DNA is inherited from both of our parents; we get 23 chromosomes of DNA from our father and 23 chromosomes of DNA from our mother at our conception. Through the interaction of dominant and recessive genes, nuclear DNA gives us the traits that make us who we are biologically.

- Every cell in your body contains the same nuclear DNA—which is important to forensics—and each cell in your body has only one copy of your nuclear DNA. In addition, we each have a unique set of nuclear DNA that belongs to nobody else in the world unless we have an identical twin.

- Because we each only get 1/2 of our mom's chromosomes and 1/2 of our dad's chromosomes, we share some of our DNA with them but not all. The closer we are related to people, the more nuclear DNA we share in common with them.

- Mitochondrial DNA is inherited completely from our mother. Because of this, we share 100% mitochondrial DNA identity with her—and not only with her, but also with every other child she has—and the same mitochondrial DNA is found in all of our mother's siblings.

DNA and Forensic Science

- Long before DNA was used in forensics, scientists knew it could be found in body cells, so any source of living or dead cells—as long as the cells aren't too badly degraded—is a potential source of either nuclear or mitochondrial DNA.

- Lots of early forensic DNA research involved trying to figure out the best sources of crime-scene DNA. Blood, semen, and other body tissues are obvious sources, but eventually scientists figured out that DNA is left behind on things like cigarette butts, licked envelope seals, hair follicles, and latex gloves.

- Biological evidence is perishable, and even though DNA is a durable molecule, it will degrade over time and fragment. In general, fresh tissues yield more nuclear DNA than older tissues, but when a nuclear DNA profile isn't possible, analysts may still be able to get mitochondrial DNA out of an old sample.

- At a crime scene, possible sources of DNA have to be handled carefully. Anything wet, such as a piece of cloth with blood on it, should be air-dried and put into a container that is open a little to stop moisture buildup. It also should be kept at a low temperature—or at least nothing higher than room temperature—to help prevent the growth of bacteria and fungi, which have their own DNA.

- Sometimes, you can't avoid environmental contamination, such as when a body decomposes in a lake or some other body of water. Once the body is in the morgue, DNA analysts can figure out how to minimize cross-contamination with the many creatures that live in bodies of water.

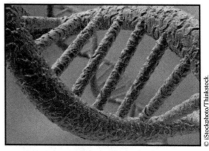

DNA is one of the oldest biologically active molecules on the planet.

- If the DNA sample is on a surface that is portable—such as a coffee mug or a piece of chewed gum—then the whole thing should be sent to the lab. However, if the whole thing isn't easily transported, then a sample that contains the questioned DNA can be taken from it.

- Evidence technicians not only have to be careful with samples to preserve the DNA in them, but they also have to think about their own safety because body fluids can carry infections. Scene and lab workers also have to make sure that they don't contaminate crime-scene evidence with their own DNA from their hair, dandruff, skin cells, or saliva.

- When investigators need a known sample from a particular person to compare to unknown crime-scene samples, they can use blood, but most often, known samples—called reference samples—are taken with a buccal swab, which is a sterile cotton swab that is rubbed over the inside of someone's cheek and then put into an envelope.

- In the morgue, DNA samples are often taken from unknown persons to help get them identified. If investigators have a pretty good idea of who they think the victim is, then they can find relatives to take reference samples from for comparison, but if no relatives are available, then a reference sample might come from the victim—in the form of a toothbrush or stored medical tissues, such as donated blood in a blood bank.

DNA Profiling

- At the lab, DNA scientists can extract genetic material from crime-scene or reference samples. To find and capitalize on the tiny fractions of DNA that differ among people—rather than the over 99% of our DNA that we have in common—scientists use sequence and length polymorphisms to develop someone's DNA profile, or DNA fingerprint.

- The first successful method of DNA profiling was restriction fragment length polymorphism (RFLP) analysis, which uses a restriction enzyme to cut DNA at polymorphic places to create DNA fragments that differ between 2 people. After using gel electrophoresis, which sorts the RFLP fragments by size, the resulting DNA fingerprint can be compared to other DNA samples.

- RFLP is problematic because it requires a fairly large sample, and the results aren't compatible with the major DNA computer databases.

- In 1983, a technique for mass-producing copies of DNA was developed called polymerase chain reaction (PCR), which amplifies a small sample of DNA so that there's plenty of it to analyze in a forensic case.

- RFLP typing of DNA has been replaced by short tandem repeat (STR) analysis, which uses PCR and some of the same principles as RFLP but is quicker and doesn't require as much sample DNA.

- The profiles generated by STR are sets of numbers that can be entered into the combined DNA index system (CODIS) database, which lets agencies easily compare the DNA profiles they obtain to those from other cases—and even to missing persons and offender databases.

- Another advance in DNA technology is the fairly recent ability to tell whether a sample is from a woman or a man by looking at DNA from the sex chromosomes.

Suggested Reading

Butler, *Advanced Topics in Forensic DNA Typing.*

————, *Fundamentals of Forensic DNA Typing.*

Hunter, *DNA Analysis.*

Questions to Consider

1. About how long has DNA analysis been a part of forensic science?

2. What is the difference between nuclear DNA and mitochondrial DNA?

3. How do we inherit the 2 different types of DNA within our cells?

4. Is nuclear DNA or mitochondrial DNA more unique?

The Forensic Analysis of DNA
Lecture 10—Transcript

You know, I always have to laugh when I hear people talk about how forensic science was different "quote" before DNA. Come on, DNA is one of the oldest biologically active molecules on the planet. Its history goes back at least as long as the 3.5 billion years that life has been on earth. And that's just part of its charm. At least as far as we know at this point, living organisms have always contained the genetic molecule DNA; it's just that until the mid-1980s, we didn't know how to use it in forensic casework.

You almost can't talk about DNA and forensic science without covering the case of a British guy by the name of Colin Pitchfork. He was the first man ever to be convicted using DNA evidence. Not only because he turned out to be a rapist and murderer, but also because he did something really stupid in his effort to cover his tracks.

In November of 1983, in Leicestershire County in central England, the body of a 15-year-old girl named Lynda Mann was found. She had been raped and strangled and left on a path in the woods. After a semen stain was found on her clothes, the UK's Forensic Science Services Lab did a standard serology exam and figured out that the semen came from a guy with type A blood. They also did an enzyme analysis which showed a protein pattern that would likely match about 10% of the male population. Without anything else to go on, though, the case went cold.

Almost 3 years later, in July of 1986, in the same county, a second 15-year-old girl named Dawn Ashworth was also found raped and strangled in the woods. Serology showed that the blood type and enzyme profile from the semen stain in this case was the same as the 1983 case. Police honed in on a 17-year-old local kid named Richard Buckland, who worked at a psychiatric hospital near where the second body had been found.

Buckland, it seems, knew some details about the body that hadn't yet been released. He also had the same blood type and serology profile found in the semen. During questioning, Buckland said that he did kill Dawn

Ashworth, but denied having anything to do with the 1983 murder of Lynda Mann. But investigators weren't fully satisfied with the reliability of Buckland's confession.

At nearby Leicester University there was a professor named Dr. Alec Jeffreys who was studying DNA. Jeffreys had figured out that there were some repeated sequences in the genetic code that varied from person to person. He thought these "hypervariable regions," as he called them, were different enough to sort out people using their DNA sequences, and Jeffreys even predicted his findings would someday have forensic applications.

The Forensic Science Services brought Jeffreys the semen samples from the 2 murders and the DNA from the confessed killer, Buckland. Jeffreys figured out that the DNA profile from the semen on the 2 little girls was identical, but it didn't match up to Buckland. Now here's where things get really weird: Once they found out that Buckland was not a match, the police decided to ask every 17- to 34-year-old guy in the county, who didn't have an alibi for the murders, to come in and give a blood and saliva sample. After analyzing 4000 samples, they still found no match. They even expanded the search to include men who did claim to have an alibi, but after another 1000 samples, still nothing.

Eventually, a woman contacted police because she overheard a friend of hers saying that he was paid 200 pounds to submit a sample in the name of his buddy, Colin Pitchfork. Pitchfork claimed that he couldn't give a sample himself, because he had already given one for some other guy who was a known flasher—you know, some guy who exposes himself in public. You already see where this is going, right?

When the cops find Pitchfork, sure enough, his DNA matches the semen from both of the murder victims. By the way, Pitchfork, himself, was already the convicted flasher he incorporated into his story. So, not only was this the first case of conviction through DNA evidence, it was also the first case of exoneration when Buckland was shown not to have been the murderer, despite his false confession.

Let's talk about DNA. DNA is an abbreviation for deoxyribonucleic acid. It's the genetic molecule that makes up our chromosomes and basically encodes the instructions for when and how to make proteins in a living organism. All standard cells have DNA, from bacterial cells to the cells of the most complicated creatures like us. Even some viruses are made of DNA, but viruses are not cells, and currently they're not considered alive.

The DNA molecule is kind of like a twisted ladder where the uprights of the ladder are made out of phosphates and sugars, and the rungs of the ladder are made out of pairs of smaller molecules called nucleotides. What's really amazing to me is that the alphabet that makes up our genetic code—and the genetic code of all living things—has only 4 letters. We even abbreviate those 4 molecules with letters: A, C, G, and T. So, in spite of all the genetic diversity on earth—from bacteria, to insects, plants, humans— the instructions for making us what we are is a code made up of only 4 repeating nucleotide molecules that are strung between the phosphates and sugars I mentioned.

Living things are much more similar when they share more of their genetic code in common and less similar when they don't. So we're very different from, say, fruit flies because they have only 6 chromosomes, and we don't share many genes with them, but we're very much like our closest living relatives, chimpanzees, because we share about 97% of our genes in common with them. And when you think about that, just imagine how closely all people are genetically related to each other. That always makes me think of how absolutely absurd racial prejudices really are.

Anyway, it's not the major genetic recipes of humans that make a difference in forensics, because we share so many functional genes in common with one another. It's estimated that we differ from our fellow humans by less than 1% of our DNA. That's because most of our DNA is devoted to making basic body structures and controlling standard functions, like making skin and hormones, stuff like that. We all do those things in pretty much the same way, with only a little variability related to our family history.

But over the course of evolution, as gene mutations have occurred, lots of randomly repeated and apparently unnecessary sequences have accumulated in our DNA. And these sequences aren't rare—they make up about 30% of our entire genome. But since these sequences don't have any real genetic function, the fact that they tend to almost stutter or stammer in certain regions of our DNA, really doesn't cause any genetic problems. It does, however, create a certain amount of uniqueness in that small fraction of our genetic code that differs from other people.

When DNA differs in a group like humans, the difference is known as a polymorphism. That word basically means having many forms. There are really 2 kinds of polymorphisms in human genes: The first one is called a sequence polymorphism, where there's a difference in the order of the nucleotide base pairs in a stretch of DNA. The other kind of polymorphism in human genes is what's called a length polymorphism. That basically means that something we could call a phrase in the genetic code gets repeated over and over a number of times—you know, the stammering I mentioned earlier.

Scientists have figured out some of the more standard genetic repeats, and call them variable number tandem repeats, or VNTRs. They use these VNTRs to categorize, or type DNA. But, it wasn't until they could really figure out how often these VNTRs occur in populations, that forensic scientists got a hold of the real power of DNA profiles.

The mathematical science called population genetics has given us information about the probabilities that any 2 people could have the same VNTR pattern just by coincidence. And when they look at multiple stretches of DNA at the same time between 2 people, the statistical probabilities get even narrower. In fact, they get strong enough to let genetic comparisons link a single person to a DNA profile, at the exclusion of anybody else—except an identical twin.

Now, because I'm not sure what kind of background you may have in biology, we probably need to talk a little bit more about DNA and its inheritance before we go on. As I first mentioned in the lecture about hair, we have 2 types of DNA in our cells: We have nuclear DNA inside—you guessed it—the nucleus of our cells, and we have another type of DNA, called mitochondrial DNA, inside the small energy-producing organelles called mitochondria that are inside our cells.

Nuclear DNA is the typical double-stranded, twisted ladder molecule that I talked about earlier. Within the nucleus of each of our cells it's packed into units called chromosomes. Nuclear DNA is inherited from both of our parents; we get 23 chromosomes of DNA from our father and 23 chromosomes of DNA from our mother at our conception. This is the type of DNA that, through the interaction of dominant and recessive genes, gives us the traits that make us who we are, biologically speaking.

Remember that mitochondrial DNA, though, is inherited completely from our mother. This is because a woman's egg is a big, fat, juicy cell that not only contains a nucleus with a half set of chromosomes, but also all the cellular organelles that do energy production, nutrient processing, and the cell division that's going to take place right after the egg gets fertilized. But a sperm is really not much more than a tiny, genetic missile. It's a nucleus with a half set of chromosomes, packed into a free-swimming cell with a propeller-like tail called a flagellum.

At fertilization, the male chromosomes are more or less ejected into the female egg and the flagellum drops off. The sperm has the right stuff to get to the egg, but really, the male sperm cell gives nothing else to a new offspring but a package of nuclear DNA. And as soon as that male DNA and female DNA partner up in a fertilized egg, the new offspring's first job is to begin to divide and make identical copies of its cells as it grows. This cell division, called mitosis, makes sure that each new cell contains the identical full set of chromosomes from conception—except in the occasional cases of random mutations. That's why any cell in the body contains the same nuclear DNA—which is really important in forensics.

Back to mitochondria. Mitochondria are basically the tiny energy factories in all of our cells. They're actually descendent from primitive bacteria that got incorporated into larger cells, which then ultimately evolved into plant and animal cells. Mitochondria have their own DNA, and they can reproduce themselves when our bodies need to produce more energy. So, if you start an exercise program, the mitochondria in your cells will multiply to help give you the energy your new workout routine demands.

Mitochondrial DNA is like bacterial DNA in that it's not housed in a group of chromosomes. Mitochondrial DNA and bacterial DNA both consist of a single circular molecule that looks kind of like a round ladder. Anyway, the 2 most important things to know about mitochondria for our purposes here, is that first, there are way more mitochondria in each body cell, compared to a single nucleus, and, secondly, that the mitochondrial DNA in every single cell of our body came from our mother through her mother and her mother and her mother, and so on.

So, let's quickly summarize both types of DNA, especially as it relates to forensics: We each have a unique set of nuclear DNA that belongs to no one else in the world unless we have an identical twin. Fifty percent of that nuclear DNA came from our mother, and 50% of it came from our father when they created us. And at this point in my class I always add, "La-la-la-la, don't make me think about my parents having sex!" That always gets a laugh.

But, since we each only get half of our mom's chromosomes and half of our dad's chromosomes, we share some of our DNA with them but not all of it. If we have full blood siblings, we share 50% of our genes with them. Because of the way sperm and eggs are made, our brothers and sisters don't get the same half set of chromosomes we got from either of our shared parents. We share a fourth of our DNA with our grandparents, aunts, and uncles. The amount drops down to an eighth with cousins. So, the closer we are related to people, the more nuclear DNA we share in common with them.

Since all of our mitochondrial DNA came from our mother, though, we share 100% mitochondrial DNA identity with her (and, not only with her but with every other child she had—in other words, all of our brothers and sisters from our mother, regardless of whether or not they had the same father that we did). And ours is the same mitochondrial DNA that our mother got from her mother, so that same mitochondrial DNA would be in all of our mother's siblings—whether they are our aunts or our uncles. As long as they came from our same maternal grandmother, they have the same mitochondrial DNA that we do. In fact, when you think long term, the only mitochondrial DNA differences in humans on earth relate to the occasional mutations that happen when DNA is copied to make new mitochondria.

The second thing about the 2 types of DNA that I should reiterate for forensic purposes is that each cell of our body has only one copy of our nuclear DNA. But since our cells contain many, many mitochondria, each body cell can yield a lot of mitochondrial DNA. And because our mitochondrial DNA molecule is a lot smaller, it seems to be much more stable over time than nuclear DNA is.

Now, long before DNA was used in forensics, scientists knew it could be found in body cells, so any source of living or dead cells—as long as they aren't too badly degraded—are a potential source of either nuclear or mitochondrial DNA. Lots of early forensic DNA research involved trying to figure out the best sources of crime-scene DNA. Some things, like blood, semen, or other obvious body tissues were a no-brainer, pardon that pun, but eventually scientists figured out that DNA was even left behind on things like cigarette butts, soft drink cans, toothbrushes, a licked envelope seal, hair follicles, tampons, latex gloves, even on the inside brim of a well-worn hat.

But, biological evidence is perishable, and even though DNA is a pretty durable molecule, it will degrade over time, and it will fragment. So, the chances of getting DNA from fresh blood are way better than the chances of extracting it from something like dinosaur bones. Some of the things that can cause DNA to degrade are strong UV light, strong acids, and things like bleach and hydrogen peroxide, things that can oxidize biological molecules. Almost any extreme environmental condition—like heat or fire, or even high humidity—can damage DNA samples, but scientists have still gotten DNA from some pretty ancient sources—maybe not a whole genome, but definitely enough to be analyzed.

A general rule of thumb is that fresh tissues are going to yield more nuclear DNA and older tissues are going to have less. But when a nuclear DNA profile isn't possible, analysts may still be able to get mitochondrial DNA out of an old sample. In my own skeletal cases, the forensic lab can often get mitochondrial DNA from cases that are decades old, even if they can't get a nuclear profile—and there's been a renewed interest in cold cases since DNA technology has improved, as you probably know.

At a crime scene, possible sources of DNA have to be handled carefully. Anything wet—like a piece of cloth with blood on it—should be air dried and put into a container that can breathe a little to stop moisture buildup, something like a paper bag. It also should be kept at a low temperature or at least nothing higher than room temperature. This'll help prevent bacterial and fungal growth because those cells have their own DNA, and you don't want to be extracting bacterial or fungal DNA instead of human DNA in the crime lab.

Sometimes, you can't avoid environmental contamination, like some of my cases where a body has decomposed in a lake or some other source of water. That's because those water sources contain lots of other creatures than just my victim—and most of those are microscopic. But once we get the body back to the morgue, DNA analysts are pretty good at figuring out how to choose the best tissues and minimize cross-contamination.

If the DNA sample isn't a body, but something on a surface that's portable—like a coffee mug, a pair of panties, or a piece of chewed gum—then the whole thing should be brought to the lab. But if the whole thing isn't easily transported—like spit on the sidewalk—then a sample that contains the questioned DNA can be taken from that.

Evidence techs not only have to be careful with samples to preserve the DNA in them, they also have to think about their own safety, since body fluids can carry infection. Scene and lab workers also have to make sure that they don't contaminate crime-scene evidence with their own DNA from their hair, dandruff, skin cells, or saliva. Anybody who has direct contact with DNA evidence might be asked for what's called an elimination sample of their DNA to make sure that the genetic profile from a crime scene isn't accidentally that of a lab person or an evidence technician.

When investigators need a known sample from a particular person for comparisons, they can use blood, but most often these days, known samples—called reference samples—are taken with a buccal swab. That just means a sterile cotton swab gets rubbed over the inside of somebody's cheek and then put into an envelope.

Remember, putting that in a vial or other air-tight container is bad, because that holds in moisture and encourages other life forms—like the bacteria in our mouths, which have their own DNA—to grow. If you tried this buccal yourself, you wouldn't see a thing, but under a microscope, there would be plenty of cells with a big nucleus in them. Anyway, these types of known reference samples can be taken from a suspect or a victim and then compared to unknown crime-scene samples.

In the morgue we often take DNA samples from unknown persons to help get them identified. But where do you start when it comes to comparisons if you're dealing with a body that's unknown? It really boils down to a couple of ways: First, if investigators think they have a pretty good idea of who they think the victim is, then they can find relatives to take reference samples from for comparison.

And what if no relatives are available? Well, then a reference sample might actually end up coming from the victim themselves. Say, we think a body in the morgue is John Q. Smith, well, maybe a death investigator can go back to Mr. Smith's home, and get his toothbrush, hairbrush, electric razor, or something else that only his DNA is likely to be on. Reference samples have even been taken from stored medical tissues, like a woman's Pap smear slide that might be years old, or donated blood sitting in a blood bank, things like that. The other major way to get people identified is by using DNA databases, and I'll talk more about that later.

So, back at the lab, DNA scientists have to extract the genetic material from crime scene or reference samples, and DNA extraction techniques have been around for a long time. Heck, there are even high school lab activities that let students get DNA out of bacterial cells. Extraction isn't the tough part. The difficult part of DNA analysis has been figuring out how to find and capitalize on the tiny fractions of DNA that differ among people, rather than the over 99% of our DNA we have in common. Remember the stretches of variable and relatively inconsequential DNA I mentioned? The ones we called sequence and length polymorphisms? That's what they use to develop someone's DNA profile—or as it is sometimes called, their DNA fingerprint.

The first really successful method of DNA profiling was what's called restriction fragment length polymorphism, or RFLP, analysis. This uses the equivalent of a molecular scissors, called a restriction enzyme, that's literally been designed by scientists to cut DNA at specific places wherever 2 particular nucleotides sit next to each other in those variable number tandem repeat—or VNTR—parts of the genetic code, I talked about. Like wherever the enzyme finds a T-A combination next to a C-G combination, it will cut the DNA.

These restriction enzymes are used on particular areas of human DNA that are known to be polymorphic. When they cut between specific places, what's left are a bunch of smaller DNA fragments. And since one person's variable regions are different from another's in these polymorphic areas, the resulting fragment sizes will differ between 2 people. So, even though the same molecular scissors could be used on your DNA and my DNA, the lengths of the DNA fabric they cut will end up being different.

A method called gel electrophoresis is then used to sort out the RFLP fragments by size. During electrophoresis, the DNA gets put in a gel with a chemical buffer that gives the DNA fragments a slight negative charge. And then the gel is put in an electric current bath, where one end is negative and the other is positive. Since the DNA has been given a slight negative charge, it's going to be attracted to the positive end of the electrophoresis chamber.

Now, because the smaller pieces of DNA are lighter and can move faster than the larger ones in the gel—after the electric current is turned off, and the fragment race is over—the result will be a separation of the fragments by size. In the same electrophoresis gel, they'll also run calibration controls called ladders to make sure everything is working OK and to give some standards for comparison. After electrophoresis, the resulting DNA fingerprint can then be compared to other DNA samples.

RFLP began being phased out of forensics in about the mid-'90s, but not before it tied the stain on Monica Lewinsky's dress to then President Bill Clinton. RFLP is problematic because it requires a pretty large sample, and the results aren't compatible with the major DNA computer databases.

In 1983—which, remember, was the same year Colin Pitchfork's first known victim was discovered—a technique for mass-producing copies of DNA was developed. The process is called PCR, which stands for polymerase chain reaction. It amplifies a small sample of DNA so there's plenty of it to analyze in a forensic case. Basically, PCR takes advantage of the double-stranded nature of the DNA molecule and the simplicity of its code to essentially clone the DNA. The machine used is called a thermal cycler, because it heats up the DNA to open up the double helix for copying, and then with each cycle it then doubles the amount of DNA present. So in a couple of hours, a single target piece of DNA can be copied about a trillion times. That means a little crime-scene sample can go a long way in testing.

Today, RFLP typing of DNA has been replaced by something called STR analysis. It uses PCR and some of the same principles as RFLP, but STR is quicker and doesn't require as much sample. STR stands for short tandem repeat, because it focuses on the smaller repeating units in DNA. STRs are essentially the shortest examples of that stuttering or stammering sections of DNA that I mentioned earlier—consisting of only maybe 3 to 7 repeating base pairs, compared to 15 to 35 for RFLP.

STRs have been shown to have a lot more variability among people, too. And because STR focuses on really small stretches of DNA, found all throughout the human genome, it can be used on much smaller and more degraded samples. One estimate I read said only about 18 cells are needed to get a DNA profile using STR technology—that's a tiny fraction of the estimated 50 to 100 trillion cells in the human body! Electrophoresis is still used to separate STR fragments, but there have been advances there, too—they now use what's called capillary electrophoresis, which is done in a tiny column, not a flat gel.

STR typing is also the most sensitive of all types of DNA testing. Scientists have settled on 13 different core locations within human DNA that capture much of our STR variability. Each one of these 13 locations has its own established probability, and then when you combine the results of STR typing at all 13 of those locations, the statistical probabilities of 2 people having the same DNA winds up jumping in the quadrillions—that's 10 to the 15th—or even higher than that!

Better still, the profiles generated by STR are sets of numbers that can be input into the CODIS database—which is the acronym for the Combined DNA Index System—that was developed by the FBI and others in the late 1990s. CODIS lets agencies easily compare DNA profiles they obtain to those from other cases, and even to offender databases, and that has the potential to pinpoint suspects and link cases. And, when DNA from an unknown person is put into CODIS, it can be compared with DNA profiles from missing persons in the effort to identify John and Jane Does.

Other advances in DNA technology have been the fairly recent ability to tell whether a sample is from a woman or a man by looking at DNA from the sex chromosomes. Those are the chromosomes called X and Y that you might remember from biology class. There is a gene called amelogenin on the sex chromosome that is a mere 6 nucleotides longer in males than females, but that's enough to produce a different genetic signature. In addition to that, the Y chromosome has its own standard tandem repeats—meaning its own STR's—that are especially useful in focusing in on the male fraction from a mixed sample of DNA that might contain sperm.

We'll revisit DNA in a couple of other lectures, including some case examples. But at least we've covered the basics, and a little bit about the technology used in forensic science to generate DNA profiles. You can see that DNA has some similarities to other kinds of evidence we've already talked about, in that it relies on comparisons between samples taken from people—whether they are known individuals, unknown persons, or crime-scene samples.

But unlike hair and serology, DNA has risen to be the gold standard in both victim and perpetrator identification because it's one of the rare pieces of evidence that can be statistically linked to a single person at the exclusion of all others. Because DNA can be found in all body tissues and fluids, we see that it has even greater ID potential than fingerprints. The field of chemistry has played a huge role in the way we analyze some types of evidence, so let's continue to explore body chemistry and see how it's used in forensic science.

Forensic Toxicology of Drugs and Poisons
Lecture 11

F orensic labs examine a variety of body fluids and tissues to extract and analyze the DNA molecule—which, of course, is native to our cells—but there are many other types of tests that are conducted in forensic labs to look for chemicals or drugs that are introduced into our bodies. Toxicology is the study of how animals, including humans, are affected by drugs and poisonous substances. The science of forensic toxicology is important because many drug and poison issues have legal ramifications.

Forensic Chemistry and Toxicology Labs

- Many forensic labs have 2 chemistry sections within them: a forensic chemistry lab that analyzes contraband, abused substances in dosage or seized form, and a toxicology lab that looks for drugs or other chemicals in biological samples such as urine, blood, or other body tissues—in other words, after people have a chemical in their system.

- The reason that there are 2 chemistry sections in forensic labs has to do with the huge differences in concentrations between a drug on the street and a drug in someone's body. The forensic chemistry lab analyzes grams and kilograms of drugs, but the toxicology lab looks for drugs in nanogram and microgram amounts.

- These 2 sides of forensics use different supplies and different analytical instruments housed in separate locations because of the potential for cross-contamination that would taint drug and poison results in the toxicology lab.

- A drug is a single chemical, or mix of chemicals, that has psychological and/or physiological effects on the body. Therapeutic drugs—such as aspirin and antibiotics—are taken for various ailments while other drugs are recreational. Some, such as alcohol and caffeine, are legal while others are not.

- Many drugs or chemicals that are typically innocuous—or even helpful to the body—can be toxic in excess. This is even true for substances normally found in the body, such as the hormone insulin, which will lower blood sugar to the point of death if given in high enough dosage.

- A poison is something that has life-threatening effects, which are often collectively known as toxicity. Both legal and illegal drugs can be poisonous if not taken in the right amounts or if taken in combination with other substances. Legal drugs and even prescription drugs can also have unanticipated toxic side effects that might affect some individuals—even when those drugs are taken properly.

The Science of Pharmacokinetics

- The way drugs act in the body and the effects they have on the body are studied within the science of pharmacology, which can be broken down into 2 areas: pharmacokinetics and pharmacodynamics.

- Pharmacokinetics is the study of the way drugs move—including how they get into and out of the body—which can be organized into 4 main areas: absorption, distribution, metabolism, and elimination.

- Although drugs can enter the body in a variety of ways, blood is the superhighway that drugs use once they're inside. Most drugs don't affect people indefinitely because they're metabolized, after which most drugs—but not all—are removed from the body in a few different ways.

- Absorption is how a drug gets into the body. Drugs can be injected directly into the blood intravenously—which means right into a vein—or injected into a muscle or under the skin where they'll enter the blood a little more gradually. Drugs can also be introduced orally or rectally, where they'll have to cross the mucous membrane lining of the gastrointestinal tract to reach the bloodstream.

- Some drugs enter the extensive network of blood vessels of the lungs by being inhaled while others can cross the skin by being applied topically. Some drugs, especially those used on the skin to treat the skin—including some anesthetics—might not end up in significant levels in the circulatory system, so they are said to act more locally.

- In terms of distribution, if a drug is not intended to act only locally, it's the circulating blood that carries the drug to almost all parts of the body. Depending on the size or chemistry of the drug, it may not reach all parts of the body. Therefore, when a person takes a drug, it may end up at different concentrations in different parts of the body.

- Metabolism is the way in which a drug is broken down within the body into other substances, which can be called metabolites, and usually takes place in the liver. Sometimes, there are multiple steps in the process of metabolism for a given drug so that even metabolites can be further broken down into other chemicals in a series of body reactions.

- The breakdown of a drug has 4 main possible outcomes.

  o First, it deactivates the drug, which ultimately limits or lessens its effects on the body.

  o Second, metabolism of a drug usually makes it easier for the body to get rid of it because metabolites are smaller and usually more water soluble than the parent drug they come from.

  o Third, metabolism can convert the drug into a substance that's usable for energy.

  o Fourth, a parent drug can be metabolized to the active drug.

- The final step in pharmacokinetics is elimination. Most drugs leave the body in urine because the bloodstream carries them to the kidneys, where blood is filtered. This puts the drug and/or its metabolites into urine, which is why most drug tests involve urine testing.

- Other drugs and/or metabolites can exit the body in feces and sweat, through respiration when people exhale, by being deposited in hair that is growing in a follicle, or through lactation in nursing mothers. These are all sources of forensic testing.

The Science of Pharmacodynamics

- The reason that a drug can exert an effect on the body is because drugs and other substances, such as our body's hormones, are like chemical keys. The locks that those keys may fit are called receptors, which are some of the many types of proteins found on the surface of cells. There are even some types of receptors that are inside of cells.

- Even though a drug may be coursing through the bloodstream, the only cells that are targets for that drug are those that have the matching receptors for it, and when a drug key finds one of its matching receptor locks, it will bind to that receptor, and in turn, the cell will react in some way.

- There are 2 main ways drugs interact with cells in the body: Some drugs chemically tell a cell to perform a certain function when they bind to a receptor on that cell, and some drugs interact with other drugs, which is known as synergism—when 2 or more drugs are taken together, they sometimes have a greater effect than either would have if taken individually.

- The science of pharmacodynamics also has allowed an understanding of drug dependence and drug addiction, which are not the same.

- Dependence is a psychological need for a certain drug; if a person stops taking that drug, he or she does not have physical symptoms of withdrawal.

- When someone is addicted to a drug, his or her body physically needs the drug to continue functioning. If the addicted person stops taking the drug, he or she goes into withdrawal, which can include symptoms such as high temperature, pain, seizures, and even death.

- The phenomenon of tolerance occurs when the body adapts to a drug. As tolerance builds up, increasingly higher quantities of the drug need to be taken to achieve the same effects. Tolerance occurs with most drugs to some degree—even with some prescription drugs—but tolerance is especially pronounced for substances such as morphine, heroin, cocaine, alcohol, and barbiturates.

- Reverse tolerance, or sensitization, occurs when users experience heightened effects from the same dose of a drug, which can occur with stimulants such as methamphetamine or cocaine.

Forensic Drug Testing
- Forensic drug testing can be divided into 2 main areas: testing on the living and testing on the dead. Tests on living people involve looking for illegal, banned, or abused substances. Reasons for drug tests on the living include preemployment drug tests and random drug tests to help ensure public safety or to make sure that athletes compete fairly.

- The postmortem forensic drug testing of body fluids and body tissues involves poisoning cases, which can be accidental, suicidal, or homicidal. When looking for and at toxicity, forensic toxicologists work in conjunction with forensic pathologists, who are medical doctors that specialize in the study of disease and trauma in the morgue.

- In order for toxicologists to discover whether a poisoning was accidental or intentional, they need to take a number of things into account. If possible, this includes getting personal information about the victim from family members or medical professionals. Forensic toxicologists can use that information in conjunction with instrumental tests that are run on body fluids and tissues and possibly by testing substances found at the scene that may relate to the incident.

- In a living person, signs of poisoning may include nausea, vomiting, respiratory issues, abnormal coloration of the skin, mental confusion, seizures, and—when severe enough—loss of consciousness. The effects depend on the type of drug involved and the amount and duration of exposure.

- In order to identify one or more drugs in a victim's body, there are 4 main steps: sampling, screening, extraction, and confirmation.

- In sampling, body fluids and/or tissues are taken from the victim to search for drugs or other chemicals. In antemortem testing, the choice of the sample is determined by what the lab thinks it is looking for or how long the drug or chemical has been in the body.

- The most typical samples for antemortem drug testing are blood and urine. In postmortem testing, in addition to blood and urine, vitreous fluid from the eye, stomach contents, bile, brain, and liver tissue are commonly collected.

- Once the toxicology lab has obtained samples, screening tests are conducted that are similar to presumptive tests—except they're done in the lab. These preliminary tests indicate that a drug may be present, which then

In poisoning cases, postmortem forensic drug testing can be done to analyze body fluids and body tissues.

© iStockphoto/Thinkstock.

allows the toxicologist to know what direction to go in for further testing.

- Screening tests can sometimes be problematic because some drugs mimic naturally occurring substances, and vice versa. Examples of common toxicology screening tests include gas chromatography and enzyme-multiplied immunoassay testing.

- Then, the toxicologist needs to extract the drugs for confirmatory testing. The purposes of extraction are to clean up the drug so that there aren't other substances present that could contaminate the testing instruments and to concentrate the drug so that it will be easier to detect. The extraction method that is chosen depends on the drug and the body fluid or tissue sample being used.

- When investigators need to know precisely what substances are in a mixture and in exactly what quantities, the current state-of-the-art confirmatory test for most chemicals and drugs is mass spectrometry, which can be calibrated with known standards to measure a drug's quantity in a sample.

Suggested Reading

Trestrail, *Criminal Poisoning*.

Questions to Consider

1. What is toxicology?

2. What is the difference between a drug and a poison?

3. What different types of forensic cases might involve toxicology testing?

4. What are some sources of tissues or body fluids that can be used for drug and poison testing?

Forensic Toxicology of Drugs and Poisons
Lecture 11—Transcript

We've just seen how forensic labs examine a variety of body fluids and tissues to extract and analyze the DNA molecule—which, of course, is native to our cells. But there are lots of other types of tests done in forensic labs to look for chemicals or drugs that are introduced into our bodies.

In this lecture we'll talk about toxicology, which is the study of how animals, including humans, are affected by drugs and poisonous substances. And since many drug and poison issues have legal ramifications, we'll more specifically address the science of forensic toxicology.

Let me first mention that many forensic labs really have 2 chemistry sections within them. A forensic chemistry lab that analyzes contraband abused substances in dosage or seized form—in other words, before somebody ingests or smokes them—we'll talk about those in the next lecture. And they have a toxicology lab that looks for drugs or other chemicals in biological samples like urine, blood, and other body tissues—in other words, after people have a chemical in their system. That's what we'll talk about in this lecture.

The reason behind the 2 chemistry lab sections in forensic labs has a lot to do with the huge differences in concentrations between a drug on the street and a drug in someone's body. The forensic chemistry lab deals in grams and kilograms, but the toxicology lab looks for drugs in nanogram and microgram amounts.

These 2 sides of forensics use different supplies and different analytical instruments. They're even housed in separate locations—that's because of the potential for cross-contamination that would taint drug and poison results in the toxicology lab.

Now, what's the difference between a drug and a poison? We all have an intuitive sense of what those terms mean, but by definition, a drug is a single chemical or mix of chemicals that have some kind of psychological and/

or physiological effects on the body. There are therapeutic drugs that we take for various ailments, like aspirin or antibiotics, and other drugs that are recreational. Some are legal, like alcohol and caffeine, while others are not.

But a poison is something that has life-threatening effects, which are often collectively known as toxicity. And as we know, both legal and illegal drugs can be poisonous if not taken in the right amounts or taken in combination with other substances. Legal drugs and even prescription drugs can also have unanticipated toxic side-effects that may affect some individuals, even when those drugs are taken properly.

Let's start off by learning a little bit about how drugs enter and act within the living body, and then we'll cover more about poisonings. Some of you might know a lot about this, if you're in a medical field, but others of you probably use medications all the time without really knowing much about how they behave once you take them. The way drugs act and the effects they have is the science of pharmacology, but we're going to break that down further into 2 areas: pharmacokinetics and pharmacodynamics—those are your 2 big words of the day.

Pharmacokinetics is the study of the way drugs move—including how they get into and out of the body—and we can organize that into 4 main areas: absorption, distribution, metabolism, and elimination. We'll see that although drugs can enter the body in a variety of ways, the blood is the superhighway that drugs use once they're inside. And the reason most drugs don't affect people indefinitely, is that they're metabolized, after which, most drugs—but not all—end up being removed from the body in a couple of different ways. Now, let's add some detail.

Absorption is how a drug gets into the body, and we're all pretty familiar with absorption routes: Drugs can be injected directly into the blood intravenously—which means right into a vein—or injected into a muscle or under the skin where they'll enter the blood a little more gradually. But drugs can also be introduced orally or rectally, where they'll have to cross the mucous membrane lining of the gastrointestinal tract to reach the bloodstream.

Some drugs enter the extensive networks of blood vessels of the lungs by being inhaled, while others can cross the skin by being applied topically. Some drugs, especially those used on the skin to treat the skin—including some anesthetics—might not wind up in significant levels in the circulatory system, so they are said to act more locally.

Now, in terms of distribution, if a drug is not intended to act only locally, it's the circulating blood that carries the drug to almost all parts of the body. I say "almost" because sometimes, depending on the size or chemistry of the drug, it may not get to all parts of the body. For instance many drugs can't cross what's called the "blood-brain barrier"—which means that they can't get into the brain. That's because the blood vessel networks of the brain are less permeable than those of the rest of the body, especially to certain sizes and types of molecules. So, when a person takes a drug, it may end up at different concentrations in different parts of the body.

Here are some other examples: Some organs, like the heart and liver, have a richer blood supply than other organs, so they can hold higher concentrations of a drug that's in circulation. Also, the chemical structure of some drugs makes them preferentially collect in certain body parts.

For instance, some pesticides tend to collect in fatty tissue, specifically called adipose tissue, and it's hard to get rid of them. Over time, the build-up of those chemicals can cause health issues or even death. This is also important in nature's food chain, like when fish swim in polluted waters, because when a person eats that fish, they're also ingesting all of the pesticides that have collected in that fish over its lifetime.

Now, let's move on to metabolism—that's when a drug is broken down within the body into other substances, which can be called metabolites. Sometimes there are multiple steps in the process of metabolism for a given drug, so that even metabolites can be further broken down into other chemicals, in a series of body reactions.

The breakdown of the drug has generally 4 main possible outcomes: First, it deactivates the drug, which ultimately limits or lessens its effects on the body. Secondly, metabolism of a drug usually makes it easier for the body to get rid of it. This is because metabolites are smaller and usually more water-soluble than the parent drug they come from.

And the smaller and more soluble they are in the blood, the easier the bloodstream can, for instance, carry them to the kidneys where they can be excreted in urine. The third thing metabolism of a drug can do is convert it into a substance that's usable for energy. There's also a fourth outcome where a parent drug can be metabolized into the active drug; drugs like this are called pro-drugs.

Usually, drug metabolism takes place in the liver. For instance, the ethyl alcohol in alcoholic beverages is a drug; remember a drug is any chemical that has psychological or physiological effects on the body. Specifically, ethyl alcohol, also called ethanol, also called grain alcohol, or just good, old "drinking alcohol," is what's called a psychoactive drug. But in terms of its metabolism, ethyl alcohol is broken down within the liver into a chemical called acetaldehyde, which is then further metabolized into acetic acid.

The intermediate metabolite acetaldehyde is more toxic than ethanol itself and contributes to liver damage. But because ethanol produces both physical and psychological dependence—and people with that dependence consume large quantities of ethanol—alcoholism ends up affecting all systems of the body and producing toxicity in many organs, not just the liver. We'll talk a lot more about drugs of abuse, including alcohol, in our next lecture.

The final step in pharmacokinetics—which, remember, is the movement of drugs in the body—is elimination. Most drugs leave the body in urine, because the bloodstream carries them to the kidneys where blood is filtered, and this puts the drug and/or its metabolites into urine. That's the basis for urine testing to look for drug use. But other drugs and/or metabolites can also exit the body in feces, sweat, through respiration when people exhale, or by being deposited in hair that's growing in a follicle, or through lactation in nursing mothers. So all of these are sources of forensic testing.

Now, remember our second big word of the day was pharmacodynamics, which is the science of how drugs act in the body, including their interactions with other drugs. The reason a drug can exert an effect on the body is because drugs and other substances, like our body's own hormones—which can also be taken as drugs—are like chemical keys. The locks that those keys may fit are called receptors. Receptors are some of the many types of proteins found on the surfaces of cells. We talked about other proteins found specifically on the surface of red blood cells when we talked about blood type. There are even some types of receptors that are inside of cells.

So, even though a drug may be coursing through the bloodstream, the only cells that are really sensitive to it, or maybe I should say the only cells that are targets for that drug, are those that have the matching receptors for it. And when a drug key fits into one of its matching receptor locks, it will bind to that receptor, and in turn, the cell will react in some way.

Today, many of our recent drugs have been scientifically designed to bind to specific receptors; but all throughout human history other drugs have been discovered by accident—like when it was first realized that willow bark relieved pain—which goes back thousands of years. We now know that's because the plant contains salicylic acid, which is the active ingredient in aspirin.

Aspirin is a drug that acts by suppressing the formation of body chemicals called prostaglandins, which, among their many other functions, are cell mediators involved in pain and inflammation. We all realize that if we have a terrible headache, and we take aspirin for it, the aspirin doesn't just rush straight to our aching head—it courses throughout our bloodstream and would also relieve pain, say, in our finger if we have a bad hangnail, too. This reminds us that the distribution mechanisms we just talked about in our discussion of pharmacokinetics mean a drug doesn't necessarily just affect one body tissue or organ—it can affect any cell, or any other drug or body chemical it interacts with.

There are 2 main ways drugs interact with cells in the body: Some drugs chemically tell a cell to perform a certain function when they bind to a receptor on that cell. For instance, when a diabetes drug binds to receptors on the pancreas, it can promote the secretion of insulin by the pancreas into the bloodstream. We call these types of drugs agonists. Morphine is an agonist because it mimics endorphins in the central nervous system.

On the other hand, drugs called antagonists are those tell that a cell to stop performing a certain function when they find and bind to that cell's receptors. Like some drugs that bind to the receptors in stomach cells to stop the cells from producing the acid that causes heartburn and ulcers.

Some antagonists work by simply blocking the receptor site so the drug that normally binds there cannot. This is how the opiate dependence treatment called naltrexone blocks opiate receptors in addicts who are trying to stop using. Some poisons are toxic because they act as antagonists and block normal functions.

And we all know that drugs can interact with other drugs, which is known as synergism. Sometimes when 2 or more drugs are taken together, they have a greater effect than either would give if taken individually. For instance, the combination of barbiturates and alcohol magnify each other's effect to the point where typical sub-lethal doses of each, when taken together, can cause death. This was apparently the cause of death for both Jimi Hendrix and Janis Joplin, among countless other famous and less famous people.

The science of pharmacodynamics also has allowed an understanding of drug dependence and drug addiction—which are not the same thing. Dependence is a psychological need for a certain drug, such that if that person stops taking that drug, they don't have physical symptoms of withdrawal.

On the other hand, when someone is addicted to a drug, the body physically needs the drug to continue functioning. If the addicted person stops taking the drug, he or she goes into withdrawal, which can include symptoms like high temperature, pain, seizures and, in some cases, like with a severe addiction to barbiturates or alcohol, a sudden withdrawal can even cause death.

Related to that is the phenomenon of tolerance where the body adapts or gets used to the drug. As tolerance builds up, higher and higher quantities of the drug need to be taken to achieve the same effects. Tolerance occurs with most drugs to one degree or another, even some prescription drugs, but tolerance is especially pronounced for things like morphine, heroin, cocaine, alcohol, and barbiturates. But there's also something called "reverse tolerance"—or sensitization—which is when users experience heightened effects from the same dose of drug, which can occur with stimulants, such as methamphetamine or cocaine.

Now, forensic drug testing can be basically boiled down to 2 main areas: testing on the living and testing on the dead. Tests on living people look for illegal, banned, or abused substances. This includes things like pre-employment drug tests, and random drug screening that help ensure public safety, whether on the job, or in the military, or to make sure athletes are competing fairly.

Human performance testing also can be prompted by a specific incident or crime, like when people are tested to see if one or more drugs have affected their abilities, such as driving under the influence—or whether a drug has incapacitated them, like when a victim of sexual assault alleges a date rape drug—we'll talk about those issues more in future lectures.

But for the remainder of this lecture, let's look at the postmortem forensic drug testing of body fluids and body tissues in poisoning cases, whether they're accidental, suicidal, or homicidal. When looking for and at toxicity, forensic toxicologists work closely in conjunction with forensic pathologists, who are medical doctors that specialize in the study of disease and trauma in the morgue.

We've all heard horrible incidents of accidental poisonings that harm or even kill people. Examples are all too familiar: A child accidentally drinks a toxin like drain cleaner or gets into and ingests prescription drugs. That's what happened to one of my nephews, leaving him brain damaged and legally blind. But similar accidents can happen to adults, too, especially when drugs are not labeled or stored properly—like somebody putting weed killer in an old whiskey bottle, storing it in the basement, and then old uncle George decides to take a nip one day.

People can accidentally take the wrong medication from a shared bathroom cabinet, or take too much of a prescription, especially if they are forgetful and thought they already took it that day. It can also be accidental poisonings related to adverse drug interactions. Or in some cases, a medical condition can lead to organ damage—particularly the liver or kidneys—and a drug taken at normal levels can become toxic because it can't be properly metabolized or eliminated by the body.

Other accidental poisonings can have environmental causes, like carbon monoxide or radon gas accumulations in homes or somewhere else. Carbon monoxide can come from faulty heaters and engines but is also produced in house fires. The discharge of lots of different toxic chemicals, including nuclear poisonings, can come from industrial and even sometimes natural sources; we'll cover examples of those in our lecture about mass disasters. These toxins can harm other creatures in the environment, as well as humans.

But, the environment can "bite back" since accidental poisonings also include attacks by venomous animals, like spiders and snakes—although I'm not sure exactly how you'd classify such a death in a snake handler. I mean, wasn't it practically inevitable? Many people know that some plants, like hemlock, and certain fungi, like toxic mushrooms, are poisonous parts of the natural world, too.

Sadly, some poisonings happen because people decide to take their own lives by intentional drug overdoses—usually involving random prescription drugs including tranquilizers and morphine, or different over-the-counter drugs, especially analgesics (or combinations of the 2). Suicide attempts from drug overdoses are only fatal about 2% of the time, but the resulting organ damage may ultimately take the person's life sooner or later.

And of course, there are countless stories throughout ancient and modern history of killings committed by poisonings, using substances like strychnine, ricin, heavy metals like arsenic and cyanides—like the hydrogen cyanide gas Zy-klon B, used in the Nazi gas chambers of World War II, which is said to cause death in less than a minute.

In order for a toxicologist to figure out whether a poisoning was accidental or intentional, they may have to take a number of different things into account. If possible, this includes getting personal information about the victim that a health-care worker or death investigator might gather from family members or medical professionals, things like the victim's medical history, drug use or abuse pattern, and their physical condition at the time of the apparent poisoning. The forensic toxicologist will then use that information in conjunction with what are called instrumental tests run on body fluids and tissues, and possibly by testing substances found at the scene that may relate to the incident.

In a living person, signs of poisoning may include nausea, vomiting, respiratory issues, abnormal coloration of the skin, mental confusion, seizures, and—where severe enough—a loss of consciousness. The effects depend on the type of drug involved and the amount and duration of exposure. Medical professionals or clinical toxicologists can sometimes have a head start on identifying the poison involved, if there are good clues as to its source—like, for instance, a snakebite.

Here's an example of a pretty confident head start on a source: When I was 4 years old, I handed 2 empty bottles of baby aspirin to my mother, saying that my older sister gave them to me and told me that if I wanted to grow up to be big and strong, I had to eat them. That's pretty much the last thing I remember about the incident, as my little blonde head began to spin—though there was a certain amount of poetic justice in that they pumped my sister's stomach, too, because they couldn't be sure she hadn't taken the aspirin, as well.

As you can see, there are lots of situations that call for toxicological testing, including in hospital and other clinical lab settings—on people and nonhuman animals—but let's return to the forensic lab's involvement in fatal human poisonings. In order to identify 1 or more drugs in a victim's body, there are 4 main steps: sampling, screening, extraction, and confirmation. Let's take those one at a time.

In sampling, body fluids and/or tissues are taken from the victim to search for drugs or other chemicals. In ante-mortem testing, the choice of the sample is determined by what the lab thinks it's looking for or how long the drug or chemical has been in the body. The most typical samples for ante-mortem drug testing are blood and urine. In postmortem testing, in addition to blood and urine, vitreous fluids from the eyes, stomach contents, bile, brain, and liver tissue are commonly collected.

Liver is important because it's the site of metabolism for so many types of drugs, and the bile that's released by the liver and gallbladder into the gastrointestinal tract concentrates many kinds of drugs. Spinal fluid can be tested, as can brain tissue. And as I mentioned earlier, fatty tissues can warehouse pesticides like DDT and marijuana. The stomach can be opened to look for signs of what was ingested, such as actual pills or remnants of undigested pill capsules.

But what if the body is putrefying and tissues are already breaking down? Sometimes it's still possible to find toxins in the vitreous humor since the eye is somewhat more resistant to decomposition. However for some drugs, the amount that diffuses into the eye is so much less than that in the rest of the body, that it's not always a helpful specimen. Urine can sometimes be withdrawn from what's left of the bladder.

Some drugs and toxins can even be found in embalmed or exhumed bodies long after death. And, as I mentioned earlier, hair is a long-standing warehouse of body chemistry. Not only is it resistant to decomposition, but hair can also be used to capture drug-use history, since some drugs can get incorporated into hair as it grows.

Once the toxicology lab has obtained the samples, they do screening tests. These are the kind of like the presumptive tests we talked about in serology, only they're done in the lab, not the field. These preliminary tests indicate a drug may be present, which then allows the toxicologist to know what direction to go in for further testing. These screening tests can sometimes be problematic, though, because some drugs mimic naturally occurring substances and vice versa. Examples of common toxicology screening tests include what's called gas chromatography and enzyme multiplied immunoassay testing.

Chromatography tests separate mixtures into their chemical constituents based on their interactions between 2 different phases. Gas chromatography uses a solid to a gas phase as it separates drugs and chemicals, but it also destroys them as it does so. Immunoassay tests rely on the same types of antibody/antigen reactions we talked about in serology, like looking for the type and concentration of a hormone in a body fluid by using the antibodies to that hormone.

Next, the toxicologist will need to extract the drugs for the actual confirmatory testing. The purposes of extraction are really twofold: First, to clean up the drug or its metabolites so there aren't other substances present that could contaminate the testing instruments. And secondly, extraction concentrates the drug or metabolite so it will be easier to detect. Scientists have honed in on a number of different extraction methods. The one that's chosen depends on the drug and the body fluid or tissue sample being used.

When investigators need to know precisely what substances are in a mixture and in exactly what quantities, the current state-of-the-art confirmatory test for most chemicals and drugs and metabolites is what's called mass spectrometry. Often coupled with gas chromatography, mass spectrometry sends a vaporized sample, through an ionization method, to charge the molecules in the sample, creating ions. Then, an electromagnetic field is applied, which will separate the resulting ions by what's called their mass-to-charge ratio. The ion signals that are created are captured as an image called a mass spectrum that shows peaks representing the chemicals or drugs or metabolites that were in the original mixture.

Qualitative and semi-quantitative data can be then obtained from the mass spectrum, in that the chemicals in that the mixture can be identified by their mass-to-charge ratio, and the amount present can be determined by the strength of the signal. Toxicologists know the spectrum "signatures," if you will, for all types of drugs, including their metabolites, as well as several types of poisons. These signatures are different for each type of chemical or drug, and in that sense, they are like drug fingerprints. A mass spectrometry method can be calibrated with known standards to measure a drug's quantity in a sample.

Now, let's talk a little more about some poisons and how they affect the body using some specific case examples. As I alluded to earlier, many drugs or chemicals that are typically innocuous—or even helpful to the body—can be toxic if they are in excess. This is even true for substances normally found in the body—like the hormone insulin. If given in high enough dosage, insulin will lower blood sugar to the point of death.

The first murder conviction for insulin poisoning happened in England in 1957, when the 32-year-old pregnant wife of a nurse named Kenneth Barlow was found dead in her bathtub, of what was initially suspected to be a drowning. After investigators found an injection site in each cheek of her buttocks, the surrounding tissue was excised and removed, and it yielded 84 units of insulin—and that's just by extraction from the tissue immediately around the wound sites. Now, Mrs. Barlow was not diabetic, and one estimate I read said the amount of insulin found just in those small tissue samples alone would have been enough of a therapeutic dose of insulin to last 2 diabetics for a full day.

Experts assume that Mrs. Barlow probably actually died from drowning, but only either after losing consciousness from the insulin coma that Barlow induced or because he drowned her. In fact, Barlow might have actually "gotten away with murder" to use that well-worn phrase, if he had left his wife in the couple's bed, rather than putting her in the bathtub—which is what he apparently did. Police found vomit in the couple's bed sheets and the woman's sweat-soaked pajamas in the laundry hamper, and both of those symptoms were likely due to the insulin toxicity.

But, insulin has a very short "half-life," which means it doesn't stick around in the body for very long before being metabolized—I mean literally on the order of minutes—so, the only reason all that insulin was able to be extracted from Mrs. Barlow's buttocks was because her death stopped her metabolism, leaving it in her tissues for toxicologists to find. Oh, and one other thing: During the investigation, coworkers revealed that Mr. Barlow had said for years that death by insulin would be the perfect murder. Wonder if he was still saying that during his subsequent 26 years in prison?

Here's another notorious case: Many people know that acetaminophen—better known by the brand name, Tylenol—causes acute liver damage in high doses. But far worse than its potential toxicity was the 1982 case of intentional product tampering in Chicago, Illinois, that cost the lives of 7 people. A person who is still unknown to authorities—so is still potentially at large—apparently purchased packages of Extra Strength Tylenol, took them somewhere, and introduced potassium cyanide into some of the capsules. Then the perpetrator took the containers back to retail stores, put them back on store shelves, and others purchased them. Investigators quickly figured that was the killer's M.O., which means the method of operations—because the tainted capsules were of different lots from different manufacturing plants.

The first victim was a 12-year-old girl, and then an adult man. Tragically, when that man's relatives gathered for his funeral at the family home—before the source of the poisonings was known—the deceased man's brother and sister-in-law both took tainted Tylenol from the same bottle, and they also died. Another 3 women also perished before investigators figured out that product tampering was to blame.

This vicious act of poisoning—known as the "Chicago Tylenol murders" or simply as "Ty-murs" by the FBI—prompted new anti-tampering legislation, as well as many changes to product packaging that we've become accustomed to today. Like so many other lessons we've learned from forensics, this case illustrates another way in which science, society, and the legal system move hand in hand.

Now, let's turn our attention to another chemical issue that also has strong relationships to forensics, and that's substance abuse.

The Forensics of Substance Abuse
Lecture 12

I t's difficult to find accurate statistics for substance-abuse deaths because the problem is so insidious and so intertwined with deaths from other causes, such as alcohol-related traffic accidents and drug-related criminal acts. In addition, deaths are just the tip of the iceberg in forensic substance-abuse issues. By far, the largest part of the day-to-day operations in crime labs is the chemical testing of contraband substances that are potentially illegal drugs. In fact, drug evidence accounts for more than 50% of all the evidence that ends up in forensic labs—including fingerprints, hair, fibers, and blood.

The Forensics of Substance Abuse
- In general, drugs of abuse can be classified into 4 major categories by source.

  o First, some come from naturally occurring plant and fungal origins and are smoked or ingested in basically their original form, such as marijuana, peyote buttons, and some mushrooms.

  o Secondly, some drugs of abuse are extracted from plants, such as cocaine, morphine, and codeine.

  o A third classification is semisynthetic drugs that are manufactured from a naturally occurring substance, such as heroin or LSD.

  o The fourth category of abused drugs is synthetics, which are entirely man-made, such as barbiturates, amphetamines, and oxycodone.

- Drugs are more commonly classified by the effects they typically have on those who take them, such as depressants, stimulants, narcotics, and hallucinogens. Despite common belief, alcohol is a depressant, and marijuana is a hallucinogen.

Depressants

- Depressants, which are often called sedatives in low doses, are drugs that generally decrease brain activity, reduce muscle activity, lower respiration and heart rate, induce sleep, and reduce anxiety—sometimes to the point of mild euphoria.

- Overdoses of depressants kill people by paralyzing the respiratory center in their brain, and when people are addicted to these types of depressants, a sudden withdrawal can be lethal as well. Street names include downers and barbs—which is short for barbiturates, the most common class of depressants in the United States.

- Benzodiazepines and related drugs make up a large family of synthetic depressants, which are especially known for their antianxiety and sleep-inducing effects. Many of these have familiar brand names, such as Xanax, Klonopin, and Ativan.

Stimulants

- Stimulants are drugs that are known to elevate mood, reduce depression, raise blood pressure, elevate heart and respiration rates, and produce intense euphoria and energy. Caffeine is a common and unregulated stimulant, but some illicit and very dangerous stimulants have been manufactured from relatively benign substances—such as lithium—in clandestine labs, such as meth labs.

- The class of stimulants known as amphetamines was originally developed to relieve the symptoms of asthma and hay fever but went on to be used to treat narcolepsy or hyperactivity and to suppress appetite. Adderall and Dexedrine are a few familiar brand names.

- Cocaine is a stimulant that resembles amphetamine in its potential for abuse and its pharmacology. Cocaine is extracted from the coca leaf grown in the Andes Mountains. It is extracted with hydrochloric acid to form the compound cocaine hydrochloride and is also known by the street names snow, flake, and blow. When cocaine hydrochloride is treated with a base and extracted into an organic solvent, it forms freebase, or crack, cocaine, which can be smoked, resulting in a greater effect but also in an increase in the chance of death.

Narcotics

- The term "narcotic" is a catchall for many drugs that are considered highly dangerous. Narcotics are still used legally as painkillers and sleeping aids. The opium resin from the poppy plant has been used traditionally for over 5000 years to relieve pain, to decrease diarrhea, and as a recreational drug in many cultures.

- Codeine has long been used in cough suppressants—and mixed with aspirin, or more recently with acetaminophen, which is Tylenol—to boost their pain-management capabilities. Morphine also has a long history as an analgesic and is still used to control pain, in particular after surgery. Heroin is derived from morphine but is about 10 times more potent; it's used as a painkiller in some other countries but not in the United States.

- Methadone is a synthetic opiate substitute used in the United States to help wean addicts off of heroin under medical supervision. There are many other narcotics used as pain relievers today that are frequently abused and illegally trafficked. This includes a large group of synthetic and semisynthetic compounds, such as Dilaudid, Vicodin, Lortab, and Demerol.

- Oxycodone is a narcotic that has been put in a time-released form called OxyContin or combined with aspirin in Percodan or with acetaminophen in Percocet. Fentanyl is another narcotic that is about 100 times more potent than morphine.

Hallucinogens

- The fourth class of typically abused drugs is hallucinogens, but these have no accepted medical uses in the United States, with the recent exception of some states allowing medicinal marijuana usage. Hallucinogens have perception-altering effects and include 4 subcategories: psychedelics, deliriants, disassociatives, and cannabinoids—each with slightly different mind-bending properties.

- Psychedelics, the classical hallucinogens, include semisynthetics, such as lysergic acid diethylamide (LSD), and naturally occurring mescaline and psilocybin mushrooms. A huge problem with psilocybin abuse is the extra risk of poisoning because people mistakenly ingest toxic lookalike mushrooms and die.

- The deliriant forms of hallucinogens are also called true hallucinogens because people taking them will have conversations with people who aren't there, for example. Deliriants are part of a group of compounds known as anticholinergics because of their effects on the nervous system and include derivatives from mandrake plants as well as MDMA, or ecstasy.

- Phencyclidine, abbreviated PCP and known as angel dust, is a powerful hallucinogen of the dissociative variety. The manic behavior and feelings of strength, power, and invulnerability seen in people on PCP make them formidable opponents for law enforcement. Other dissociatives include ketamine (special K), nitrous oxide (laughing gas), and some derivatives of the salvia plant.

- Cannabinoids are the last class of hallucinogens, but they don't fit neatly into any category. Marijuana has mild analgesic and sedative properties but also causes perceptive alterations, memory impairment, mood swings, euphoria, and hallucinations. Heavy use can promote delusions and paranoia.

The History of Drug Regulation in the United States
- In the late 19th century, there really was no drug control in the United States, but—prompted by an increase in patented medicines, cocaine use, and public reaction to opium smoking by Chinese railroad workers—the Pure Food and Drug Act was passed in 1906.

- This became part of a history of regulating the use of drugs of all kinds and linked drug use to the Treasury Department through taxes. Alcohol prohibition happened at the federal level in 1920 with the 18th Amendment of the U.S. Constitution—followed by the repeal of prohibition in 1933.

- In 1956, the Narcotic Drug Control Act was created, which increased penalties for illicit drug use, including that dealers who sold drugs to minors could face the death penalty. Concurrent with this came the responsibility for controlling any substance that had the potential for abuse by the Food and Drug Administration, expanding the sphere of dangerous drugs beyond only narcotics.

- In 1970, the Comprehensive Controlled Substances Act updated or abolished previous dangerous drug laws. This also moved enforcement from the Treasury Department to the Justice Department and marked the beginning of the Drug Enforcement Administration (DEA). Tobacco and alcohol were excluded from the DEA's jurisdiction and instead are regulated by the Bureau of Alcohol, Tobacco, Firearms, and Explosives.

- Ultimately, the U.S. Congress became responsible for scheduling potentially abused substances by dividing them into 5 groups. Drug scheduling is based on the potential for abuse, addiction, and any legitimate medical value the drug has. The lower the schedule number, the higher the potential for abuse and addiction.

Drugs and Toxicology
- Forensic toxicologists are responsible for trying to determine the identity and quantity of drugs in the body—possibly by looking for drug metabolites. They also have to determine whether there are drug interactions if more than one drug is present. Furthermore, they have to relate all of this—if they can—to the history and patterns of drug abuse by the person involved, including whether dependency or tolerance issues played a role. They have to figure out whether a drug was simply in a person's body or whether it contributed to, or was, the cause of death.

- The most common drugs of abuse that toxicologists see in drug deaths are heroin, morphine, and the opiates—but not marijuana and hallucinogens because people don't die even from overdoses of these drugs.

- Whether toxicology is done after an injury or fatality where substance abuse could be involved or during a preemployment or workplace screening, the most common specimens used are blood and urine. Blood tests are typically used when looking for cannaboids or when alcohol use is suspected. Urine tests are better for other suspected substances, especially those that tend to hang around in the body.

© iStockphoto/Thinkstock.

The contraband drug section of forensic labs tests substances that are on the street and being sold.

- Part of the reason that forensic chemists have to analyze, quantify, and identify seized substances is because that's part of the basis for determining what charges will be brought against the suspects involved. In some jurisdictions, a larger amount of drug will mean a harsher punishment, but weight isn't everything.

- Many drugs—especially the closer they get to the street-sale level—are usually "cut" with something else. For most states, the total weight of the drug plus the cutting agents count toward the penalty determination. In some states, in the case of small amounts of a drug, there needs to be a usable quantity of the drug—more than a trace—to officially break the law.

- Some forms of the same drug have harsher penalties than another. For example, the U.S. federal government gives out worse punishments for crack cocaine as compared with an equal amount of flake cocaine, so toxicologists have to determine which version it is.

- At the state level, most states don't require impurities to be identified, but in federal cases, cutting agents are identified for intelligence purposes. Knowing what a drug was cut with can make tracing its trafficking and distribution trail easier.

- In the case of large quantities of drugs, sampling is an issue. For example, if a large brick of marijuana comes into the crime lab, analysts will take multiple samples from multiple places on the brick to determine whether the whole package really is marijuana.

- Many of the same toxicological techniques are used to identify potential substances of abuse in the crime lab—such as gas chromatography, mass spectroscopy, and radioimmunoassay. High-performance liquid chromatography (HPLC) and Fourier transformation infrared spectroscopy (FTIR) are also used as confirmatory tests.

- There are also preliminary screening tests available, and some are even used by officers in the field. These can be as simple as looking up the identity of manufactured pills or using quick chemical spot-testing methods. These field tests are sometimes done to be able to get a search warrant, but as with other preliminary tests, they have to be confirmed later by another method.

Questions to Consider

1. About how long have there been governmental drug control entities in the United States?

2. What are the major classes of the typical drugs of abuse?

3. When a huge quantity of a suspected substance is encountered, is every bit of that quantity subject to chemical testing?

The Forensics of Substance Abuse
Lecture 12—Transcript

Actress Marilyn Monroe, comedian Lenny Bruce, singer Elvis Presley, author Jack Kerouac, *Saturday Night Live* comedians John Belushi and Chris Farley, pop icon Michael Jackson, writer Truman Capote, singer and actress Judy Garland, big band leader Tommy Dorsey, Senator Joe McCarthy, musician Kurt Cobain, entrepreneur Howard Hughes, Jim Morrison of The Doors—that list could go on and on, and sadly it does. And you probably recognize the commonality there—like Jimi Hendricks and Janis Joplin, mentioned in our last lecture, all these high-profile people died either directly or indirectly from substance abuse.

Some cases were related to alcohol, others to prescription drugs, some died from illegal drug use, and for many, it was a combination of abused substances. Some died from acute toxicity, either through accident or suicide, while others from a lifetime battle with drugs and/or alcohol. In the grip of the downward spiral associated with substance abuse, some chose to end their lives by other means of suicide.

Now consider this: That list only includes celebrities, so just imagine how many substance abuse–related deaths occur each day in the U.S., not to mention elsewhere. In the year 2006, one source attributes 26,000 deaths in the United States to drug overdoses.

In fact, it's difficult to find accurate statistics for substance-abuse deaths because the problem is so insidious and so intertwined with deaths from other causes, like alcohol-related traffic accidents, and drug-related criminal acts, such as drug-deal murders and killings during robberies that are intended to support a drug habit. And deaths are just the tip of the iceberg in forensic substance-abuse issues.

Statistics from the early 2000s, compiled by the U.S. Bureau of Justice, indicate about 1/4 of all prisoners landed in jail because of crimes committed to try to raise money to support a drug habit. In the UK it's estimated that over 50% of robberies, over 70% of burglaries, and 85% of shoplifting crimes are committed to get money for drugs.

Alcohol abuse has been implicated in about 3/4 of U.S. violent crimes, like rape, domestic violence, child abuse, and other physical attacks. And, the trafficking of commonly abused drugs profoundly impacts both law enforcement and forensic science.

Did you know that by far, the largest part of the day-to-day operations in crime labs is the chemical testing of contraband substances that are potentially illegal drugs? In fact, of all the many types of evidence we've talked about—fingerprints, hair, fibers, crime-scene blood, and the rest—drug evidence accounts for more than half of all the evidence that winds up in forensic labs.

The chemistry section is usually the largest part of the lab in terms of personnel and expenses; and it's been that way since the 1970s. In fact, U.S laws allow for the seizure of money and property involved in drug trade—like boats, cars, and motorcycles, and then that confiscated property is usually sold. Why? So the funds can go to the law enforcement agency that caught the criminals, to help fund their chemistry lab.

So let's take a closer look at the forensics of substance abuse, starting with drugs that are either illegal or highly controlled in the United States. In general, drugs of abuse can be classified into 4 major categories by their source. First, are those that come from naturally occurring plant and fungal origins and are smoked or ingested more or less "as is," like marijuana, peyote buttons, and some mushrooms. Secondly, some drugs of abuse are extracted from plants, like cocaine, morphine, and codeine. A third classification would be semi-synthetic drugs that are manufactured from a naturally occurring substance, like heroin or LSD. And the fourth category of abused drugs is synthetics, which are entirely man-made, like barbiturates, amphetamines, and oxycodone.

Drugs are more commonly classified, though, by the effects they typically have on those who take them. Most of us are familiar with the terms depressant, stimulant, narcotic, and hallucinogen, and could probably name a couple of drugs in each of those classes. The classification of alcohol and marijuana usually stumps my students, though. Do you know which of those 4 classes alcohol fits into?

Most of my college-age students believe that alcohol is a stimulant, probably because they are stimulated to get stupid when they drink too much. But alcohol is actually a depressant. And do you know how marijuana currently is categorized by its effects? It used to be considered a narcotic, but is now considered a hallucinogen; it really doesn't fit into that 4-part scheme as well as most other drugs do.

Depressants, which in low doses are often called sedatives, are drugs that generally decrease brain activity, reduce muscle activity, lower respiration and heart rate, induce sleep, and reduce anxiety—sometimes to the point of mild euphoria. Overdoses of depressants kill people by paralyzing the respiratory center in their brain. Street names include downers and barbs—short for barbiturates, the most common class of depressants in the United States. These include over 2500 synthetic drugs that were developed as pharmaceuticals, like sleep aids, anti-epileptic drugs, and surgical anesthetics.

Phenobarbital is a barbiturate you may have heard of. Mixing alcohol and barbiturates has serious consequences, often including death, and when people are addicted to these types of depressants, a sudden withdrawal—also called "cold turkey"—can be lethal, too.

Benzodiazepines and related drugs make up a large family of synthetic depressants, especially known for their anti-anxiety and sleep-inducing effects. Many of these have familiar brand names, like Xanax, Klonopin, and Ativan. Two that are known for their amnesic affects are Versed—used during medical procedures where the patient is awake, like colonoscopies—and Rohypnol, which has unfortunately become one of the date-rape drugs (although my toxicologist friend tells me alcohol is still the most common date-rape drug).

Historically, other depressants were popular drugs of use and abuse. Some have been discontinued or replaced, including methaqualone, which was better known in the '60s and '70s by the brand names Quaalude and Sopor, and another drug marketed as Librium back in the '60s—but ultimately these were replaced by the more potent, and still abused, Valium. We'll return to the depressant alcohol later in this lecture, because—although it's regulated—it's not a scheduled substance in the U.S., so it's not covered under drug laws.

Stimulants are drugs known to elevate mood, reduce depression, raise blood pressure, elevate heart and respiration rates, and produce intense euphoria and energy. Caffeine is a common and not regulated stimulant, but some illicit and very dangerous stimulants have been manufactured from relatively benign substances in what are called clandestine labs, like the meth labs of the past couple decades.

Methamphetamine can be made from lithium, which clandestine producers often get from rechargeable batteries, ammonia, and pseudoephedrine, which is an over-the-counter allergy medication. Meth labs are the reason that pseudoephedrine allergy medications are now only available at the pharmacy window in U.S. retail stores.

The class of stimulants known as amphetamines was originally developed to relieve the symptoms of asthma and hay fever, but they went on to be used to treat narcolepsy or hyperactivity, and to suppress appetite. Brand names you may have heard of include Adderall and Dexedrine.

Amphetamines grew in popularity as drugs of abuse during the 1960s, especially when users began to take them by intravenous injections instead of oral doses. The latest craze in stimulants of abuse are synthetic amphetamine-like drugs commonly called "bath salts" that can found for sale in gas stations, truck stops, and on the Internet. As their dangers have become known, they've begun to be outlawed.

Cocaine is another stimulant that resembles amphetamine in its potential for abuse and its pharmacology. Cocaine is extracted from the coca leaf grown in the Andes Mountains. It's extracted with hydrochloric acid to form the compound cocaine hydrochloride, also known by the street names snow, flake, and blow. When cocaine hydrochloride is treated with a base and extracted into an organic solvent, it forms what's called "freebase" or crack cocaine.

Crack and freebase have a lower boiling point so it's possible to smoke them. Smoking allows the large surface area within the lungs to rapidly absorb the drug, resulting in a greater effect, but these forms also increase the chances of death in the user. Cocaine is still used legally in some medical procedures, and—as many of you know—was the original stimulant in Coca-Cola and some other soft drinks before being replaced with caffeine.

We're not going to talk extensively about drug trafficking, but since cocaine is a huge drug of abuse, let me give you some rough ideas of the kind of money that can be involved in its sale. One source I consulted estimated that more than 110 million pounds of coca leaves—that's about 50 million kilograms—are produced annually in South America. A drug processor can purchase about 500 pounds of coca leaves for about $250, and from that will net about one pound of pure cocaine. So, there's about a 500-to-1 ratio between the amount of coca leaves needed, and the amount of cocaine that results.

Now, a pound of pure cocaine can be sold for about $1000. But a drug trafficker will dilute that and put it into smaller packages of, say 5 pounds. That 5-pound block of street-grade cocaine will sell for about $25,000 in the U.S. All told, that's a 100-fold increase in value, from the original cost of the coca leaves, to the street price of the drug. And in the pyramid scam that is drug dealing, a smaller dealer can adulterate or dilute—they use the term "cut"—they can cut that cocaine even more, to make their own profit, as long as they can find a buyer.

Let's get back to classifying drugs by their effects The term "narcotic" is really a catch-all for many drugs that are considered highly dangerous. Narcotics are still used legally as painkillers and sleeping aids. The opium resin from the poppy plant has been used traditionally for over 5000 years to relieve pain, to decrease diarrhea, and as a recreational drug in many cultures.

Codeine has long been used in cough suppressants—and mixed with aspirin, or more recently acetaminophen, which is Tylenol—to boost their pain management capabilities. Morphine also has a long history as an analgesic, and is still used for to control pain, after surgery, in particular. Heroin is derived from morphine, but it's about 10 times more potent—it's used as a painkiller in some other countries, but not in the United States.

Here's a side note related to heroin: You probably heard of the French Connection, maybe from the movie starring Gene Hackman and Roy Scheider that won the Academy Award in 1971. In its heyday, the French Connection supplied almost all white heroin being brought into the United States. This network started in the 1930s when farmers in Turkey had legitimate licenses to grow opium poppies and sell them to legal drug companies.

When farmers grew more than the drug companies needed, some sold the extra poppies on the black market. The morphine was taken out of the poppies in Turkey, and the morphine "paste" was then sent to Marseille, France, where it was converted into heroin. The heroin, in turn, was then smuggled into the U.S., mainly through New York, by organized crime gangs.

In the late 1940s, the battle between the heroin importers and law enforcement intensified, especially at U.S. ports. But still, by the 1960s, somewhere in the neighborhood of 1 1/2 to 2 1/2 tons of heroin each year was coming into the U.S. from France. Finally, in 1971, after years of negotiations with the Turkish government, opium farming was banned in Turkey. French and U.S. authorities also stepped up efforts to intercept heroin shipments, leading to more heroin seizures and arrests.

A notorious incident happened in the early '70s in the U.S. where a group of New York police officers was arrested and charged with corruption. Investigators discovered that some of the cops had allowed New York mobsters to steal heroin from a police storage room and replace it with flour and cornstarch. The switch was discovered after insects were found eating the flour.

Once all aspects of the French Connection had been targeted, the whole heroin pipeline from France fell apart, marking the end of the French Connection. But as we know, when one door closes, another one opens, and today most heroin comes from Central and South America, and from Mexico. Since it's processed differently than the heroin from France, it's sometimes called "Mexican Mud" for its off-white or light brown color.

Methadone is a synthetic opiate substitute that's used in the United States to help get addicts off of heroin under medical supervision. And there are many other narcotics used as pain relievers today that are frequently abused and illegally trafficked. This includes a large group of synthetic and semi-synthetic compounds, like Dilaudid, Vicodin, Lortab, and Demerol.

Oxycodone is another narcotic, which has been put in a time-released form called OxyContin, or combined with aspirin in Percodan, or with acetaminophen in Percocet. Fentanyl is another narcotic about 100 times more potent than morphine. These are all very common drugs of abuse.

The fourth class of typically abused drugs is hallucinogens, and—unlike the others I mentioned—these have no accepted medical uses in the United States—with the recent exception of some states allowing medicinal marijuana use. Hallucinogens have perception-altering effects, and include 4 subcategories: psychedelics, deliriants, disassociatives, and cannabinoids—each with slightly different mind-bending properties.

Psychedelics, the classical hallucinogens, include semi-synthetics, like LSD, and naturally occurring mescaline and psilocybin mushrooms. As you might imagine, a huge problem with psilocybin abuse is an extra risk of poisoning, because people mistakenly ingest toxic look-alike mushrooms, and they die.

Mescaline is structurally similar to the stimulant amphetamine, but because of slight chemical differences, mescaline also has hallucinogenic effects. It's found in the peyote cactus that grows in the southwestern U.S. and Mexico. The cactus crown is sliced into wafers called buttons, which are softened in the mouth, rolled into balls, and then swallowed, after which hallucinations can last for a half a day. Because the peyote cactus has been a part of Native American religious ceremonies for hundreds of years, the U.S. government has granted special dispensation for certain Native American groups to continue that practice as part of what's called "The American Indian Religious Freedom Act of 1978."

Lysergic acid diethylamide, better known as LSD or simply acid, comes from a natural substance derived from a fungus that grows on grain. As an aside, if an infected grain is used in bread, people get the disorder called St. Anthony's fire, which may have caused some symptoms of those accused in the Salem witch trials of the late 1600s.

Very small doses of LSD, smaller than a period on a written page, which is about 50-micrograms, can cause auditory and visual hallucinations that can last up to 12 hours. LSD is not known to be addictive, but can cause psychosis and flashbacks, meaning residual hallucinations, that happen months or years after taking the drug.

LSD has been distributed in many forms: liquefied and put into paper, made into tablets, or dissolved in small pieces of dry gelatin—which has led to some creative distribution, like being put behind a postage stamp and mailed to another user. Because LSD can be absorbed through the skin, investigators need to be exceptionally careful when they handle it.

The deliriant forms of hallucinogens are also called "true hallucinogens" because people taking them will actually have conversations with people who aren't there and things like that. Deliriants are part of a group of compounds known as anticholinergics, because of their nervous system effects. They include derivatives from mandrake plants like Nightshade, as well as 3, 4-Methylene-dioxy-methamphetamine, abbreviated MDMA, but more commonly called ecstasy.

Ecstasy is derived from amphetamine, and was actually used in certain forms of psychotherapy until the mid-1980s when Congress stepped in. Among other effects, ecstasy induces euphoria and a sense of intimacy, which turned it into the rave club drug that peaked around the world in the '80s and '90s.

Phencyclidine, abbreviated as PCP, known as angel dust, is a powerful hallucinogen of the dissociative variety. The manic behavior and feelings of strength, power, and invulnerability seen in people on PCP make them really formidable opponents for law enforcement officers. Other dissociatives include ketamine (known in drug culture as "special K"), nitrous oxide (or "laughing gas"), and some derivatives of the salvia plant.

Cannabinoids are the last class of hallucinogens, but as I mentioned earlier, they don't fit neatly into any category. Marijuana has mild analgesic and sedative properties, but also causes perceptive alterations, memory impairment, mood swings, euphoria, and hallucinations. Heavy use can promote delusions and paranoia.

Marijuana comes from the cannabis sativa plant; the psychoactive compounds in that plant are collectively known as cannabinoids, with the major active ingredient tetra-hydro-cannabinol, abbreviated THC. The oily extract of the cannabis plant has a higher THC content, and so a greater effect, and is called hashish. Medicinal marijuana has an active ingredient that's structurally identical to THC, but less potent.

I should also mention the type of substance abuse called huffing—this is when kids inhale a variety of legal chemicals to get high. For instance, some hydrocarbons found in petroleum and its distillates can cause erratic behavior because of effects on the brain. This "high" makes people do stupid things, like engage in dangerous behavior and not notice hazards around them—leading to serious injury or death. The practice of huffing, itself, can also cause death due to oxygen deprivation.

Now, let's talk a little about the history of drug regulation in the United States. In the late 19th century there really was no drug control in the U.S., but prompted by an increase in patented medicines, cocaine use, and public reaction to opium smoking by Chinese railroad workers—the Pure Food and Drug Act was passed in 1906.

This became part of a history of regulating the use of drugs of all sorts, including the Harrison Act of 1914, which required the registration and taxation of individuals involved in the opium drug trade in the United States, and actually linked drug use to the Treasury Department through taxes. Alcohol prohibition happened at the federal level in 1920, with the 18th amendment of the U.S. Constitution—followed by the repeal of Prohibition in 1933.

After World War II, by the late 1940s, it was estimated that half of all crime in cities in the U.S. was related to illegal drug use. So in 1956, the Narcotic Drug Control Act was created, which increased penalties for illicit drug use, including that dealers who sold drugs to minors could face the death penalty. Concurrent with this came the responsibility for controlling any substance that had the potential for abuse by the Food and Drug Administration, expanding the sphere of dangerous drugs beyond only narcotics.

In 1970, the Comprehensive Controlled Substances Act updated or abolished previous dangerous drug laws. This also moved enforcement from the Treasury Department to the Justice Department and marked the beginning of the Drug Enforcement Administration, abbreviated DEA.

Tobacco and alcohol were excluded from the DEA's jurisdiction, and instead are regulated by the Bureau of Alcohol, Tobacco, Firearms, and Explosives. When you actually put together a mini-history like this, you really begin to see the patchwork quilt nature of drug regulation in the U.S.

Ultimately, the U.S. Congress became responsible for what's known as "scheduling" potentially abused substances, by dividing them into 5 groups. Drug scheduling is based on the potential for abuse, addiction, and any legitimate medical value a drug has. The lower the schedule number, the higher the potential for abuse and addiction. Schedule 1 drugs have no currently accepted medical use in the United States, while schedules 2 through 5 have recognized medical uses. Related criminal penalties are linked to those schedules.

Schedule 1 drugs currently include heroin, LSD, marijuana, PCP, and methaqualone, which remember are Quaaludes. Examples of schedule 2 drugs are morphine, cocaine, methadone, and methamphetamine. Into schedule 3 fall codeine, hydrocodone, some barbiturates, and the anabolic steroids that have been abused by dirty athletes. Valium and Xanax are schedule 4 drugs.

Examples of schedule 5 controlled substances are things like cough medicines that have codeine in them. The Comprehensive Controlled Substances Act of 1970 is still in use today in the U.S., but individual states may legislate to modify scheduling, as well as the penalties for distribution and possession of some of these controlled substances.

Now, let's relate all this back to the toxicology lab. Remember that forensic toxicologists are responsible for trying to determine the identity and quantity of drugs in the body, and maybe by looking for drug metabolites. They also have to sort out whether there are drug interactions, if more than one drug is present. And they have to relate all this—if they can—to the history and patterns of drug abuse by the person involved, including whether dependency or tolerance issues played a role.

They have to figure out whether a drug was simply "on board" in a person's body, or whether it contributed to, or was, the cause of death. The most common drugs of abuse that toxicologists see in drug deaths are heroin, morphine, and the opiates—but not marijuana and hallucinogens, because people don't die from those, not even from what some could call "overdoses."

Whether toxicology is done after an injury or fatality where substance abuse could be involved, or during a pre-employment or workplace screening, the most common specimens used are blood and urine. Blood tests are typically used when looking for cannabinoids or when alcohol use is suspected. Urine tests are better for other suspected substances, especially those that tend to hang around in the body.

For example, PCP stays in urine for about a week after it's been used. One of the cocaine metabolites can be found in urine about 3 days after cocaine use. And heavy marijuana users can show a THC metabolite in their urine for up to 2 months. So, as we talked about in the last lecture, toxicology labs are busy each day analyzing blood, urine, and sometimes other body tissues for evidence of drug use. These include forensic labs investigating criminal matters or suspicious deaths, but others are private labs selected by companies or athletic organizations for drug screening.

I also mentioned the other section of a forensic chemistry lab, where seized substances are analyzed—they see a very different picture of substance abuse. That side of the lab is dealing with bricks of cocaine and sometimes bales of marijuana, not minute amounts in blood or urine samples.

The contraband drug section of the lab most commonly sees marijuana, heroin, and cocaine as the 3 biggest types of samples—at least according to my local crime lab in Cincinnati. They're testing what's on the street and being sold, while the toxicology section is looking for what impairs or kills people.

Part of the reason forensic chemists have to analyze, quantify, and identify seized substances is because that's part of the basis for determining what charges will be brought against the suspects involved. And that isn't as straightforward as you might think. In some jurisdictions, a larger amount of a drug will mean a harsher punishment, but weight isn't the whole story.

Remember that many drugs—especially the closer they get to the street-sale level—are usually "cut" with something else. For most states, the total weight of the drug plus the cutting agents counts toward the penalty. For instance, there could be one gram of cocaine in 650 grams of sugar, but the penalty would be based on the total 651 grams.

This works the other way, too—in some states, in the case of small amounts of a drug, there needs to be a "usable quantity" of the drug to officially break the law—like there has to be more than a trace. For example, even though the remnants of a marijuana joint, or a bloody syringe suspected in heroin use, could be found by law enforcement officials, if there's not a "usable quantity," there might not be enough to prosecute somebody for possession. One reason that is, is there might not be enough of the drug to analyze.

Some forms of the same drug will have a harsher penalty than another. For instance, the U.S. federal government gives out worse punishments for crack cocaine as compared with an equal amount of flake cocaine, so toxicologists have to determine which version it is. And at the state level, most states don't require impurities to be identified, but in federal cases cutting agents are identified for intelligence purposes, because knowing what a drug was cut with can make tracing its trafficking and distribution trail easier.

In the case of large quantities of drugs, sampling is an issue. If a large brick of marijuana come into the crime lab, analysts will take multiple samples from multiple places on the brick to make sure—as best sampling will allow—that the whole package really is marijuana. Or, if a large shipping box is confiscated, and in it are 1000 large Ziploc bags, each with 50 small baggies of what looks like cocaine in them, sampling will be needed—that entire quantity just can't be analyzed. A few small baggies from a random number of the larger Ziplocs will be sampled and tested, and then the total weight of all of the packages would be determined.

Many of the same analytical techniques mentioned in the toxicology lecture are also used to identify potential substances of abuse in the crime lab—like gas chromatography, mass spectroscopy, and radioimmunoassay. For those of you who know a bit more about chemistry, high-performance liquid chromatography, or HPLC, is also used as a confirmatory test.

But, there are preliminary screening tests available, too, and some are even used by officers in the field. These can be as simple as consulting the *Physician's Desk Reference* to look up the identity of manufactured pills, or quick chemical spot-testing methods. For example, something called a marquis reagent turns purple in the presence of heroin. These field tests are sometimes done to be able to get a search warrant—but as we've seen with other preliminary tests, they have to be backed up later by another method.

In terms of preliminary field analysis for substance abuse, though, one test is king—know what it is? Hopefully, you don't have any first-hand experience, but by far the most common field test for abused substances is, of course, the breathalyzer. All U.S. states and many other parts of the world have laws intended to curb drunk driving. And many use some form of sobriety field-testing that includes a chemical analyzer to detect alcohol levels using expired air.

Because alcohol is volatile, it comes out of the blood that flows through the lungs, and then mixes with air. The machine itself is actually a form of a spectrophotometer that measures how ethanol—which, remember, is drinking alcohol—participates in chemically induced color changes inside the machine.

And in the case of a breathalyzer, science is really taking advantage of what's called a surrogate mechanism to estimate or infer the actual effects of the drug. After all, the alcohol coming off a person's breath isn't what's making them drive poorly, but rather what's going on their brain. But, since brain alcohol levels can't be tested, and actual blood alcohol levels can't be tested in the field, when somebody tests over the legal limit—although they call the result blood alcohol content—it's really a scientifically derived estimate devised for forensic purposes.

Alcohol is the most commonly abused substance in the world. Later in the series, you'll get a chance to use a little math to figure out how much a person can drink before going over the legal limit, including yourself—if you're willing to admit your body weight.

Handwriting and Forgery Analysis
Lecture 13

Q uestioned documents can include anything from a forged check to graffiti scrawled on a wall, and questioned-document experts have just as many techniques for analyzing them. Some, such as handwriting and linguistic analysis, are a bit subjective; others, involving chemical and mechanical analysis, are more objective, but they can also be destructive to the evidence.

What Is a Questioned Document?

- Questioned documents include all sorts of computer-manipulated and hand-altered documents. Questioned-document examiners might look at money, checks, forms, credit cards, stamps, concert and sports tickets, wills, contracts, deeds, ship's logs, passports or other identification, insurance forms, medical records, suicide notes, threatening letters, bank hold up notes, ransom demands, or words written on a wall, a mirror, or even a body at a murder scene.

- Any type of written material could prompt investigation by a questioned-document specialist for both handwriting clues and the materials used to create the document. This includes papers and inks of all sorts; toners used in photocopiers; and print produced by word processors, fax machines, and typewriters.

- Lots of large law-enforcement agencies have document examiners on staff or police officers trained in document analysis. The FBI; the CIA; the Secret Service; the Bureau of Alcohol, Tobacco, Firearms, and Explosives; the Internal Revenue Service; and the U.S. Postal Inspection Service all have questioned-document labs. Military forensic labs and some large private corporations employ document examiners, too.

Handwriting Analysis

- The 2 major areas for questioned-document analysis are handwriting comparisons, which are much more subjective, and materials examination, which are far more objective. Handwriting analysis is not at all the same as graphology—the pseudoscience that alleges you can tell somebody's personality by their handwriting.

- Handwriting analysis involves looking at the class and individual characteristics in a person's writing, usually by comparing the evidence to another writing sample. As we mature in our writing, most of us develop individual characteristics—variations that depend on things like how often we write, how fast we write, and even deliberate changes in style.

- Handwriting also changes with experience, age, and sometimes physical condition. Culturally, styles of cursive writing have changed over time. There may be some minor differences between the handwriting of those who are writing in their native language and a second language as well.

- Casual writing, like a grocery list, might look very different from formal writing, like what you might put on a form in the doctor's office or the address on an envelope. But generally, there are consistencies that mark our handwriting as our own. However, things like someone's sex, race, age, health status, or mental condition cannot be decisively determined from handwriting.

- When a document examiner wants to compare handwriting, a known sample called an exemplar is needed—just as with comparisons of bullets, hair, DNA, and other types of evidence. The more exemplars an examiner has to work with, the better.

- There are times when the examiner might need an exemplar from someone who is no longer alive. Other problems arise when the person providing the exemplar is a suspect in a crime; that person might try to disguise his or her handwriting style.

- There is a standard protocol for obtaining a good requested exemplar: The investigator should make the subject comfortable and provide optimum lighting. The same type of writing instrument and paper should be used as used in the questioned document. The same style of writing should be requested—like print or cursive.

- Most importantly, the writer should have the material dictated for transcription, rather than looking at the questioned document and being asked to copy it. Dictation not only means the writer cannot deliberately try to mismatch the evidence; dictation also tends to make it harder for a person to concentrate solely on the act of writing, making it harder to hide one's natural quirks. For best results, the needed words or phrase should be inserted into some longer passage.

- Features a document examiner would look for include letter size and shape—for example, are they more rounded or tall and thin? Is the handwriting consistently small or large? What about the relative heights of letters? The typical depth below the line of *j*, *g*, or *y*? How about slant? With unlined paper, does the writing tend to creep upward or downward on the page? Finer points include the direction and shape of beginning and end strokes, the letter connections, and quite literally how someone dots *i*'s and crosses *t*'s.

- Pen pressure reveals a lot about a document. Genuine writing shows smooth, rapid, nonstop, free-flowing motions and the absence of any repair and correction strokes. Generally, jerky starts and stops can be signs that someone is trying to duplicate somebody else's handwriting by looking at a copy of it. Fakes include awkward and inconsistent pen movements and inconsistent letter formations throughout as forgers slip back into their own penmanship.

- Analysts cannot always determine who a forger is, since the individual and class characteristics of the forger are not usually present. Investigators can really only say that a document was made by somebody other than the person who wrote the exemplar. Essentially, what investigators are looking for—using no more advanced technology than magnification—are significant similarities or significant differences.

Mechanical Analysis—Typewriters

- Historically, the only printing methods commonly available to people outside the printing industry were typewriters. Although not in common use today in developed countries, document examiners may need to analyze older pieces of writing produced on them.

- Because there were many different kinds of typewriters, examiners have reference files for type styles for different models and manufacturers. From these, they could narrow some fonts down to a specific brand or time period.

- Like other tools, individual typewriters typically had manufacturing defects, like a small notch in a letter's face that would not hit the typewriter ribbon or, conversely, a small bit of extra metal that would give that particular letter a little bump when it appeared on the paper. As a typewriter aged, it could also develop use-wear patterns, like any other tool. The older and less cared-for a typewriter was, the more unique features it would have.

- Next-generation electric typewriters used interchangeable metal spheres, rather than type bars, to strike the ribbon, which meant type could not be traced to an individual machine. It would be impossible for an examiner to get a match between a typewriter and a questioned document unless they were able to locate the exact typewriter ball that was used.

- Investigators had ways to tell if everything on a page was typed at the same time or if, for example, a will had been altered after it was written. Examiners could look for type alignment by using a glass plate with a grid etched on it. They would also compare the ink color—a newly inked ribbon would make darker type than an older ribbon.

Mechanical Analysis—Printers and Photocopiers

- Older dot-matrix printers formed characters by putting down small dots of ink in various patterns. Sometimes, an individual pin could have a defect that might be unique to that machine, but this was not nearly as common as defects on typewriters.

- Ink jet printers, like the name implies, shoot ink onto paper to produce an image or characters. They can sometimes have slight individualizing features, but not often or many. Investigators cannot use fonts to determine printer manufacturers, since many brands have all the same font options. It is thus almost impossible to determine if a document was printed on a specific ink jet printer.

Today's printers and copiers have revolutionized the way documents are produced.

- Laser printers work sort of like photocopiers; the text and images are electronically created on the printer's drum. The toner sticks to the electronic image and is transferred onto the paper. Sometimes it is hard to figure out whether a document was produced on a laser printer or a copier—or if a document is an original from a printer or a photocopy. Like inkjets, you cannot use fonts to determine manufacturer or if a document was printed on a specific printer.

- The machinery that moves paper through a photocopier can sometimes leave small indentations and other marks that can point to a manufacturer. Individual copiers can also have defects that will appear repeatedly on copies; these can link a document to a specific copier—at least until the machine is fixed. Examiners call these trash marks.

- Each time a page is run through a copier, it can pick up new defects, and it is hard to determine whether a questioned document is an original or a copy—or even a copy of a copy. A second-generation photocopy will show the defects of both copiers, and it is nearly impossible to tell which came first.

Mechanical Analysis—Paper

- Questioned-document examiners can also look at the composition and other identifying features of paper. Chemical watermarks are put in after the paper is made, but mechanical watermarks are impressed on the paper during manufacturing and are sometimes coded for quality control. If you have such a mark, not only can the brand be determined, but also when the paper was made.

- Different types of paper vary in how they fluoresce under ultraviolet light and have a variety of fiber types and fiber contents. Two pieces of paper can look identical to the unaided eye, but under the microscope or in the lab they can look or react very differently.

- If somebody tries to insert a new page into a stapled, multipage document like a contract, investigators can look at the staple holes for alignment and the paper type—even its thickness. There are measuring tools called micrometers that can judge the differences in paper thicknesses down to the thousandths of an inch. If a page does not match the rest of a document, that may be suspicious.

- Multiple pages, as in a notebook, can show indented writing. In the movies, a detective will rub the side of a pencil over indented writing; that will not only ruin the paper for fingerprinting, but it can actually smooth out the indentations. Side lighting and photography work much better. An electrostatic device, as used in obtaining shoe prints, is the latest technology for recovering indented writing.

Mechanical Analysis—Ink

- Different inks contain different chemicals, and examiners have all kinds of analytical methods for detecting them, but many chemical tests are destructive, and you cannot just destroy a bunch of evidence to validate your suspicions. Therefore, investigators start with the least damaging methods.

- Ultraviolet and infrared light can show whether any part of the writing on a page was done with different ink. Certain photographic techniques can be useful, too. These types of nondestructive tests can also detect mechanical or chemical erasures. Investigators might not be able to see exactly what was erased, but they can see that something was altered.

- Chemical tests do not always mean destroying a whole page. Examiners can use a hypodermic needle to take a tiny punch out of a piece of inked paper. They can then subject that punch to chromatography and spectrometry tests.

Linguistic Analysis
- Forgeries are common and no doubt as old as writing itself. In fact, during the Middle Ages, a forgery called the Donation of Constantine changed the course of history as we know it. Allegedly written in the 4th century by Constantine the Great, it gave the pope and his successors dominion over all of Italy and the Western Roman Empire, as well as Judea, Greece, Asia, and Africa.

- The document's authenticity was questioned even as early as 1054, but it was officially shown to be a fake in 1440, when Italian humanist Lorenzo Valla exposed it by a detailed linguistic examination—illustrating that because language changes over time, linguistic discrepancies are yet another way forgeries can be exposed.

Suggested Reading

Ellen, *Scientific Examination of Documents.*

Seaman Kelly and Lindblom, *Scientific Examination of Questioned Documents.*

Slyter, *Forensic Signature Examination.*

1. What are some examples of documents that may be of questioned authenticity?

2. Can sex, age, or personality be determined from a handwriting sample by a forensic document examiner?

3. In addition to handwriting analysis, what other types of testing might be done in the analysis of a questioned document?

Handwriting and Forgery Analysis
Lecture 13—Transcript

In 1981, the Gruner and Jahr publishing house in West Germany paid the U.S. equivalent of about 2 million dollars for previously undiscovered writings of Adolph Hitler. Hitler was known to keep diaries during World War II, and it was alleged these writings were kept in a locked metal box, that was being transported by air to Berlin, when the plane carrying them crashed near Dresden in 1945. There were historical accounts of such a crash to back up this possibility.

The 27-volume Hitler diaries, along with other writings—including what was alleged to be the third copy of *Mein Kampf* in existence—were later smuggled out of East Germany. They had been held by a wealthy collector until being offered to Gruner and Jahr by one of its employees, newsman Gerd Heidemann, who broke the story to his boss.

The publishing company decided to authenticate the documents, before showcasing them in their German news magazine, *Stern*, and then selling the rights to other publishers, including *Newsweek* in the U.S., and the *Times Newspapers* in the U.K.

They had 2 experts look at the diaries, comparing them to supposedly "known" documents of Hitler's handwriting. Both the diaries and the exemplars were confirmed as having been written by the same person.

The cover story in the April 1983 issue of *Stern* announced that the magazine's parent company was in possession of Hitler's diaries. But, since *Stern* had provided both the diaries and the exemplars for comparison, some people remained skeptical, so further testing was done.

Ultimately, Dr. Louis Werner of the German police conducted analytical tests that exposed the hoax. He determined that the paper used in the diaries contained a whitening agent that only came into use in 1954—but Hitler had committed suicide in 1945. Plus the ink used was less than a year old.

The alleged diaries and exemplars were written by the same person—but it was not Adolf Hitler—it was actually a small-time criminal named Konrad (Kujau) who provided them to newsman Heidemann. Both ended up serving nearly 4 years in jail for embezzlement and forgery. A handwriting expert who later compared the forgeries to some of Hitler's known writing said Kujau had not even done a very good job.

In this lecture, we're going to look at what are called questioned documents—this includes forgeries by tracing, disguised handwriting, computer manipulation of images, and examinations of documents that have been altered. Questioned-document examiners look at money, checks, forms, credit cards, stamps—even concert and sports tickets. They may also be asked to examine things like wills, contracts, and deeds for their authenticity. Document examiners may look for potential falsification of records, like a ship's log, a passport or other ID, maybe an insurance form or a medical record.

Questioned-document examiners also analyze suicide notes, threatening letters, bank holdup notes, and written demands for ransom. A murder scene could have written evidence—sometimes even in blood—on a wall, a mirror, or even a body. Really, any type of written material could prompt investigation by a questioned-document specialist for both handwriting clues—and, as we saw with the Hitler forgeries—the materials used to create the document. This not only includes papers and inks of all sorts, but also toners used in photocopiers, print produced by word processers, fax machines, and in the old days, primarily typewriters.

Lots of large law enforcement agencies have document examiners on staff, or police officers trained in document analysis. At the federal level, the FBI, the Central Intelligence Agency, the Secret Service, the Bureau of Alcohol, Tobacco, Firearms, and Explosives, the Internal Revenue Service, and the U.S. Postal Inspection Service all have questioned-document labs. Military forensic labs and some large corporations in the private sector employ document examiners, too.

The 2 main areas for questioned document—often just called QD—analysis are handwriting comparisons, which are much more subjective, and materials examination, which are far more objective. Let's start by talking about handwriting analysis. Which, by the way, is not the same thing at all as graphology—you know, the pseudoscience that alleges you can tell somebody's personality by their handwriting? Handwriting analysis involves looking at the class and individual characteristics in a person's writing, especially when comparing 2 writing samples.

All of us who learned to write the same language have similar class characteristics in our handwriting. Especially in the past, schools in the U.S. were fond of what's known as the Palmer method of penmanship, and kids were praised and graded on how precisely their own writing matched the Palmer copybooks.

But as we mature in our writing, most of us develop individual characteristics—these are variations in our handwriting that depend on things like how often we write, how fast we write, and even deliberate changes in style as we develop our own writing flair—I remember the junior high days when girls, in particular, would add their own little frilly tweaks to their writing.

Handwriting also changes with experience and age, and sometimes, physical condition—for instance, elderly people may show shakier handwriting than they did when younger. Culturally, styles of cursive writing have changed over time—as you might notice if you see a sample of writing from the 1700s, like the U.S. Declaration of Independence. I've also noticed some minor differences in the handwriting of friends and colleagues who didn't grow up writing English as their first language, too.

We all know that our casual writing—maybe like a grocery list—might look very different than what we might put on a form in the doctor's office or the address on an envelope we intend to mail. But generally, there are consistencies in the quirks that mark our handwriting as our own. Still, I should point out things like someone's sex, race, age, health status, or mental condition really cannot ever be decisively determined from handwriting. After 25 years of college teaching, I often think a handwritten paper is from a guy or a girl just by its appearance, and I'm often surprised.

When a document examiner wants to compare handwriting, a known sample called an "exemplar" is needed—just as we've seen with other comparisons of bullets, hair, DNA, and other types of evidence. And the more known writing examples a QD-examiner can get, the better able they will be to see the full range of class and individual characteristics, as well as somebody's normal variations.

Exemplar writing can be requested writing, but there are times when the known sample might need to come from someone who's no longer alive— like we saw in the Hitler diaries. To get known exemplars in cases like that, investigators look for pieces of writing that were executed in the course of everyday life, like checks, memos, personal letters, business forms, a diary, a lab journal, or other kind of work log. But, as we saw in the case of the Hitler forgeries, a QD examiner has to be sure that the known sample is authentic.

The other problem with requested exemplar writing is that if the person the writing sample is being taken from happens to be a suspect in a crime, that person is not likely to be very genuine in his or her handwriting style. For instance, when somebody is in a police station being asked to give a writing sample for comparison to a ransom note—and he was the author—he'd be foolish not to try to disguise his handwriting. And I don't even think I have to say I'm making smarter criminals there, since anybody should be able to figure that out!

There's a standard protocol for obtaining a good requested exemplar: The investigator should make sure the subject is comfortable and provide optimum lighting, and the same type of writing instrument needs to be used—like a blue gel pen if that's what it appears was used in the questioned document. The same style of writing should be requested—like print for printed questioned documents, and cursive for cursive. The exemplar should also be executed on the same kind of paper, as much as possible, especially if it was lined paper.

And this is important: The writer should have what's supposed to be written dictated for transcription, rather than looking at the questioned document and being asked to copy it. Dictation not only means the writer can't try to alter his handwriting from what he'd see, but dictation tends to make it harder for a person to concentrate solely on the act of writing.

If a bank holdup note said, "Put all the money in your drawer in an envelope and don't hit the alarm," the investigator should read that same phrase to the person whose writing is being sampled. But, for best results, that phrase should really be inserted into some longer passage—and then maybe even just put bits and pieces of the holdup note here and there in a longer piece of dictation—so the writing is already "flowing" when the desired passages come along. And if the questioned document is a check where there's not a lot of text, the subject should be asked to fill out 10 or 20 checks in a row so comparisons can be made regarding signature, spacing, and things like that.

You might want to make your own handwriting sample and check for things that a document examiner would look for—and maybe get a friend or family member to write the same passage for comparison. Or grab some paper now and transcribe some of what I'm saying right at this moment. Look to see whether your letters are more rounded or tall and thin. Is your handwriting consistently small or is it large?

What about the relationships of heights of letters—do the "tall" letters tower over the "short" letters, or are they all roughly the same height; do letters with a "bottom loop" such as a lower case "J," "G," or "Y" consistently go to the same "depth" below what would be the line on lined paper? How about slant; are the letters pretty much straight up and down, do they slant to the left or the right? And with un-lined paper, do the lines of writing tend to creep upward or downward on the page?

Now how about some finer points, like the direction and shape of beginning and end strokes—do yours consistently start at the bottom and loop up for some letters like a lower case "L" or "F," or do you start at the top and "omit" the first half of the loop? What about letter connections; do you continue from one letter to the next, or do you sometimes have "breaks" in the middle of a word? Do you stop to dot your "I"s and cross your "T"s immediately after you write them, or do you come back after the word's completely written?

QD examiners also look at things like indentations to see pen pressure, which can vary depending on the writing instrument and the thickness of the paper or what's under it. Some people show very smooth pen movements, but again, that may depend on the writing tool. Genuine writing shows smooth, rapid, nonstop, and free-flowing motions, and the absence of any repair and correction strokes. But we all probably knew kids in grade school that got pretty good at their mom or dad's signature on their papers, right?

Generally, "jerky" starts and stops can be signs that someone's trying to duplicate somebody else's handwriting by looking at a copy of it. Features of fakes include awkward or inconsistent pen movements—as well as letter formations that are inconsistent throughout, as forgers slip back into their own penmanship.

QD analysts can't always determine who a forger is, since the individual and class characteristics of the forger are not usually present when they're trying to forge something—investigators can really only say that a document was made by somebody other than the person who wrote the exemplar.

This doesn't hold true if someone's deliberately changing their handwriting, like writing with opposite hand, or intentionally changing letter construction or slant—but there may still be clues. If a person has some type of impediment, it can also change their writing—if they're drunk, or they're in an unnatural or awkward writing position—like tied up, or writing on a wall—or if they have some injury or illness.

Essentially, what investigators are looking for—really using no more advanced technology than magnification—are significant similarities or significant differences. The more similarities and the fewer differences, the more likely the writer of both documents is the same person. But they can't usually eliminate a suspect unless they're physically not capable of producing the writing, as in the case of a child, or an adult who's too ill to hold a pen.

Now, let's get on to the more scientific ways that documents are examined which are more objective, and require more sophisticated testing equipment.

Historically, the only "writing" methods commonly available to people outside the printing industry were typewriters. Although they're not in common use today in developed countries, document examiners may need to analyze older pieces of writing. And before photocopiers and computers, typewriting was the bulk of the non-handwriting analytical work QD specialists did.

Because there were many different kinds of typewriters, examiners have reference files for type styles for different models and manufacturers. From these, they could narrow some fonts down to a specific brand or time period—for example, evidence could show a font style or typewriter wasn't in existence at the time something was supposedly typed.

Like other tools, individual typewriters typically had manufacturing defects in some of their letters—like a small "notch" in a letter's face that wouldn't hit the typewriter ribbon, so no ink would be transferred to the page in that little spot. Gosh, I guess if you're much younger than me, you probably don't have any idea of what I'm talking about, but each letter on a typewriter had to be pressed on the keyboard, sending a little bar called a typebar with a raised version of that letter forward, to strike a ribbon full of ink, that would then transfer the inked image of that letter onto the paper.

Anyway, sometimes that raised letter on the typebar would have a defect— either a notch out of it that would leave a void in the printed letter, or maybe a small bit of extra metal from the manufacturing process that would give that particular letter a little "bump" or a "tail" when it appeared on the paper.

As a typewriter would age, it could also develop use-wear patterns, like any other tool—like if a kid played with the typewriter and hit a bunch of keys at once, it would send a whole flock of typebars crashing into each other—I'll bet some of you remember doing that—and as a result, the older and less cared-for a typewriter was, the more unique features it would have.

Analysts would use these unique characteristics to eliminate a typewriter, and in theory its owner or user—or keep a typewriter, and possibly a person, in a list of suspects. These defects were more common with the older manual typewriters that used those typebars. The next generation typewriters were electric and used a small metal sphere with all of the letters on it that would spin to the correct spot and then imprint the letter on the page when a key was pressed.

Those typewriter balls could be easily changed out on a typewriter, though, and if that happened, it would be impossible for a QD examiner to get a match between a typewriter and a questioned document—unless they were able to locate the exact typewriter ball that was used.

Investigators also had ways to tell if everything on a page was typed at the same time—for example, to determine if a will had been altered after it was written. Examiners could look for alignment issues on the page using a glass plate with a grid etched on it. Since paper was fed manually into typewriters, it would be difficult to insert the same page into the machine 2 different times with perfect horizontal and vertical alignment. Examiners could also check how lines of ink matched—a newly inked ribbon would make darker type than an older ribbon.

Today printers and copiers have revolutionized the way documents are produced. Not only has this changed the way words are put on a page, but it has also enabled people to add images to a document, unlike a typewriter. Many of us have seen generations of computer printers go from dot matrix, to inkjet, and then laser printers.

With the old dot-matrix printers, characters were formed by putting down small dots of ink to form each letter. You could easily see the dots in what was called a 9-pin dot matrix printer, since they were larger and farther apart. But with the more advanced 24-pin dot matrix printers, it was harder to see the individual dots. In either case, sometimes an individual pin could have a defect that might be unique to that one machine, but this wasn't nearly as common as defects on typewriters.

Inkjet printers, just like the name implies, shoot ink onto a page to produce an image or characters. They can sometimes have slight individualizing features, but not often and not many—some might have a slight "spattering" of ink that happens when the ink comes out of the cartridge. But paper texture can affect the amount of spatter too, so that really complicates looking at a spatter pattern as a "signature" defect to identify a specific inkjet printer.

Investigators can't use printer fonts to determine manufacturers, since many brands have all the same font options that we can select on our computers. As a result, it's almost impossible to determine if a document was printed on a specific inkjet printer.

Laser printers work sort of like copiers; the image of the text, or whatever else, is electronically created on the printer's drum. Then toner sticks to the electronic image, and then is transferred to paper, and heated briefly so it will stick to the paper. Sometimes it's hard to figure out whether a document was produced on a laser printer or a copier—or if a document is an original from a printer or a photocopy. Like inkjets, you can't use laser printer fonts to determine manufacturer or determine if a document was printed on a specific printer. So, there I go making smarter criminals again!

The machinery that moves paper through a photocopier can sometimes leave small indentations and other marks that can point to a manufacturer. Individual copiers can also have defects that will appear repeatedly on copies; these can link a specific document to a specific copier—at least until it's fixed. If you work in an office, you've seen these defects, like black or white lines across the pages, smudges, or black specks, that QD examiners called "trashmarks."

One complicating thing is that each time a page is run through a copier it can pick up new defects, and it's hard to determine whether a questioned document is an original or a copy, or even a copy of a copy. A second-generation photocopy will show the defects of both copiers and it's nearly impossible to tell which came first.

As with the alleged Hitler diaries, questioned-document examiners can also look at the composition and other identifying features of paper, too. We've all seen fancy paper that has a watermark on it. Chemical watermarks are put in after the paper is made, but mechanical watermarks are impressed on the paper during manufacturing, and are sometimes coded for quality control—

if that's the case, not only can the brand be determined but also when the paper was made.

Also different types of paper vary in how they fluoresce under UV light, and have a variety of fiber types and fiber contents in them. The fiber content will affect the way paper absorbs ink and the way it reacts to certain chemical tests. Two pieces of paper can look identical to the naked eye, but under the microscope or in the lab they can look or react very differently.

Say somebody tries to insert a new page into a stapled, multi-page document, like a contract. Investigators can look at the staple holes for alignment and they can look at the paper type and even its thickness. There are measuring tools called micrometers that can judge the differences of paper thicknesses down to the thousandths of an inch. And although there are standard width and height sizes to papers—like 8.5 by 11—there can actually be very slight differences in the true size based on the machinery that cut the paper into reams. If a page doesn't match the rest of a document, that may be suspicious.

Multiple pages, as in a notebook, can show indented writing. You've probably seen that yourself on a pad of paper, where you tear off the sheet you wrote on and see the indentations of what you wrote on the sheet below it. In the movies, they always show the detective rubbing the side of a pencil over the surface to see what was written—but that will not only ruin the paper for fingerprinting, it can smooth out the indentations. As we saw with other kinds of impression evidence, side lighting and photography work much better.

An electrostatic device, like the one I talked about in the shoe-print lecture, is the latest thing for recovering indented writing. They put a thin piece of plastic and hold it onto the document by a vacuum, then, together, the paper and plastic are put into the electrostatic box. The plastic is electrically charged and then dusted with black "toner" that sticks to the plastic sheet where the indentations are. This creates a replica, and the plastic sheet can be peeled off of the paper and preserved as evidence of the indented writing.

Another key in the Hitler diaries was the ink—as you can imagine there are all types of chemicals in different types of inks. Questioned-document examiners have all kinds of analytical methods—but you have to consider that many chemical tests are destructive—and you can't just destroy a bunch of evidence to validate your suspicions—I mean, what if those were Hitler's diaries? You can't just pull a page out and put it in a vat of chemicals. So, as we've seen before, investigators start with the least damaging methods.

Alternate lighting, like UV and infrared, can show ink differences, if any part of the writing on a page wasn't done with the exact same ink. Say if an extra zero is added to a check to turn 100 bucks into 1000 bucks—or a loop added to the top of a one to turn 1 into 9. Certain photographic techniques can be useful, too. These types of nondestructive tests can also detect mechanical or chemical erasures, too. Investigators might not be able to see exactly what was erased, but they can see that something was altered.

After nondestructive tests are completed, then chemical tests can be done—and it doesn't mean destroying a whole page. QD examiners or chemists can use a hypodermic needle to take a tiny punch out of a piece of paper that has the ink on it. They can use chromatography tests, like those we mentioned with fiber evidence—that can separate the subcomponents in a chemical mixture. There are lots of chromatography procedures, but there's a simple one you can try for yourself.

You'll need a small amount rubbing alcohol as your first solvent, and 2 tall skinny containers—we use test tubes in my class, but anything will do—like a drinking glass or plastic party cup. If you have nail polish remover, that would make a cool comparison—but if not, use water as your second solvent. Next, get 3 pens that all have the same color of ink—like 3 black ink pens—maybe one with permanent ink, a gel pen, and a regular black ballpoint, but really any 3 pens of the same color ink will do. Don't put your solvents into your 2 containers yet—they'll evaporate, that's the point.

Now you'll need 6 strips of paper—you can use any paper, but a coffee filter would work well. Cut the paper into 6 strips, each about 5 inches long and maybe 3/4 of an inch wide. Now, take one of your pens, and color in a small circle of ink near the bottom of each one of those, about an inch from the bottom. Repeat that using your second pen on 2 other strips, and your third pen on your last 2 strips. And so you'll wind up with 6 strips. To keep them straight you may want to make a code for yourself by writing "pen 1" at the very top of your first 2 strips, "pen 2" at the top of your second 2, and "pen 3" on your last 2. So what you should wind up with is 2 identical sets of 3 strips each—one for each pen.

Now, separate those sets so that you have 3 ink types ready for one solvent, and your other 3 ink strips ready for your second solvent. OK. Time to put the solvents into your containers—but this is important—only put about a half-inch of the rubbing alcohol into one container, and a half-inch of the nail polish remover or water into the other one. You don't want to let the level of the solvent reach as high as the ink dots you drew on the paper.

Now, put the dot end of each strip set into each solvent, but don't let the 3 strips for pens 1, 2, and 3 touch each other—lean them up against different parts of the inside of the glass. You should quickly start to see the solvents climb up the paper, reach your ink, and then hopefully separate some of the chemicals in the ink into a fan of colors that will rise up on the paper. If so, you've seen a simple demonstration of chromatography!

Of course, forensic labs use much more sophisticated chemical analyzers, including different kinds of spectrometry devices like the ones we talked about in our toxicology discussion. But this gives you some insight into the ways papers and inks in suspected forgeries can be tested that are not subjective like handwriting analysis is.

Forgeries are common, and, no doubt, as old as writing itself. In fact, during the middle ages, a forgery called the Donation of Constantine changed the course of history as we know it. This document, allegedly written in the 4th century by Constantine the Great, and sent to Pope Sylvester the First, describes the Emperor Constantine's conversion to Christianity and gives the pope and his successors dominion over all of Italy and the Western Roman Empire as well as Judea, Greece, Asia, and Africa. The only land Constantine wanted to keep was the Eastern Roman Empire where Constantinople had been established.

Constantine's conversion is a historical fact, but the letter was probably actually written between 750 and 800 A.D. by a church official—350 or more years after it was supposedly sent. That forgery was used for many years by various popes to assert political and spiritual power, including against Charlemagne.

Its authenticity was questioned even as early as 1054, but the Donation of Constantine was not officially shown to be a fake until 1440, when Italian humanist Lorenzo Valla exposed it by a detailed linguistic examination—illustrating that because language changes over time, linguistic discrepancies are yet another way that forgeries can be exposed.

Computer Forensics and Digital Evidence
Lecture 14

D igital forensics has become an ever-more-important part of crime solving over the past few decades as computers, cell phones, and other electronics become more central to our lives. As crime has moved online, investigators have developed painstaking techniques for retrieving and analyzing digital evidence, which are used side-by-side with traditional police work.

The Age of Digital Crime

- Forensic computer science is concerned with identifying and extracting digital evidence of criminal activity not only from computers but from cell phones, 2-way pagers, cameras, GPS units, fax machines, and all types of other electronic gear. Thus, the current trend is to refer to the analysis of evidence like this as digital forensics.

- Crimes that used to require the perpetrator to commit them in person—or at least required a physical transfer of information (a bank holdup note, a ransom letter)—can now be carried out remotely. Fraud, identity theft, and embezzlement can happen online. Hackers steal corporate data over the Internet. Predators use social networking sites to lure their prey.

- For a digital crime investigation to start, somebody first needs to realize that it has happened. It may take weeks, or even months, before a person or organization becomes aware of a security issue. The initial analysis also has to show that whatever happened is really a criminal act and not a programming glitch or a simple human mistake.

- Next, investigators have to get to the source of the damage and figure out where the incident originated. They must figure out the path the perpetrator used to get to the server or the victim's computer—Was it over the Internet, a wireless network, or by physical means such as attaching a USB drive or inserting a CD into a computer?

- Investigators will also look at the victim to make sure they understand why this person or organization was attacked, which might help them figure out motive. For instance, somebody hacking into a government website might have political motivations. Targeting a single person's bank account would lead investigators down a different path than if the credit card numbers of all consumers doing business with a certain website were stolen.

Digital Forensics Investigations

- A digital forensics analysis team will always include computer experts of some type, but depending on the incident, it might include law enforcement officers who use standard investigative methods out in the community at large, like interviews. Specialists called forensic accountants might be part of the team to look for irregularities in financial records that indicate embezzlement or fraud.

- If the crime was something more like cyber bullying, investigators need to focus on the victim's daily interactions, and they often quickly point a finger at a possible suspect. If the victim has been targeted by a phishing scam, interviewing the victim and figuring out how they may have opened the door to this crime themselves is important.

- The technology itself is used to track down the suspect. The computer experts will start by performing what is called a traceback to find the source computer. In other words, they look for a trail of Internet provider addresses, or IP addresses, that can be followed back to a suspect, or at least a specific computer.

- Meanwhile, the authorities can continue to use routine policing techniques. They might interview the witnesses or check surveillance tapes. If they hone in on a suspect, officers might interview that person's associates to find out what they may know.

- Investigators also look for motive. Some computer security violations are committed simply out of curiosity; we are all familiar with the legends about teenage hackers breaking into government computers for fun. But many, if not most, computer security breaches, Internet scams, and website hacking are done for financial gain. Some digital crimes are committed for power, leverage, revenge, or emotional issues. We must still remember that motive does not equate to guilt.

- Once an investigation has led to a suspect, experts have to figure out whether that person has the knowledge and the means to carry out the digital crime. This is different from many other crimes, because it takes some real know-how to disable serious computer security measures.

- The next step in looking at the suspect is to figure out if they had the access to commit the crime, and this can be also hard to pinpoint. Some viruses have delayed effects or are dependent on certain conditions, such as another program being executed or some other software being run. Smart digital predators can also alter computer logs to give a false picture of when the security breach actually took place.

Digital Chains of Evidence

- To collect, analyze, and preserve digital evidence, authorities need search warrants for the suspect's home computer, work computer, or whatever else could be involved. A search warrant must be specific, and it will set limits on the scope of the examination. If, for example, a warrant is for searching a computer for child pornography, the videotapes in the suspect's home are not covered.

- Laws regulating and governing electronic media and the ability of authorities to monitor and investigate what people do with their digital communication devices include the Cable Communications

Policy Act of 1984, the Electronic Communications Privacy Act of 1986, the Digital Millennium Copyright act of 1998, and the USA Patriot Act of 2001.

• Collecting digital evidence can be a risky operation because data can be accidentally overwritten or lost while trying to retrieve it. Any alterations in data can change its meaning, or critical pieces of information, like the characters in a password, can be erased while mining data.

• The computer has to be left on while investigating it because a shut down can sometimes overwrite any evidence in temporary storage. Investigators have to disconnect the computer from its modem but leave both on in case the computer's owner could be monitoring the computer for intrusions.

• Investigators also need to be careful of business computers that are networked.

The science of computer forensics has expanded over the past few decades with the increase of electronic communication.

Disconnecting a computer from its network might add additional unwanted data to its memory. In advance of data collection, investigators will usually work with the company's system administrators to be sure they know how things are set up.

• If this is a clandestine search where a computer must be seized while a suspect is elsewhere, investigators have to sketch or photograph the entire computer and modem setup so they can get the information they need and reassemble everything exactly the way they found it.

- Like other forms of forensic evidence, if digital data is not handled appropriately or the legal grounds for obtaining it are not met, that evidence might not hold up in court. Proper evidence-collection procedures and a good chain of custody must be maintained every step of the way.

- The no. 1 rule for digital investigators is the same as it is for all of us who use computers: Make a backup. Since digital files can be destroyed, changed, or damaged by working with them, it is imperative that investigators work from a copy on a special-examination computer so that the original data stays intact.

- Investigators first make a working copy master, which they archive. Other copies are made from that first download, and it is those versions investigators actually work on, while the working copy master is safely stored. Investigators can make a fresh copy from the archived working copy master at any time without having to go back to the original device.

- The technology itself keeps the chain of custody for the working copy master and all versions made from it within the device they are using to analyze the digital evidence. Digital devices time-date stamp things automatically. To make sure the data in each copy generation is an exact duplicate of the original, computer analysts use a hash function.

Retrieving Hidden and "Erased" Data
- Some data can often be retrieved from computer storage even after a person thinks it has been deleted. A hard disc contains tracks, like a phonograph record, and is divided, like a pie, into units called sectors. Data itself gets written into clusters, which are series of contiguous tract sectors.

- When a disc is newly formatted, files tend to be written on contiguous clusters. But over time, the disc begins to fill up with files of all sizes. The computer will break large files up to put some of it in other available clusters, which may or may not be adjacent. When this happens, the hard drive disc is said to be fragmented.

- Any leftover space in a cluster is called slack space. When somebody tries to save a new file, the operating system will not use up the slack space in a half-full cluster; it will go to a new cluster. Computers use slack space for other sorts of internal tasks, such as temporary data storage.

- Thus, when we think data is deleted and gone, a copy may still be sitting there in slack space. Users cannot normally access slack space, but computer forensic experts have special software tools that let them access it.

- Computer forensics experts use some of the same search features that we use on our own computers, such as browsing and keyword searching, but savvy computer criminals will often use code words.

- Investigators can use metadata searches to find information about a file, like who created it, when it was created, who it was sent to, and when it was received to develop a timeline of the crime, which might show opportunity or negate a suspect's alibi. They can also use automatic log searches created by computer programs to record activity; these will show when someone was online, or when a file was moved from one place on the computer into another folder, and so on.

- It is not just property crimes that leave digital clues, so can violent acts like kidnapping and murder. The 2004 murder of Jennifer Corbin, by her husband Dr. Barton Corbin, was solved by tracing his cell phone records. Not only that, the similarities of that murder to the alleged suicide of Dolly Hearn (one of Corbin's girlfriends), 14 years earlier, led to his confession to Hearn's murder as well.

Suggested Reading

Carrier, *File System Forensic Analysis.*

Casey, *Digital Evidence and Computer Crime.*

Kranacher, Riley, and Wells, *Forensic Accounting and Fraud Examination.*

Nelson, Phillips, and Steuart, *Guide to Computer Forensics and Investigations.*

Peterson, *Understanding Surveillance Technologies.*

Questions to Consider

1. What is digital evidence?

2. How is digital evidence different from computer evidence?

3. What types of crimes might include digital evidence?

Computer Forensics and Digital Evidence
Lecture 14—Transcript

In our last lecture we looked at the way in which forensic examiners analyze suspicious documents for their authenticity. But when you think about it, so much of what used to be information on a page that you could hold in your hand, has gone digital, as they say. Sure, there are still plenty of paper documents around today, but e-mail, electronic record-keeping, and online banking have made some of what questioned document examiners do nearly obsolete, or certainly limited its use.

The science of computer forensics has really taken off over the past couple of decades, because so much of our communication traffic today happens on computers and over the Internet. Forensic computer science does concern identifying and extracting digital evidence of criminal activity, but with the proliferation of technology in this area, including cell phones, 2-way pagers, cameras, GPS units, fax machines, and all kinds of other electronic gear, the current trend is to refer to the analysis of evidence like this as digital forensics.

When you think about it, crimes that used to require the perpetrator to commit them in person, or at least by some physical transfer of information, like a bank holdup note, or a letter demanding ransom, can now be carried out remotely. Fraud, identity theft, and embezzlement, can now be accomplished using a computer and the Internet.

Hackers can break the security measures of large corporations and electronically siphon money from them, or steal their customers' bank codes or credit card numbers. Plans for a robbery or homicide could be stored on a computer, and a kidnapper could send a ransom note by a computer or other digital device.

We've all heard cases of cyber-bullying, child pornography sent across the Internet, and predators using social networking sites to lure their prey. Law-enforcement has even taken advantage of some of the anonymity inherent to these crimes, by posing as potential victims or consumers of illegal images or stolen goods in order to catch the perpetrators of these kinds of offenses. And social networking and other websites have had to enact safeguards to help their users defend themselves from abuse, but sometimes it's hard to know what somebody else is doing with your information.

In order to investigate digital crime, somebody first needs to realize that it's happened—I mean this isn't like a bank holdup, where an alarm gets instantly pushed. It may take weeks, or even months, before a person or organization becomes aware of a security issue. The initial analysis also has to show that whatever happened is really a criminal act; there's always the possibility that an error, like a programming glitch or a simple human mistake, caused something like the diversion of funds.

Next investigators have to get to the source of the damage and figure out where the incident originated; in other words what computer, phone, or other device was attacked and how. They'll have to figure out the path the perpetrator used to get to the server or the victim's computer; was it over the Internet, did they use a wireless network, or did somebody physically attach a USB drive to a computer, or put a CD in it?

Investigators will also start to look at the victim to make sure they understand why this person or organization was attacked, which might help them figure out motive, so they can start to hone in on possible suspects. For instance, somebody hacking into a government website might have political motivations, but an attack on a pharmaceutical corporation could result from something like competition or a desire to harm the company's reputation. Targeting a single person's bank account would lead investigators down a different path than if the credit card numbers of all consumers doing business with a certain website were stolen.

Of course, some major computer geeks are going to be involved in these kinds of investigations, but let me point out that they don't work alone. Depending on the incident, the analysis team might include law enforcement officers—maybe some with a background in white-collar crime—and they'll use standard investigative methods out in the community at large, like interviews. The situation might call for auditors to sift through records to figure out how money was moved from one account to another or things like that.

Did you know there are specialists called forensic accountants? They are bean counters specially trained to look for irregularities in accounting practices that might indicate embezzlement, fraud, or the kind of illegal activity that's sometimes called cooking the books. And the computer scientists involved in these investigations may be specialists in security issues, who will look at the strengths and the weaknesses of the computer systems involved, or those who can read computer code to figure out how the problem occurred.

If the crime was something more like cyber-bullying, investigators really need to focus on the victim's daily interactions, because these types of crimes usually hit very close to home, and often quickly point a finger at a possible suspect. If it's an elderly person or somebody else, who's been targeted by a phishing scam, or maybe a lonely hearts' scheme, interviewing the victim and figuring out what they may have done that opened their vulnerability to that kind of crime is important. Did the victim answer an e-mail and give their account number because they mistakenly thought the message had come from the bank, those sorts of things.

But beyond interview and other standard police investigation techniques, let's see how the technology itself is used to track down the suspect. The computer experts will start by performing what's called a "traceback" to get them to the source computer. In other words they'll see if the trail of Internet Provider addresses, called IP addresses, can be followed back to a suspect, or at least to a specific computer. They'll also check the records of the attacked computer for its system documentation and its computer logs.

Along each step in the trail of digital evidence, authorities can continue to use routine policing. They might interview the witnesses who first noticed the incident, maybe somebody at a library or school computer lab where the perpetrator might have tried to use a public computer for the attack, or they can check surveillance tapes at a facility. If they hone in on a suspect, officers might interview that person's associates or family to find out what they may know.

One of the main things investigators look for—in analyzing these and other types of crimes—is motive. Did this suspect have a motive, and if so, what was it? Some computer security violations are done simply out of curiosity; we've all heard about teenage hackers who breach government or corporate network security, just to show they can. Ironically, just as soon as they finish their criminal sentence, many of those hackers are quickly hired as computer security specialists.

This leads into another common motive, and that's money. Many, if not most, computer security breaches, Internet scams, and website hacking are done for financial gain. Maybe those young hackers realize if they disable some company's security system for kicks the first time around, that will become the first entry on their resume, and they'll ultimately make a lot of money later to prevent such breaches. Motives aren't always discrete entities.

Some digital crimes are committed for power or leverage over someone or an institution, or maybe to get revenge against them in some way. Other offenses relate to lust or other emotional issues—these can be pathological drives or normal feelings that get out of hand, just as with other criminal activity. We need to always consider, though, that just because a person has a motive doesn't mean they would do whatever happened in a case.

Once an investigation has led to a suspect, experts have to figure out whether that person has the knowledge and the means to carry out the digital crime that's been committed. This is different from many other crimes when you think about it, because anybody can theoretically walk into a bank and commit a robbery, with or without a weapon, since some holdups have been carried out with realistic-looking toy guns or just the threat of a weapon when one's not present at all. But, it takes some real know-how to disable serious computer security measures.

Investigators might need to reconstruct the technological crime to help them figure out what skill level was needed to execute it. Once they've done that, they can look into the background of the suspect to see if that person really could carry it off. Not all computer hackers have extensive formal training, though, some of these are not much more than self-taught computer jockey kids who could probably go really far in life if they were just on the right track.

The next step in looking at the suspect is to figure out if they had the access to commit the crime; and this can be also hard to pinpoint. Some of these hackers have developed viruses that have delayed effects, or things that are called logic bombs that will go off, as it were, later when some program is executed or some software is run.

Smart digital predators can also alter computer logs to give a false picture of when that security breach actually took place.

And when you consider how long it might take for a digital crime to be uncovered, there may be a lot of computer activity that will have to be waded through to get to the bottom of things. So, unless digital investigators can match a login time to an event, or maybe in the case of cyber bullying or child pornography, catch the offender when they're online and in the act, it can be very difficult to know when the crime actually took place.

As part of monitoring suspects, investigators can do surveillance, either by watching the person and his or her activities, or hanging around online conducting surveillance electronically. Let's say police suspect a certain guy is soliciting minors for sex. Well, they can sit at a computer and pretend to be the victim or another target themselves. But in the meantime, if other investigators are watching the suspect, and he's a construction worker who is up on a girder at a job site at the time, he's probably not their guy. Of course, smart phones with Internet capability can complicate assessing a person's physical location as an alibi these days. But, all these devices leave a digital trail, as we'll see in a little bit.

In order to collect, analyze, and preserve digital evidence, authorities will need to get a search warrant and then execute it by looking through the suspect's home computer, work computer, or whatever device could be involved. A search warrant must be specific, and it really sets and limits the scope of the examination.

Suppose a warrant is written looking for a computer that may have child pornography stored on it, but while they're in the suspect's house the investigators find a bunch of old videotapes—the warrant doesn't cover those. That's a Fourth Amendment thing we'll talk more about in another lecture—but search warrants have to be carefully considered and may need to be written inclusive of all digital storage devices and media, for example.

Because of the privacy issues involved, when computer technology really took off in the public, laws arose to regulate and govern electronic media, and the ability for authorities to monitor and investigate what people do with their digital communication devices. These laws include the Cable Communications Policy Act of 1984, the Electronic Communications Privacy Act of 1986, the Digital Millennium Copyright Act of 1998, and the one most of us have probably heard of, the USA Patriot Act of 2001.

You might not realize, though, that the name USA Patriot is really a 10-letter acronym that stands for Uniting and Strengthening America by Providing Appropriate Tools Required to Intercept and Obstruct Terrorism. It was a response by the George W. Bush administration to the September 11 attacks on the United States. In 2011, Barack Obama granted a 4-year extension of certain aspects of the Patriot Act, including surveillance of suspects, wiretaps, and business-record searching in any situations where terrorist activities are suspect.

So once legal constraints to search are met, digital investigators can begin collecting evidence off of source and target computers, or from a computer network. Collecting digital evidence can be a risky operation, because data can be accidentally overwritten or lost while trying to retrieve it. Any alterations in data can change its meaning, and critical pieces of information, like the characters in a password, can be erased while mining data. Now I'm no computer expert, but here's the way it's been explained to me.

The computer they are working on has to be left on while investigating it, because a shut down can sometimes overwrite any evidence in temporary storage, as we'll see in a bit. Investigators have to disconnect the computer from its modem, but leave both of them on; that's because of the chance that the computer's owner could be monitoring things and see that a remote session is happening on his computer.

If the modem is left connected to the computer, the suspect could dial in or come in through the network and destroy evidence in real time. We've seen that on TV shows and the movies. The phone that's connected to a modem might contain the last number dialed, a list of commonly called numbers, or other digital evidence, that might be important too.

Investigators also need to be careful of business computers that are networked. Disconnecting one computer from its network might cause that computer to start hunting around, and potentially add additional unwanted data in its memory. In advance of data collection, investigators will usually work with the company's system administrators and IT people to ensure they know how things are set up and what might happen when they start tinkering with a victim or suspect computer.

And if this is a really clandestine search where investigators want to look at a suspect's computer, maybe in the case of terrorism, but don't want to tip their hand, they might review a guy's computer while he's off doing something else. If they are doing that kind of investigation, they'll have to sketch or photograph the entire computer and modem setup at the guy's house, or wherever it is, so they can get the information they need, and then reassemble everything exactly the way they found it. Heck, that sounds like a good idea whenever you take something electronic apart; I can never figure out which cable jack was supposed to go in what port sometimes, myself.

Remember, like other forms of forensic evidence, if digital data isn't handled appropriately or the legal grounds for obtaining it aren't met, that evidence might not hold up in court under scrutiny some day. Proper evidence collection procedures and a good chain of custody must be maintained every step of the way for digital evidence, just as with more tangible things like fingerprints, fibers, or questioned documents. But how do you do that on something like a computer?

Well, the number 1 rule for digital investigators is pretty much the same as it is for all of us who use computers, and that's to make a backup copy of whatever you're working on. So the first step of forensic analysts, who need to look through computer files for evidence, is to make themselves a working copy. Since digital files can be destroyed, changed, or damaged—either on purpose, or as some of us know all too well, completely by accident—it's imperative that the original data stays intact while investigators work from a copy.

This way if something does happen, they always have the original data files to go back to, to create another working copy. Keeping the original data intact also allows it to be presented later in its original condition, if that's necessary in court someday. This is really analogous to taking photographs of the crime scene, when you think about it.

In order to make a working copy, the digital media has to be first placed on a special examination computer, or linked to a device that prevents any new data from being added, whether it's on a computer hard drive or another storage device. Investigators have different ways to copy the data off a drive, but they're the same types of data transfer technologies the rest of us use: USB connectors, computer FireWire's, and what are called scuzzies, which is really just the pronunciation of the acronym S-C-S-I, which stands for small computer system interface. I mean, there are only so many ways in or out of today's computers, right?

After the digital forensic people copy or as they say "image" the evidence, that first copy is what they call their "working-copy master," which they archive. Other copies are made from that first download, and it's those versions investigators actually work on, while the working copy master is safely stored. If one of the versions they are analyzing gets corrupted in the process of going through the evidence, investigators can make a fresh copy from the archived working copy master, without having to go back to the original device where the evidence came from in the first place.

Essentially the technology itself keeps the chain of custody for the working copy master and all versions made from it, right there, within the device they are using to analyze the digital evidence. Digital devices time and date stamp things automatically and we're used to that in our own personal computer use. As we'll see in a bit, this is the same technology that allows police to follow the chain of events in digital crimes.

To make sure the data in each copy generation is an exact duplicate of the original, computer analysts can use what's called a hash function. That's a special computer program that converts the data into whole numbers and adds those numbers up. If the hash sum that's generated matches between a copy and the document it was made from, investigators know the copy is a true and identical reflection of the original file.

Now, we've all heard that data, at least some data, can often be retrieved from computer storage even after a person thinks it's been deleted. That's because of the way data is written to a hard drive. So, to understand that, let's talk about how data is stored, using the example of a typical MS-DOS type file system hard drive. Computer systems differ slightly, but the basics are the same.

The storage disc in the hard drive is kind of like an old record album that records data on a circular track. But the entire disk drive is divided, like a pie, into units called sectors. The area where a circular track of data is contained in a particular sector is called a track sector. But the actual data itself gets written in what's called a cluster, which is a series of contiguous tract sectors.

When the disc is newly formatted, files tend to be written on contiguous clusters. But over time the disc begins to fill up with files of all sizes, some large and some small. If the computer attempts to store a large file and there's not enough room in a cluster to fit all the information in, the computer will break the file up to put some of it in other available clusters, which may or may not be adjacent to the first cluster the computer used for the first part of the file. When this happens the hard drive disc is said to be "fragmented," since the files are fragmented over the storage space.

Now any unfilled clusters that have smaller files in them have leftover space that computer jockeys call slack space. When somebody tries to save a new file, the operating system won't use up the slack space in a cluster; it will go to a new cluster. Now we can't generally find or access our slack space, to see what's in it or put things in it, but our computer can.

It dumps all kinds of stuff into slack space when it tries to clear its memory, and do its other internal tasks, that are way beyond my understanding of computers. But, that's the reason, when we think data is deleted and gone, it may really still be sitting there in some piece of slack space. Computer forensic experts have special software tools that let them access computer slack space and see what's in it.

That same slack space can also be a security risk on a computer, because it might hold something like the original unencrypted version of some text or numbers that a security software package would encrypt before sending over the Internet. So computer slack space might be a great place for forensic investigators to search for files somebody thought were gone from the computer memory, but it also may be a place where hackers can find unsecured data to exploit, like people's credit card numbers.

Slack space on a computer hard drive is also where a computer automatically saves temporary versions of files. As computer users, these are a great resource to many of us if there's a system crash, since the computer can go back to its slack space and recover the last version of a document or spreadsheet data it held in temporary memory—even if we were unable to save—or we can't retrieve—that final version. But again, if that temporary version of the computer file held important or sensitive data, that information may still be in slack space for a digital criminal to find, even if the document or spreadsheet was password-protected.

That's just one example of the ways computers store information that we can't see or access. The way computers use their storage space, things that we think we've deleted a while back, may actually still be completely intact, if that portion of the disk space wasn't ultimately rewritten over by a new file.

The general user can't necessarily easily get to the deleted document or spreadsheet; but that doesn't mean the information is really gone. Computer forensic experts—just like some savvy computer techs at businesses and other institutions—know different ways to get information out of storage, even sometimes after it's been intentionally deleted, but, so do computer hackers and other data thieves.

Back to the investigation: To find data on a piece of computer hardware or get into a file that's in slack storage, computer forensics experts use some of the same search features that we would on our own computers. They can search their working copy of the computer files by browsing, which is opening up individual files to see what's in them, or they can do a keyword search that will look for things within documents. But savvy computer criminals and terrorists will often use code words to deflect these kinds of keyword searches.

Investigators can use what are called metadata searches; these find information about a file, like who created it, when it was created, who it was sent to, when it was received. Metadata information can also help develop a timeline of the crime, which might show opportunity, or negate a suspect's alibi.

Automatic log searches are searches created by computer programs to record activity; these will show when someone was online, or when a file was moved from one place on the computer into another folder, things like that. But for metadata and automatic log searches, the forensic investigators will need to check the time-date stamp on the computer's internal clock matches.

But computers, as I said earlier, are only one part of the digital picture. Some of the same investigative tools are used to look for crimes involving credit card readers, electronic banking, and the piracy of software, music, and videos. Offenses committed electronically can include money laundering, identity theft, and altering medical records or insurance claims. But it's not just property crimes that leave digital clues, so can violent acts like kidnapping and even murder. So, in the time we have left, let's look at another way that digital evidence from the latest technology can help solve crimes.

In the Atlanta, Georgia suburb of Buford, in December of 2004, a 7-year-old boy awoke to find his mother shot in her bed. Alone in the house with his

5-year-old brother, he went to a neighbor. The deceased woman was 33-year-old Jennifer Corbin, whose husband, dentist Dr. Barton Corbin, had filed for divorce just a few days before, indicating he wanted custody of their 2 sons and the family home.

When police contacted Barton Corbin, he claimed to be nowhere near the house when his wife had been shot, which death investigators estimate happened around 2 in the morning. The case looked potentially to be the suicide of a woman about to lose everything she loved.

Corbin said he had been at a restaurant the night before with some of his friends, and then went to his brother's house by 1:30 in the morning, where he stayed the rest of the night. But digital forensic experts pulled the records of Corbin's cell phone, and were able to see that 2 calls were made from Corbin's phone around 2 in the morning. And because of the global positioning satellite chip each cell phone carries, the calls could be shown to have bounced off of a cell phone tower in the vicinity of the Corbin family home where Mrs. Corbin was found dead.

Not only that, but investigators were able to use cell-phone tracking to hone in on a couple of other calls that were placed later that same night from Corbin's phone. This time, the cell signals had used a tower near his brother's house.

It wasn't a great distance between the home where Jennifer Corbin had been shot and where Corbin's brother lived, but because there were a few cell-phone towers in between the 2 locations, investigators were able to see that there was no, what they call, "handoff" or "bleed" of the cell signal from either of those implicated towers to the other.

That evidence really threw Corbin's alibi into a tailspin. But the digital forensic experts weren't finished in this case. They went back further into Corbin's cell phone logs, and using the GPS records of the towers his phone was hitting off during the days before, learned that Corbin had traveled to Alabama a few days prior to his wife's death.

Next, using the log of the calls Corbin placed in Alabama, they checked who the phone numbers belonged to, and the digital trail led them to an old friend of Corbin's who he had gone to see. When Corbin's Alabama buddy was questioned, he admitted to giving Corbin a handgun on that visit. That gun turned out to be the murder weapon.

And that's not even the end of the story. Investigators learned that Barton Corbin had also been questioned 14 years before the death of his wife in another apparent suicide. This time the victim, who apparently shot herself, was a young dental student named Dolly Hearn, who incidentally had just broken up with Corbin, while the couple was in dental school. When faced with questioning again, Corbin admitted to Dolly Hearn's murder and, because of the digital evidence in his wife's killing, and the similarity to the 1990 offense, he pled guilty to both of those crimes.

Investigators at the time of Dolly Hearn's murder said that Corbin also had an alibi that involved making phone calls from a certain place at a certain time, but, back in 1990, this type of digital tracking wasn't available to law enforcement, and Corbin couldn't be definitively linked to Hearn's death. So, what has the digital age brought forensics? It's shown criminals that when it comes to computers, you can delete, but not always destroy. And when it comes to cell phones, you can run, but you can't hide.

Structure Failure—Forensic Engineering
Lecture 15

orensic engineering specialists are responsible for determining what went wrong in the event of major disasters that result in the collapse of man-made or natural structures. Engineers and builders have a legal responsibility to meet certain standards and plan for worst-case scenarios. When a storm or an earthquake takes out a bridge, or when a group like the September 11th terrorists cause a building collapse, forensic engineers can determine why the builders best-laid plans have failed.

The Purpose of Design Standards

- Good design is no accident, and ensuring that the things we need to work for us are functional and safe cannot be left to chance. A civil lawsuit prompted by negligent construction or poor manufacturing might carry huge financial penalties. It is difficult for a judge or jury to put a dollar amount on the loss of life, health, productivity, or state of mind, but decisions like that are made every day.

- We have standards that govern the production of the objects around us. As consumers and users of things made by others, we need to be able to trust that those who construct and produce the things in our environment do so carefully, ethically, and to the standards society has agreed on.

- When that trust is broken by negligence, carelessness, or maliciousness—or corners are cut to save money, giving consumers less than what they have coming to them—we have agreed as a society the manufacturers of those products are liable for the damage they cause.

- Unforeseen issues of planning, implementation, and use can arise. Even rigorous testing may not have uncovered a design flaw in a product or vehicle. And of course, accidents happen for all kinds of reasons, from weather-related incidents to malicious acts like sabotage and terrorism.

- The science of figuring out the cause of material, product, and structural failures is known as forensic engineering. Forensic engineers use the principles of physics, chemistry, biology, design, and construction, among other things, to analyze fault and mechanism when things go wrong.

Structural Integrity
- The collapse of the Tacoma Narrows Bridge, colloquially known as Galloping Gertie, in a wind storm in November 1940 is a classic case used in nearly every physics or forensic engineering book. Some theories attributed its failure to mechanical resonance—that is, the wind shook the bridge at a frequency matching the bridge material's natural frequency, called its resonance frequency. Other sources attribute the structural failure to aeroelastic flutter, in which winds caused fluttering waves of motion that ultimately tore the structure into pieces.

- Structural integrity refers to how soundly a structure is built for its purpose and, as a result, how well it holds up in the variety of conditions to which it might be subjected. The root causes of poor structural integrity usually boil down to 2 types of support inadequacies—static load deficiencies and dynamic load deficiencies.

- Static includes the basic weight of a structure; in other words, the structure has to be strong enough to withstand gravity and hold itself up. Static load is often broken down to 2 components, called dead load and live load.

- The dead load is the actual weight of the materials that make up the structure. The live load is the part of the weight that changes, including factors like people, furnishings, machinery, weather, and how that weight is distributed throughout the space.

- Dynamic load relates to forces that change over a short period of time. In the case of a bridge, for example, an increased dynamic load could result from a lot of trucks that are over the weight limit repeatedly traveling over it. Dynamic loads also include natural forces like earthquakes, tornados, tsunamis, and high winds.

- Like people, buildings, bridges, and other structures age. Over time, the ability of a structure to support its static and dynamic loads decreases because of factors like corrosion and weathering. Structures are therefore engineered to support static loads that are much heavier than the actual loads expected in regular use, and are regularly inspected over time.

- Designers and architects refer to this bonus engineering as the structure's margin of safety. A structure can collapse, even under normal use and expected dynamic loads, if the margin of safety was miscalculated.

- Some buildings have lasted many centuries or more, and some materials and design styles are just inherently better than others. Then again, acts of nature or other attacks can level even the most well-built structures.

When Engineers Cut Corners

- In January of 1919, in Boston, Massachusetts, in a warmer than normal winter, a 2.3-million-gallon molasses storage tank towering 50 feet in the air suffered complete structural failure and sent a flood of molasses barreling through the city streets at about 35 miles an hour. It almost sounds comical until you realize that 21 people were drowned or crushed to death, and over 150 were injured.

- The precise cause of the tank's failure will never be known. Some theorize that fermentation of the molasses—which could have been accelerated by the warm weather—caused carbon dioxide pressure to rapidly build within the tank, causing a fatigue crack in the base of the tank to propagate. There was little doubt in the minds of many that the true fault rested with the construction of the tank, during and after which there was apparently no safety testing.

- Because the quality of design and how structures function over time and temperature is something that may not be understood until accidents happen, construction methods and standards evolve. Numerous building and manufacturing codes have come into existence to protect the public and consumers from danger by setting minimum construction standards.

- In 1981, a dance party on the skywalks of the Hyatt Regency Hotel in Kansas City, Missouri, led to their collapse, killing 114 people and injuring 200 others. Investigators studied both the original building plans and the structure as built and discovered an unexpected design change: The contractor that made the rods that suspended the skywalks asked to change the one-piece rods to 2-piece rods to make them easier to manufacture and hang.

- This change in fabrication shifted the way the static and dynamic loads were carried by the skywalk. Investigators also determined that the raised walkways were designed for a modest amount of foot traffic, not a large number of people dancing. They estimated that the total load at the time of the collapse was more than double the weight architects had designed them to hold—notwithstanding the design flaw.

The World Trade Center Collapse
- In the United States, the National Bureau of Standards was developed in 1901 and became known as the National Institute of Standards and Technology in 1988. Its engineers, scientists, and other technology experts are charged with identifying and promoting appropriate measurements, calibration standards, and quality-control benchmarks for all kinds of manufacturing and construction.

- One of the bureau's subcommittees, the National Construction Safety Team Advisory Committee, was charged with the monumental task of analyzing the 2001 collapse of the World Trade Center's twin towers.

- When designers conceived the towers, they actually took airplane impacts into consideration, because in 1945 a U.S. Army B-25 bomber had hit the nearby Empire State Building. Their most probable worst-case scenario for the World Trade Center used a single Boeing 707, which was—at the time—the largest aircraft in the world. The designers also assumed an accidental impact during takeoff or landing at speeds around 180 miles an hour.

- On September 11, 2001, the towers were struck by 2 Boeing 767s, each weighing almost 30 tons more than the Boeing 707 and carrying 10,000 gallons more jet fuel and traveling at a cruising speed of 530 miles an hour—almost 3 times faster than the takeoff and landing speed of the worst-case projections.

- The initial horizontal impact on the North Tower severed about 2/3 of the steel supports on the tower's north side. Six floors were damaged directly but did not collapse at this point. The resulting fire burned for 102 minutes before the North Tower collapsed.

- A short time later, the next Boeing 767 flew into the South Tower. This time, 9 floors were damaged during the impact at a lower point on the building. The impact

A domino effect of collapsing floors is what ultimately brought down the World Trade Center's twin towers.

285

caused similar structural damage to the steel supports, and after only 56 minutes of burning, the South Tower came down.

- Structurally, those towers were technically able to withstand those impacts, even though the hits each took were much greater than the expected worst-case scenario. What doomed the towers to collapse was the fire. In the case of the South Tower, each floor was covered in about 9 ounces of jet fuel per square foot, with a potential to burn at 3140°F (although the actual fire temperature was several hundred degrees lower).

- The major effect of the fire on the structural integrity of the World Trade Center towers was on the steel supports and the concrete around that steel. Steel-reinforced concrete degrades and cracks at temperatures over 120°F. At 1000°F, the structural steel supports lose about half their tensile strength. At 1300°F, steel is no longer even viable in its support capabilities.

- When the structural components of steel and concrete failed on the 6 floors in the North Tower and the 9 floors in the South Tower, they could no longer carry their loads. The South Tower fell first, even though it was struck second, because there were 16 floors above the impact zone weighing down on the 9 damaged floors, compared to the North Tower, which had 11 floors bearing down on the 6 damaged floors.

- The undamaged part of each building came crashing down, as one unit, with all of its weight, onto the damaged area—a direct vertical dynamic load. Their mass was too much for the floors below to hold, and then each floor gave way in turn, causing the pancaking collapse we all witnessed, until the entire tower was gone.

- Figuring out what went wrong in any type of catastrophe like this is the responsibility of forensic engineering specialists. Even in natural disasters, like Hurricane Katrina, the expertise of forensic engineers is called on, for example, to try to determine whether or not faulty construction was to blame for the many levees that failed during the storm surge.

Suggested Reading

Carper, *Forensic Engineering*.

Delatte, *Beyond Failure*.

Noon, *Engineering Analysis of Fires and Explosions*.

―――, *Forensic Engineering Investigation*.

―――, *Introduction to Forensic Engineering*.

Ratay, *Forensic Structural Engineering Handbook*.

Why the Towers Fell.

Questions to Consider

1. What are some possible uses of engineering in forensic science?

2. What types of sciences and technologies are used in forensic engineering analyses?

3. Can you think of specific instances or cases—besides those in the lecture—in which forensic engineering has been used to explain a sequence of events?

Structure Failure—Forensic Engineering
Lecture 15—Transcript

The increasing sophistication of document production and computer equipment, and the tremendous array of digital devices available to us today, illustrate just some of the uses of engineering in developing new technologies. But human design and manufacturing undoubtedly go back beyond even the first stone tools created by our ancient ancestors millions of years ago.

Even some of our closest living primate relatives are inventive. Humans are uncanny engineers, able to figure out how to manipulate what's around us to create the things we desire.

Along the route of design and implementation, come both trials and errors. We fashion prototypes and test them to see if they fit our needs. And when we come up with things that seem to work for us, and improve our quality of life, they catch on. What was once an idea turns into mass production.

We've created structures, clothing, ways to process food, weapons, machines, medicines, vehicles, and all sorts of other products that fill our world. Many of those things work pretty darn well, and those that don't are improved over time. But good design is no accident; and ensuring that the things we need to work for us are functional and safe, can't be left to chance.

Around 1780 B.C.E., the code of Hammurabi was created; it's still the fundamental idea behind building codes around the world today, and it reads as follows: "If a builder makes a house and does not properly construct it, and the house falls down and kills the owner, the builder shall be put to death. If it kills the son of the owner, the son of the builder shall be put to death. If it kills the owner's slave, the builder shall pay for the slave. If it ruins goods, the builder shall pay for all that was ruined. Since he did not construct it properly, the builder shall rebuild the house at his own expense. If a builder makes a house and the walls are shaky, the builder must strengthen the walls at his own expense."

Today the penalties are not as severe as to put a builder to death, but a civil lawsuit prompted by shoddy construction might carry an even greater financial penalty than only paying for all that was ruined. Negligent construction or poor manufacturing that cause harm to others, may result in a settlement with damages paid out far in excess of what a structure or its contents may have cost to replace. It's difficult for a judge or jury to put a dollar amount on the loss of life, health, productivity, or state of mind, but in civil cases around the world each day, decisions like that are made.

That's because we have standards that govern the production of things we operate, purchase, and utilize. As consumers and users of things made by others, we need to be able to trust that those who construct and produce the things in our environment do so carefully, ethically, and to the standards that society has agreed on.

And when that trust is broken by negligence, carelessness, or maliciousness—or corners are cut to save money, giving consumers less than what they have coming to them—we have agreed as a society the manufacturers of those products are liable for the damage they cause.

There are also unforeseen issues of planning, implementation, and use that can arise. Even rigorous testing might not have uncovered a design flaw in a product or vehicle. A bridge could have been built to specifications to hold a certain number of cars and trucks each day, but increasing population density and the traffic that results from it, could push that bridge beyond its limits. A perfectly functional and safe tool or vehicle could be used or operated in a manner not intended or recommended by the manufacturer.

And of course, accidents happen for all kinds of reasons that unrelated to the products or vehicles involved. Along that line, natural disasters like earthquakes, floods, tornadoes, snowstorms, can all cause buildings, bridges, dams, highways, and electrical and other energy systems to fail. Malicious acts like sabotage and terrorism have also destroyed both natural and man-made things around us.

The science of figuring out the cause of material, product, and structural failures is known as forensic engineering. Forensic engineers use the principles of physics, chemistry, biology, design, and construction, among other things, to analyze fault and mechanism when things go wrong. This can include anything from a short in a faulty appliance to the metal fatigue that might cause a bridge collapse, and everything in between.

Have you heard of Galloping Gertie? That was the name given to the Tacoma Narrows suspension bridge, which was built beginning in 1938 to cross part of Puget Sound in Washington State. The construction workers called the bridge Galloping Gertie because of the way the structure would sway up and down any time there were strong winds.

At the time it was made, it was the third longest suspension bridge in the world. The bridge was opened to the public in July of 1940, but immediately engineers realized the bridge was dangerous and moved to correct the design errors, but just a short 4 months after it opened, during a November morning full of high winds, Galloping Gertie collapsed into Puget Sound.

Surprisingly, only one car went into the Tacoma Narrows, and only the dog in it perished. The reason for the significant lack of human and property loss was that the bridge took literally hours of swaying before it finally gave way, and only a few foolhardy people used it that morning—though it was open to the public. Because of Gertie's slow death, her final hours—and all the galloping she did in them—were captured on film.

Oh, and for you dog-lovers, 2 people did try to save Tubby, the little cocker spaniel who had been left on the bridge in his owner's car, after the driver literally crawled to his safety. But the dog was apparently so scared he bit one of the guys who tried to rescue him. And remember I talked about civil lawsuits? The settlement in this case was $450 for the man's vehicle, and $364.40 for its contents, including little Tubby.

The Tacoma Narrows Bridge collapse is a classic case that's used in nearly every physics or forensic engineering book. Some theories attributed it to the phenomenon called mechanical resonance—where a structure takes on more and more energy when it's moved at oscillations that match the frequency of the vibrations inherent to its own material makeup, which are called its resonance frequencies.

According to this theory, when the wind drove Gertie at just the right frequency, the total energy of the oscillations increased to a level she could not stand. But other sources say this structural failure was due to what's called aeroelastic flutter, in which steady winds, coupled with the bridge's inherent resonance frequencies, were sufficient to cause the fluttering waves of motion that ultimately tore the structure into pieces.

Now, I don't think the term forensic engineering was really in use back then, but engineering principles have always been used to figure out how to build things, how to make things better, how to gauge what happened when they don't work right, and how to fix things, if possible. And, to focus this discussion, let's just talk in general terms about one facet of engineering called structural integrity. That essentially means how soundly a structure is built for its purpose and, as a result, how well it holds up to the variety of conditions to which it might be subjected.

When it comes to problems with a structure's integrity, the root causes usually boil down to 2 types of support inadequacies—static load deficiencies and dynamic load deficiencies. So let's talk a little about each, in turn. Static load has to do with the basic weight of a structure; the structure has to be strong enough to withstand gravity and hold itself up, without causing problems for its occupants or other contents. Static load is often broken down into 2 components called a building's dead load and its live load.

The dead part of a static load is the actual weight of the materials that make up the entire structure itself. For a building—like each of the World Trade Center towers—that means the weight of the steel girders, the exterior and interior walls, elevator housings, floors, plumbing, and roofing materials. For a bridge, like Gertie, it's the weight of the pylons that hold her in place, the bridge supports, and the driving deck.

The live part of a static load is the part of its weight that can change over time. It includes factors of weather—like excessive rain or snow on the roof of a building or the deck of a bridge. Live load also includes occupancy, such as the weight of all the people in a building, which might seem pretty negligible in the twin towers, but given 25,000 people worked in each of the 2 towers, estimating 180 pounds per person, that's 4.5 million pounds or about the weight of 1125 cars—about 10 cars per floor.

Live load would also include the weight of all the vehicles on a bridge, which could be a pretty massive amount of weight depending on traffic at any given time. Live static load also relates to the weight of a building's furnishings and machinery, and how that weight's distributed throughout the space.

So that's static load. Dynamic load in terms of structural integrity relates to forces that change over a short period of time. Factors that influence dynamic load are things like heavy construction machinery working in or near the structure. Or in the case of a bridge, an increased dynamic load could be from lots of trucks that are over the weight limit repeatedly traveling over it. Dynamic loads also include natural forces like earthquakes, tornados, tsunamis and, as happened to Galloping Gertie, high winds.

Like all of us, buildings, bridges, and other structures age and grow weary. Over time, the ability of a structure to support its static and dynamic loads decreases because of factors like corrosion, and the inherent aging and weathering of the materials used in it. Since this aging is expected and owners want their constructions to last a long time, structures are engineered to support static loads that are much heavier than the actual loads expected in regular use, and they are regularly inspected as they age. Designers and architects refer to this bonus engineering as the structure's margin of safety.

A structure can collapse, even under normal use and expected dynamic loads, if the margin of safety was miscalculated—for instance, if architects underestimated the static or dynamic loads. A building or bridge can founder, too, if there was an error in design or construction, or the structure wasn't put together according to what were well-made plans.

But one of the issues with structural collapse is a phenomenon we're all familiar with—and that's the domino effect. That's what ultimately happened with Galloping Gertie, and it's what happened to bring down the World Trade Center, in that "pancaking" effect we all witnessed. In domino cases, the weight of part of the structure adds stress to another part, and the net effect continues the collapse.

We all know that there are buildings and other structures in certain parts of the world that have lasted many centuries or more—and sure, there are periodic problems with aging constructions that have to be addressed. But there are also materials and design styles that are just inherently better than others. And then there are acts of nature or other attacks that can level even the most well-built structures. Let's look at a couple more structural integrity issues, starting with a historic case sometimes referred to as the Great Molasses Flood.

In January of 1919, in Boston, Massachusetts, temperatures were higher than normal for winter. Suddenly, witnesses heard a rumbling sound and an amazing wave of molasses, estimated to be between 8 and 25 feet high, and traveling at about 35 miles an hour, barreled down city streets to a distance of several blocks. It almost sounds comical until you realize that 21 people were drowned or crushed to death, and over 150 were injured.

A newspaperman wrote, "Only an upheaval, a thrashing about in the sticky mass, showed where any life was. ... Horses died like so many flies on sticky flypaper. The more they struggled, the deeper in the mess they were ensnared. Human beings—men and women—suffered likewise."

What happened? A huge storage tank that towered 50 feet high and was 90 feet in diameter, containing 2,300,000 gallons of molasses, had suffered a complete structural failure. The rumbling sounds heard were apparently all of the rivets popping out of the tank nearly at once. The structure's half-inch steel walls literally tore apart, and the flow of that sticky goo was so powerful—pressures were estimated to be 2 tons per square foot—that it collapsed nearby buildings and knocked others off their foundations. The wave even broke the uprights of the Boston's elevated railway, knocking a train off its tracks, and a truck was thrown into the Boston harbor.

What caused the collapse is complicated; and the precise failure will never be known. Some theorize that fermentation of the molasses—which could have been accelerated by a 38-degree rise in air temperature over the course of the prior day—caused carbon dioxide pressure to rapidly build within the tank. The stress is greatest at the base of a filled tank like that, and one source suggests a fatigue crack may have begun there, and then propagated.

But, there was no doubt in the minds of many, that the true fault rested with the construction of the tank, during and after which, there was apparently no testing—like checking the tank for leaks by filling it with water. Because of its thick viscosity, molasses would be a slow leak, and it's alleged that local residents would collect what oozed from the tank regularly for their home use. In fact, some say that the reason the tank was painted brown was to cover the molasses leaks in it. Regardless, in one of the first class-action lawsuits in the State of Massachusetts, the parent company paid $600,000 in an out-of-court settlement.

Because the quality of design and how structures function over time and temperature is something that may not be understood until accidents happen, construction methods and standards evolve. Due to losses of life and fines incurred, once problems are discovered, no engineer or builder wants to repeat them, unless they're negligent or trying to make a buck by cutting corners.

Historically, as the knowledge of materials and an understanding of engineering evolved, numerous building and manufacturing codes have come into existence to protect the public and consumers from danger by setting minimum construction standards.

Before we take a look at the entities responsible for building codes, let's take look a quick look at a more modern example of structural collapse—one that started with good plans, but still ended up with a design error that cost over 100 people their lives. This was the 1981 collapse of the Hyatt Regency Hotel skywalks that happened in Kansas City, Missouri. The atrium of this hotel had elevated walkways that hung from rods attached to the ceiling, and they crossed in the air on the second, third, and fourth floors. On July 17, during a party, people began dancing on these skywalks.

Suddenly, the fourth floor skywalk collapsed, took out water pipes as it fell, and landed on the second floor skywalk. The collapse—resulting in a heap of wet, twisted steel and other construction rubble—killed 114 people and injured 200 others. Claims against the hotel for the incident topped $140 million.

Forensic engineers started with 2 primary theories, both related to the dance party: The first was that the rhythmic dancing caused the same type of harmonic resonances along the decks of the skywalks that some say took down old Galloping Gertie. The second theory was that the vibrations from the dancing caused material fatigue within the skywalks. Investigators began to look deeper into the collapse, and they discovered that there was an unexpected design change, from the original plans, that ended up being used in the final construction of the elevated walkways.

The contractor that was hired to make the rods that suspended the skywalks asked to change what was to be a one-piece rod into a 2-part rod—in order to make the suspension rods easier to manufacture and easier to hang. This change in fabrication shifted the way the static and dynamic loads were carried by the skywalk.

The second factor was apparently related to the number of people dancing on the fourth floor skywalk. The raised walkways were designed for a modest amount of foot traffic, not a large number of people dancing. Forensic engineers estimated that the total load at the time of the collapse was more than double the weight architects had designed them to hold—notwithstanding the design flaw.

Tragic events like this have necessitated the continued testing of materials and design, and made it essential that overarching entities are in charge of making sure standards are in place and adhered to. Of course in the case of the Hyatt Hotel disaster, it would have taken impossible foresight to imagine all the potential circumstances to which those elevated walkways could possibly be exposed.

And undoubtedly, if anybody saw it coming—whether the designers, the hotel management, or the dancers themselves—that catastrophe would never have happened. There are many components to a disaster like this, and not all of them can be anticipated or governed, but all of them can be analyzed.

In the United States, the National Bureau of Standards was developed in 1901, and it became known as the National Institute of Standards and Technology in 1988. Prior to 1901, the U.S. Department of Treasury's

"Office of Standard Weights and Measures," was essentially the precursor agency, but its sphere was a little more limited.

The current National Institute of Standards and Technology, through its engineers, scientists, and other technology experts, has the charge of identifying and promoting appropriate measurements, calibration standards, and quality control benchmarks for all kinds of manufacturing and construction. Among its subcommittees is the National Construction Safety Team Advisory Committee. It was this group that was charged with the monumental task of analyzing the 2001 collapse of the World Trade Center's twin towers.

The way the twin towers were designed, each floor was about 3–3.5 million pounds, and at its foundation the total bearing load was about a billion pounds. When designers conceived the towers, they actually did take airplane impacts into consideration, because in 1945 a U.S. Army B-25 bomber had hit the Empire State building, killing 14 people. In the architectural vision, the most probable worst case scenario for the World Trade Center was the accidental impact of a Boeing 707, which was, at the time, the largest aircraft in the world, and commonly flew out of the 3 surrounding airports: JFK, LaGuardia, and Newark.

Engineers knew that a Boeing 707 has a maximum takeoff weight of 168 tons, a maximum cruising speed of 607 miles an hour, and contains 230,000 gallons of fuel when its tanks are full. Because of the proximity to the nearby airports, designers assumed if there was an accident, the impact velocity when an aircraft hit would be close to that of takeoff or landing, which is only around 180 miles an hour.

As you may know, most airline accidents typically take place during takeoff or landing. So, the buildings were constructed with the potential for plane crashes in mind, but who would've imagined that on September 11, 2001, not one, but 2, even larger jets, that can carry even more fuel, would be deliberately used as missiles to attack the World Trade Center.

The planes that struck the towers in 2001 were Boeing 767s, each of which has a maximum takeoff weight of 197.5 tons—that's almost 30 tons more than the Boeing 707 the building design engineers had used in their worst-case calculations. Plus, a Boeing 767 carries 10,000 gallons more jet fuel than a 707. Due to all that weight, the cruising speed of a Boeing 767 is only 530 miles an hour, but remember, design calculations used takeoff and landing speeds of only 180 miles an hour. In summary, a Boeing 767 is about 18% heavier than its smaller counterpart, and at its cruising speed of 530 miles an hour, would be traveling almost 3 times faster than the takeoff-and-landing-speed worst-case impact projections.

At 8:46 am, when the first jet impacted the North Tower, seismometers 21 miles away in Palisades, New York, recorded a ground shock Richter scale equivalent of a 0.9 earthquake. The initial horizontal impact severed about 2/3 of the steel supports on the North Tower's north side. Six floors were damaged by the impact directly, but didn't collapse at this point. The resulting fire burned 102 minutes, before the North Tower collapsed, and when it fell—which was actually after the collapse of the second tower hit—it generated the equivalent of a 2.3 magnitude earthquake.

At the time the next Boeing 767 flew into the South Tower, which was 9:03 am, the same seismometer recorded a ground shock equivalent to a 0.7 earthquake. This time, 9 floors were damaged during the impact. This was because the plane came in nose-down at about 10 degrees, and at about a 45-degree angle, so it cut a larger swath than the first plane had in the other tower.

The second jet was also at a lower altitude and impacted lower on the South Tower than the first plane did on the North Tower—that will be important in our failure analysis. The impact caused similar structural damage to the steel supports, and after only 56 minutes of burning—just about half the time the North Tower stood after it was hit—the South Tower came down first, at 9:59 am, sending with it a seismographic wave equivalent to a 2.1 magnitude earthquake.

One source I've seen says that the impact energy of just one of those Boeing 767s would be equivalent to the structure being hit by about 4439 compact cars all traveling at 100 miles an hour. Or for another comparison, the estimated force applied to each World Trade Center tower at impact was approximately 23,850,000 pounds, while a hurricane with winds of 126 miles an hour would have hit the structures with 11 million pounds, which is less than half the force of those aircraft.

Despite the tremendous damage to each building, structurally, those towers were technically able to withstand those impacts, even though the hits each took were much greater than the worst-case scenario engineers had used to design their construction. What doomed the towers to collapse was the fire involved.

Forensic engineers and fire investigators determined in their analysis that if the full amount of jet fuel in a Boeing 767 was spread evenly over 9 floors—using the case of the South Tower—there would be 9 ounces of jet fuel per square foot. This was based on each floor having an area of 40,000 square feet, times 9 floors, for the 24,000 gallons of fuel on board. Now, take a minute to imagine that—here's a square foot of floor space, and then picture a measuring cup—there are 8 ounces in a cup—so we're talking about pouring more than 1 cup of highly flammable jet fuel on each square foot of floor space.

We'll talk a lot more about fires in another lecture, but it's important to say here, the maximum temperature jet fuel burns is about 3140 degrees Fahrenheit. Now, flame temperatures don't reach this in real life, even in an uncontrolled interior building fire—but the temperatures from this jet fuel fire would only be several hundred degrees less than that. The major effect these high temperatures had on the structural integrity of the World Trade Center towers was on their steel supports and the concrete around that steel.

Steel-reinforced concrete, itself, degrades and cracks at temperatures over 120 degrees Fahrenheit. And when a fire reaches 1000 degrees, the structural steel supports, themselves, lose about half their tensile strength. Engineers know that when temperatures reach 1300 degrees, steel is no longer even viable in its support capabilities. Given the extreme amount of jet fuel per square foot in the areas where each plane hit, the fire temperatures, without a doubt, would have easily far exceeded 1300 degrees, causing a full material failure in the steel.

Now we get to the domino effect that brought each of the 110-story towers down: When the structural components of the steel and concrete failed, on the 6 floors in the North Tower and the 9 floors in the South Tower, they could no longer carry their loads. And if you remember, the South Tower actually fell first, even though it was struck second. This was because the second Boeing 767 hit lower on the South Tower, and as a result there were 16 floors above the impact zone weighing down on the 9 damaged floors, compared to the North Tower, which had 11 floors bearing down on the 6 floors that were destabilized by the fire from the first plane.

So, what happened is that the badly damaged zones—where the fires disabled the structural steel and concrete—essentially left no support for the undamaged floors above them. Then, the undamaged part of each building came crashing down as one unit, with all of its weight, into the area where the fire had burned. That took all of the mass within that undamaged portion, and turned it into a vertical impact of dynamic load that fell on the burned zone. When the upper floors hit as a unit, their mass was too much for the floors below to hold, and then each floor gave way in turn, adding its weight to the domino effect, causing the pancaking collapse we all witnessed, until the entire tower was gone.

Forensic engineers concluded that the 2 different impact altitudes also affected how quickly each building came down. The North Tower not only failed second, but also took a longer time to collapse. The North Tower's horizontal plane impact was on the 93rd floor, and although the floors above it fell from a higher point, they fell for a longer period of time, because there were more floors to pancake below that point.

The South Tower aircraft impact was on the 85th floor, so it took less time to fall because there were fewer dominos, as it were, below that level. The higher collapse energy of the North Tower is also why it wound up having a higher seismometer reading of 2.3 in its collapse than the South Tower's 2.1 magnitude.

Figuring out what went wrong in any type of catastrophe like this is the responsibility of forensic engineering specialists. Even in natural disasters, like Hurricane Katrina, the expertise of forensic engineers is called on, for example, to try to determine whether or not faulty construction was to blame for the many levees that failed during the storm surge.

We can only hope that tragedies like this are once-in-a-lifetime events—but there are other uses of materials science and physics that forensic scientists and law enforcement investigators use day-in and day-out during vehicular accidents, and we'll take a look at those next.

Forensic Analysis of Vehicle Accidents
Lecture 16

A nalysis of motor-vehicle crashes relies, fundamentally, on Newton's laws of motion, but accurate accident reconstruction is far from simple. Forensic engineers use a wide variety of evidence, from skid marks and crash-test statistics to modern innovations like black-box data. This work is not only important in understanding individual accidents, it has led to the development of safer vehicles.

Vehicle Accident Statistics

- In 1900, only about 8000 cars were registered in the United States; by 1915, there were more than 2.3 million cars on the developing U.S. road system. Today, there are over 250 million registered passenger vehicles in the United States—over half are cars and the rest are SUVs, light trucks, and motorcycles.

- The number of accidents per capita in the United States varies depending on location, with city streets being safer than country roads in terms of fatal crashes when comparing population base to miles driven. At the same time, safety improvements have decreased fatalities from motor-vehicle accidents significantly; in the last 3 decades of the 20th century, the death rate from traffic injuries was cut by 50%.

- The decline in accident fatalities seems to relate to 3 main factors: a dramatic increase in seat belt and child car seat use; a major reduction in drunk driving; and the effort to design safer vehicles by car companies. Some of those changes were due to legislation, some to social activism and driver awareness, and some because of lawsuits among insurance companies or against car manufacturers.

- The most common causes of vehicular accidents, other than driving under the influence of alcohol or other drugs, include right-of-way mistakes, failure to yield, excessive speed, following too closely, disregarding traffic signals, and otherwise "imprudent" driving styles. Interestingly, equipment failure is not a significant cause of motor-vehicle accidents.

- Almost half of fatal accidents are collisions between vehicles; about a quarter are collisions with fixed objects like telephone poles, overpass and bridge supports, and trees. A little over 10% of fatalities involve pedestrians being struck, and just over 10% are considered noncollisions—things like going off a cliff. Accidents involving bikes, scooters, and the like cause about 2% of traffic fatalities, and those with trains are about 1%. Fatalities due to collisions with deer and other animals amount to only 0.2%.

Analyzing Accident Scenes
- Analysis of motor-vehicle accidents involves Newton's laws of motion, as well as the conservation of energy and conservation of momentum principles. But the data investigators use also comes from specific and more familiar things at the scene of an accident like the length of skid marks, the positions where vehicles come to rest after the accident, the direction they were traveling before the accident, and the point of impact, if they can be figured out.

- To gather this kind of data, the law enforcement officer who documents the accident scene has to create the equivalent of a crime-scene sketch of the area, complete with accurate measurements. He or she will also have to look at the damage to the vehicles and other objects involved.

- The investigator notes the location of crash debris, looks for impact and paint transfer evidence on both cars, and assesses the road-worthiness of the vehicles both before and after the accident. The investigating team will also have to note the road and weather conditions at the time of the accident and figure out the physical and mental conditions of the drivers.

- Time and speed are difficult to judge when you are in the moment of an accident. Each driver typically underrepresents his or her own speed and overrepresent the speed of any other vehicle involved. Different people can judge any event differently, depending on their perspective or involvement, like whether the light was green, yellow, or red when a car went through it.

- Forensic engineers who reconstruct accidents are seldom, if ever, at the scene just after it occurs. They may be crunching the data weeks after the accident, or maybe even years later, if they're offering a second opinion before a trial. They use the accident report from the investigating scene officers, photographs taken by police or insurance estimators, the vehicles—or what is left of them—and statements from the drivers or witnesses.

The Mathematics of a Crash

- Kinetic energy is the energy of motion. Work, in physics, is the force needed to overcome resistance and produce change. When a vehicle is moving, it has kinetic energy, which is determined relative to its speed and mass. Stopping—whether by coasting, breaking, or hitting something—means that the kinetic energy of that vehicle has to get to zero.

- The kinetic energy of a moving vehicle, is one half of the product of its mass and squared velocity ($\frac{1}{2}mv^2$). Since velocity is squared, when speed doubles, the kinetic energy increases by a factor of 4. So, if you are going 50 miles an hour, you will need 4 times the distance to brake as you would if you were going just 25 miles an hour. The damage to a vehicle and its occupants, or a pedestrian that it hits, also increases with speed.

- The speed at the time of the accident has to be estimated after the accident. The physics principle of conservation of energy sets forth that the total energy at the beginning of the physical processes involved in the accident is equal to the total energy at the end of the physical processes involved in the accident.

- The accident includes what investigators call "irreversible work" like braking, skidding, and crushing. They use up some of the energy in an accident and cannot be converted back into energy of motion. The rubbing of the brake pads on the brake disk or drum, for example, irreversibly changes some of the energy of the moving vehicle into friction and heat.

- If you are trying to bring a car to a complete stop, that heat loss and friction will continue until all of the energy of the moving car is used up and the vehicle comes to a halt. But in an accident, the energy of the car in motion can be irreversibly changed in other ways, like by producing a skid or crumpling the bumper.

- The investigator can measure the skid mark and figure out how fast the vehicle was traveling at the time the driver first slammed his foot on the brake. To get an accurate calculation, the type of road surface and how wet or dry it was need to be considered. There are specific standards, called frictional coefficients, for different types of tires and pavement.

In plastic collisions, the car parts that hit are damaged to the point where they can't snap back to their original condition.

- The damage to a vehicle's front end can also help determine how fast it was going at the time of a crash. Crash test data produced by government and private agencies establishes crush-versus-speed relationships for different types of vehicles, called energy-to-crush depth coefficients. The average crush depth across the damaged part of the car tells the investigator how much energy that car spent when it crashed into whatever it hit. Then that, in turn, shows how fast it was going at the time.

- The driver's body is being propelled at the same speed as the car; therefore, the driver hits the inside of the car at the same speed as the car hits another object. That is why car interiors have been redesigned over the years to include not only better safety restraints and airbags but also collapsible steering columns and engines that slide beneath the car rather than through it.

- Because more than half of all collisions happen between 2 cars—both of which are usually moving—the calculations get a little more complicated. When 2 cars run into each other they exert equal but opposite forces on each other, following Newton's third law of motion. These forces sum to zero unless some other external force is applied.

- Momentum is the velocity of an object times its mass, or $p = mv$. The law of conservation of momentum states that when 2 vehicles crash into each other, their momentum just before the crash is equal to their momentum just after they have hit.

- For example, if a car is sitting still at a stop sign and someone rear-ends it, the stopped car will move forward because the moving car will slow but some of the moving car's momentum will transfer to the stopped car. If either car leaves skid marks, investigators can use a combination of skid-mark measurement and momentum calculation to figure out how fast the moving driver was going when he hit the stopped car.

Beyond the Math

- Distracted drivers often leave clues for investigators like open maps, cell phones, headphones, open makeup containers, splattered food, or a loud stereo to incriminate themselves. Accident investigators also consider evidence about a person's sobriety at the time of a crash, which might come in the form of alcohol and drug paraphernalia.

- Sometimes drunk or high drivers try to put the blame on each other—even to the point of changing seats with a sober (or deceased) passenger. Investigators use all available clues to evaluate the position of occupants at the time of the accident, like bloodstain and injury patterns, especially in crashes where the sobriety of the driver might be at issue.

- The filaments in car light bulbs can show whether exterior lights were on or off at the time of an accident. That can be used to see if the headlamps or a turn signal was on at the time of the crash, which might corroborate or refute somebody's statement.

- These days, many cars have technology that has the capability to tell its own side of the story. Black-box technology, similar to that found in airplanes, can be found in some vehicles for capturing information in case of an accident.

Learning from Accidents

- In the crash of American Eagle Flight 4184 out of Indianapolis, Indiana, which happened on Halloween 1994, the data recorder captured far more than just speed; it registered a terrifying series of events in flight. The type of plane involved—the ATR 72—had already been implicated as prone to equipment failure, particularly during icy conditions, and that is apparently what happened in this case. As a result of that accident, and other incidents involving the same type of plane, ATR-72s, are only permitted to fly in warmer climates today.

- Another tragic equipment and temperature combination apparently caused the Space Shuttle Challenger disaster in 1986, killing all 7 of its crew, including the highly-publicized first "teacher in space"— Christa McAuliffe. It was ultimately determined that the morning's cold temperatures likely caused a failure of a simple piece called an O-ring that served as a seal in a solid rocket booster. This tragedy also pointed to some major disconnects between management and science within NASA that needed to be addressed.

- These types of tragedies—from car accidents to plane crashes to space travel disasters—all have the power to promote change. As sad as these accidents are, they do promote better and safer vehicles, as well as remind us all to be more careful when we drive.

Suggested Reading

Burke, *Forensic Medical Investigation of Motor Vehicle Incidents.*

Noon, *Forensic Engineering Investigation.*

———. *Introduction to Forensic Engineering.*

Ratay, *Forensic Structural Engineering Handbook.*

Questions to Consider

1. What do you know about the analysis of vehicular accidents?

2. How has the analysis of motor-vehicle accidents changed how and what we drive?

3. What are Newton's laws of motion, and how are they relevant to accident reconstruction?

Forensic Analysis of Vehicle Accidents
Lecture 16—Transcript

Many causes of death and injury are as old as human history, like knife wounds and poisons, whether they were intentional, accidental, or suicidal. But deaths due to motor vehicle accidents are only as old as the invention of transportation methods driven by machines. Sure, there were deaths in the past from horse and buggy collisions, or falling off of a chariot, but there's no way those had the same impact—and I didn't mean that as a pun—as the crash of a 747 jet liner or a subway train. But most of today's motor vehicle accidents still involve personal vehicles like cars, trucks, motorcycles, and other recreational vehicles.

Automobile-type vehicles with steam engines go back to the late 18th century, and internal combustion engines developed shortly after the turn of the 19th century, but it wasn't until 1885 that gasoline-powered engines was introduced. By 15 years later, in 1900, only about 8000 cars were registered in the United States, but by 1915 there were over 2.3 million cars on the developing U.S. road system.

The earliest motor vehicle accidents probably involved cars running into things other than each other, like buildings and unfortunate people. But as the popularity and availability of cars increased so then did the frequency of motor vehicle accidents. Today, there are over 250 million registered passenger vehicles in the United States alone; over half of those are cars, and the rest are SUVs, light trucks, motorcycles, things like that.

The number of accidents per capita varies depending on location; with city streets being safer than country roads, but that's based on federal data involving fatal crashes when comparing population base to miles driven. Lots of factors are behind that generalization, including lower speed limits in cities, more traffic control devices—like stoplights and one-way streets—as well as shorter distances to emergency medical treatment in cities as compared to rural areas.

At the same time, safety improvements have decreased fatalities from motor vehicle accidents significantly; in the last 3 decades of the 20th century—between about 1970 and the year 2000—the death rate from traffic accidents was cut by 50%. That decline seems to relate to 3 main factors: First, a dramatic increase in seatbelt and child car seat use; second, a major reduction in drunk driving; and third, the effort to redesign safer vehicles by car companies.

Some of those changes relate to legislation, like seatbelt laws and much tougher penalties for drunk driving. Some of the decrease relates to social activism, including public service announcements and national organizations like Mothers Against Drunk Driving. And I'm sure those of you who are my age or older remember the sharp points and metal interiors of the cars of the 1950s and '60s, and so you recognize the drastic improvements in the safety features of cars, like shoulder belt seat restraints, airbags, safety glass, laminated windshields, and child car seats.

I remember my little brother's car seat was not much more than a few straps of cloth, tied to this bare metal frame that hooked over the back of the bench seat in the front of my mom's big old turquoise blue 1960s station wagon—you know, the one with the fins on the back of it. She would sit him in that little car seat right next to her in the front seat, and in hindsight, it seems like it wasn't really much more than an aiming device to send the poor kid right through the front windshield if an accident did happen!

We also have to consider that some of these changes were probably brought about because of lawsuits—among insurance companies, or against car manufacturers. One estimate I read suggested economic losses from motor vehicle accidents in the U.S. are about $200 billion a year, and a third of that is still due to crashes involving alcohol. That total considers not only all the legal, medical, and funeral costs, but also the property damage and lost wages of those involved.

Lastly, I want to mention some of the most common causes of vehicular accidents, other than impaired driving from the influence of alcohol or other drugs. These include whether people were killed, injured, or not—and those top causes are right-of-way mistakes, failure to yield, excessive speed, following too close, disregarding traffic signals, and other things they call "imprudent" driving styles. Interestingly, equipment failure is not a significant cause of motor vehicle accidents.

And while I'm rattling off statistics, let me mention a relatively recent breakdown of the kinds of car accidents that do result in fatalities: Almost half of the fatal accidents are collisions between vehicles, as you might expect, but another quarter of the fatal accidents are collisions with fixed objects like telephone poles, overpass and bridge supports, and trees. A little over 10% of the fatalities involve pedestrians being struck by a car, and just over 10% are considered non-collisions—awful things like going off a cliff. Accidents involving bikes, scooters and the like cause about 2% of the traffic fatalities, and accidents with trains are about 1%. I live in an area with a high deer population, so I was curious to see the percent of human accident fatalities due to collisions with animals, and it was only point .2%.

And because so many of us drive and have the potential to be in traffic accidents—more so than being robbed or assaulted—I think it's important that we talk about the forensics of vehicular accidents in this series, so now let's get onto the science.

Some of you math and physics geeks out there probably already realize that the analysis of motor vehicle accidents, often just called MVAs, involves Newton's laws of motion, as well as the application of some particular laws of physics—namely conservation of energy and conservation of momentum. But the data investigators use comes from specific and more familiar things at the scene of an accident—things like the length of skid marks, the positions where vehicles come to rest after the accident, the direction they were traveling in before the accident, and the point of impact—if it can be figured out.

To gather this kind of data, the law enforcement officer who documents the scene has to create the equivalent of a crime-scene sketch of the whole area, complete with accurate measurements. He or she will also have to look at the damage to the vehicles and other objects involved.

The investigator needs to note the location of any crash debris, look for impact and paint transfer evidence on both cars, and try to assess the road-worthiness of the vehicles involved both before and after the accident. The investigating team will have to note things like the road conditions and weather conditions at the time of the accident, as well as figure out the physical and mental conditions of the drivers involved.

And to complicate matters even more, all of this has to be done after any injured victims are attended to and a roadblock or safe detour is established for other vehicles in the vicinity. Think about that the next time you are sitting in traffic, cursing the fact that you are being delayed because of an accident—there's a lot going on, and a lot that needs to go on, before the scene can be released again to the general public—especially if the accident is serious and involves fatalities.

If you've ever been in or witnessed an accident, you recognize that time and speed are really difficult to judge when you're there in that moment. How many of us have thought we were driving the speed limit, only to look at the speedometer and realize—whoo—I'm 10 miles over? In accidents, it's typical that each driver under-represent his own speed, and over-represent the speed of any other vehicle involved.

And we've all seen how different people can judge the same event, depending on their perspective or their involvement; like whether the light was green, yellow, or red when a car went through it. We'll talk a lot more about eyewitness testimony in another lecture, but obviously that's going to be a factor when witnesses to an accident are being interviewed.

What's interesting to me about accident reconstruction is that the forensic engineers that actually do the calculations to reconstruct what happened are seldom, if ever, at the scene of an accident just after it occurs. They might be crunching the data weeks after the accident, or maybe even years later, if they're offering a second opinion before trial, for instance.

Forensic engineers often have to base their analysis after the fact—using the accident report from the investigating-scene officers, photographs taken by police or insurance estimators, the vehicles—or what's left of them in a junkyard or salvage lot—as well as the statements of the drivers or witnesses. And if a car is examined at the place where it ended up being towed, it can be significantly different than it was at the time of the accident. That's because doors might have to be removed to rescue victims, towing could have meant replacing a flat tire, or a break-in at the junkyard might have stripped parts off the car that could be important to the analysis.

Do you remember some of the basics of physical science? We only need a couple of them here. To start off with, we need to remember that kinetic energy is the energy of motion, and work—in physics—is the force needed to overcome resistance and produce change.

When a vehicle is not moving, it has no kinetic energy, and when it is moving it has kinetic energy related to how fast it's traveling and its mass. Now mass is not quite the same thing as weight. Mass is how much matter is in something as related to how it accelerates when a force, like gravity, acts on it. So, stopping the motion of a vehicle—whether by coasting, breaking, or hitting something—means that the kinetic energy of that vehicle has to get to zero.

The kinetic energy of a moving car, or any other vehicle, is 1/2 of the product of its mass and squared velocity, which is easier to see in symbols than hearing me say it. The reason it takes more braking power to stop at higher speeds than at lower speeds, is because—since velocity is squared in that equation—when speed doubles, the kinetic energy increases by a factor of 4. So, if you're going 50 miles an hour, you will need 4 times the distance to brake as you would if you were going just 25 miles an hour. I think all of us who have had some practical and white-knuckle experiences can relate to that! Another consequence is that the damage to a vehicle and its occupants, or a pedestrian that it hits, also increases with speed. I'm sure you've all heard the phrase speed kills, and it's really true.

But people don't look at their car's speedometer just before they hit something, right? And even if they do, that's a secret they may take to their grave. So, the speed at the time of the accident has to be estimated after the accident. To figure out the speed of a vehicle right before an accident happens, the physics principle called the Conservation of Energy has to be applied. This law sets forth that the total energy at the beginning of the physical processes involved in the accident is equal to the total energy at the end of the physical processes involved in the accident.

The accident event itself includes what investigators call "irreversible work" that happens during the accident. This irreversible work includes things like braking, skidding, and crushing—because they use up some of the energy in an accident and can't be converted back into the energy of the motion that caused them. There are a couple ways this can it be expressed mathematically, like $0 = \Delta E / \Delta T$—where E is the total energy, T stands for time, and the delta symbol means change.

When we use our brakes to stop our car when it's moving, the rubbing of the brake pads on the brake disk or drum irreversibly changes some of the energy of the moving vehicle into friction that wears off the brake drum and the pad surfaces—and that's why we eventually need new brakes, And it also converts some of that energy to heat. If we're trying to bring our car to a complete stop, that heat loss and friction will continue until all of the energy of a moving car is used up, and the vehicle comes to a halt. But in an accident, the energy of the car in motion can be irreversibly changed in other ways, like by producing a skid or crumpling the bumper.

So, without going into a whole lot of mathematical detail that I just barely understand myself, when a police investigator studies the scene of an accident, he or she can measure the skid mark and figure out how fast the vehicle was traveling at the time the driver first slammed his foot on the brakes. But in order to get an accurate calculation, the type of road surface and how wet or dry it was, need to be considered too. There are specific standards, called frictional coefficients, for different types of tires and different types of pavement.

One book I use in my class gives the example that a 100-foot skid mark on dry concrete pavement will result from a car that slammed on its brakes when it was going 47 miles an hour. The implications are obvious—if the speed limit is 35 miles an hour on that stretch of road where the accident occurred, then the math shows that the driver was speeding when he slammed on his brakes.

But not all collisions produce skid marks, right, because not everybody sees a crash coming? So, looking at the damage to a vehicle's front end can also help determine how fast it was going. Crash test data, produced by both government and private agencies, breaks cars down by their crashworthiness into several categories, like subcompact, compact, intermediate, and full-size cars, among others. Some of this data forms the basis for establishing crush versus speed relationships for different types of vehicles—although cars in each category do have their own independent safety ratings, based on how they are manufactured. For these major categories of cars, standards called "energy-to-crush" depth coefficients have been generated.

For example, subcompact cars generally have crush coefficients of about 5000 pounds of force per inch. So, by looking at the average crush depth across the front of a car that's involved in an accident, and knowing what category the car fits into, tells how much energy that car spent when it crashed into whatever it hit. Then that, in turn, will tell how fast it was going at the time.

Investigators can also use combinations of skid marks and front-end crush in the case where a skid mark leads up to the site of an impact, for example. Let's say the driver recognizes she's about to hit a concrete bridge abutment, and then slams on her brakes, but ultimately hits it anyway.

Something else to consider is that the driver's body is also being propelled at the same speed so, if there's nothing like an airbag or seat belt to take some of the kinetic energy, the driver hits whatever is in front of her at the same speed as she hits the bridge support. That's why car interiors have been redesigned over the years to include not only things like better safety restraints and airbags, but also collapsible steering columns and engines that slide beneath the car, rather than slamming through it.

Now, because more than half of all collisions happen between 2 cars—both of which are usually moving—the calculations get a little more complicated. So let's turn our focus to momentum. Momentum is the velocity of an object times its mass and can be represented by the equation $p = mv$, where p represents linear momentum—meaning something moving in a straight line—and m represents the mass of a vehicle, and v equals its velocity. We also need to think about force, since collisions involve force. Force relates to momentum and can be expressed by the equation $F = \Delta p/\Delta t$. In words that means the change in momentum divided by the change in time gives you the force that caused the change over time. Remember the Greek symbol delta means change in equations like this.

When 2 cars run into each other they exert equal but opposite forces on each other. You might remember, if you studied physics, that's basically Newton's third law of motion. And because the forces between both cars are equal and opposite, they sum to zero, unless some other external force is applied. The principle of Conservation of Momentum states that the total momentum stays the same in a system like this, regardless of the collision. So whatever momentum the 2 cars had just before they hit is equal to the total momentum they still have just after they hit.

Here's an example of how this works: If a car is sitting motionless at a stop sign, and a guy who's talking on his mobile phone and not paying any attention, smacks into the back of the stopped car, the distracted driver's car will slow down from the impact, but the stopped car will be pushed forward. The total momentum of the 2 vehicles is equal just before and after the collision, but some of the initial momentum of the idiot's car gets transferred to the bumper of the guy that was sitting at the stop sign.

And if either of them leave skid marks, say if the cell phone user sees the crash coming and slams on his brakes, or if the car at the stop sign has his foot firmly on his brakes, well, investigators can use a combination of the skid mark method and the momentum method to figure out how fast the distracted driver was going when he hit the stopped car. It takes some pretty fancy math, but it's routinely done by people who understand the principles involved. Mind you, it's not really that simple, because there's more than one dimension to the conservation of momentum—it's really a 3-D issue—but you get the general idea.

Another thing we should talk about is that there are really 2 basic types of collisions, known as elastic and plastic. In passenger cars, elastic collisions happen only at really low speeds of less than about 2 1/2 miles an hour. To call a collision like that "elastic" means that the car parts that hit each other will bounce back to their original shape after the wreck. And we know that modern bumpers and vehicle manufacturing materials are now designed so that they can now better withstand things that used to be considered fender benders. Forensic vehicle accident reconstruction really doesn't apply to these elastic collisions, since by definition they don't cause damage.

But car crashes of any real significance are always plastic collisions where the car parts that hit are damaged to the point where they can't snap back to their original condition. In other words, what gets smashed, dented, and crumpled at the time of the accident stays that way—at least until you get that monumental bill from the body shop, which hopefully you can pass to somebody else's insurance company.

That damage, though, while painful to your pocketbook and maybe even your insurance rating, has value in the accident investigation. If we go back to our previous example, remember that the crush depth on the back bumper of the car sitting at that stop sign, and the front end of the distracted driver's car, can be used to check the accuracy of the driving speed that's arrived at by using the momentum method. So it's worth something, right?

Speaking of distracted drivers, again, although they're probably too clueless to realize it, they leave clues for investigators. Things like open maps, cell phones, head phones, ladies' open makeup containers, splattered food, or a loud stereo—which investigators can check by the position of the radio knob, even if the car isn't running. Those are all things that could incriminate a driver as not paying attention at the time of an accident.

Accident investigators also need to consider a person's sobriety at the time of a crash. So in their search of a car's interior they also look for alcohol or drug paraphernalia. But, they need to be careful where they stick their hands—syringes or a loaded gun could be under the seat, especially if the car is a "thug-mobile." Where there's thugs, there's often drugs.

And sometimes these characters who are drunk or high try to put the blame on each other—even to the point of changing seats. So, if the passenger dies, the impaired driver might try to switch seats to try to implicate the dead guy as the one that was behind the wheel. Investigators have to use all available clues to evaluate the position of occupants at the time of the accident, like bloodstain and injury patterns, to make sure they make sense, especially in crashes where the sobriety of the driver might be at issue.

Here are a couple of other tidbits worth mentioning about vehicle accident analysis. Did you know that the filaments in car light bulbs can actually help show whether exterior lights were on or off at the time of an accident? That can be used to see if the headlamps, or maybe a turn signal, were on at the time of the crash. That could be used to corroborate or refute somebody's statement or show a driver's intention, in the case of a turn signal.

These days, many cars have technology that has the capability to tell the truth, despite what those involved or witnesses say. The newer "black box" technology in some vehicles can capture information in an accident. Here's an example that got a lot of attention when it happened. In 2003, South Dakota Congressman Bill Janklow ran a stop sign at a high rate of speed. A motorcyclist traveling on the cross street struck Janklow's car and was killed instantly. Janklow's Cadillac continued moving another 300 feet beyond the scene before it hit a sign, and that's what stopped his car.

The speed limit on the rural road that Janklow was traveling was 55 miles an hour, but by the evidence at the scene, the investigating state highway patrolman figured Janklow was probably going around 70 miles an hour. When the data from the black box in Janklow's Cadillac was retrieved, it showed he sailed through the stop sign at between 63 and 64 miles an hour—so although not as fast as the investigating officer suspected, he was clearly over the speed limit, and through a stop sign, no less.

At trial, Janklow said that a blood sugar issue was to blame. He said he had taken insulin that morning but hadn't eaten all day and was confused when the accident happened. But, Janklow had a history of driving offenses—although they didn't allow that to come out at trial—but he was ultimately convicted of second-degree manslaughter—mainly based on the information about speed from the car's data recorder.

Of course, we've all heard about black box technology being used in airline crashes, and in a future lecture about mass disasters, I'll talk about the work

I did in the morgue after the crash of American Eagle Flight 4184 out of Indianapolis, Indiana, which happened on Halloween in 1994. In that crash, the data recorder captured far more than just speed, it registered a terrifying series of events that happened in flight. The black box showed that the plane did a full rollover and then was able to right itself, once, but the second rollover resulted in a full-speed crash, upside down at 375 knots. That's just over 430 miles an hour or about 695 kilometers an hour—into the middle of a soybean field in Roselawn, Indiana.

The type of plane involved—which was the ATR 72—had already been implicated several times as being prone to equipment failure, particularly during icy conditions, and that's apparently what happened in this case. While the pilots were on auto-pilot in a holding pattern, pending landing in Chicago O'Hare, freezing rain caused a super fast buildup of ice on the plane. The plane's monitoring systems gave the pilots a warning that something was going wrong—the plane was going way too fast for the poor conditions. But when the pilots lowered the flaps to slow the aircraft, the plane went into that first rollover, which kicked off the auto-pilot and the plane never recovered.

68 people lost their lives in that incident: 64 passengers and 4 crewmembers. That stemmed from a really tragic combination of an equipment issue and the cold weather conditions that caused the issue to manifest itself. As a result of that accident, and other incidents involving the same type of plane, ATR-72s, are only permitted to fly in warmer climates today.

Another tragic equipment and temperature combination apparently caused the Space Shuttle Challenger disaster in 1986, killing all 7 of its crew, including the highly publicized first "teacher in space"—Christa McAuliffe—who had become somewhat of a media icon before the flight. Just a mere 73 seconds into the flight—while much of America and others elsewhere watched—the spacecraft disintegrated, leaving that huge plume of smoke that's been forever burned into many of our minds.

It was ultimately determined that the morning's cold temperatures likely caused a failure of a simple piece called an O-ring that served as a seal in a solid rocket booster. This O-ring failure set off a chain of events that ultimately let pressurized hot gasses affect the solid rocket booster and an external fuel tank, and the spacecraft broke apart.

Because of this President Ronald Reagan formed the Rogers Commission, which included famed physicist Dr. Richard Feynman, to investigate the accident, and shuttle missions were put on a 32-month hold. Many of us probably recall the sad and simple news video footage in which Dr. Feynman elegantly explained the cold failure of this small and seemingly innocuous object in his hands. You can find that online if you're interested. Feynman's role in the investigation also pointed to some major disconnects between management and science within NASA that needed to be addressed.

As we can see, these kinds of tragedies—whether car accidents, plane crashes, or space-travel disasters—they all have the power to promote change. These include modifications in the way all manner of vehicles are designed and manufactured, as well as changes in policies and procedures. It's a shame that awful things often have to happen before these kinds of faults are revealed. But as sad as these accidents are, however, they do promote better and safer vehicles, as well as remind us all to be more careful when we drive, so maybe in that sense, the victims of vehicle fatalities do not completely die in vain.

Fire Science and Explosion Forensics
Lecture 17

Fires and explosions can occur naturally, so forensics experts look for specific clues to determine when arson and deliberate bombing have taken place. Investigators collect evidence about a fire or explosion's point of origin, the chemical composition of the materials involved, the spread of damaged objects and debris, even standard forensic evidence like fibers, fingerprints, and DNA to create a complete picture of an incident's cause.

Arson Facts and Statistics

- Fire happens when oxygen combines with some fuel in the presence of heat. The dancing flames we observe are gases burning as the combustion takes over one substance after another in its path.

- Some fires, and even some explosions, are truly accidents. But how do investigators determine this? Unlike in the courtroom where innocent until proven guilty is the rule, since any incident could be a crime scene, suspicious until proven otherwise is the way all cases of fire and explosion are approached.

- Investigators look for accelerants, igniters, bomb fragments, and explosive residues. They also look for the point of origin in a fire; multiple origins nearly always rule out an accident. Other evidence of a fire that was intentionally set could include signs of a breaking and entering.

- The most common motive for arson is to destroy evidence of some other crime—like murder, burglary, or embezzlement. Another common reason is insurance fraud. Intimidation, extortion, terrorism, or sabotage can also drive people to arson, as can emotions like revenge, jealousy, or hatred. Some arson is caused by vandalism, and it is estimated that half of all arson arrests involve juveniles.

- Occasionally, an arsonist will set a fire and then "discover" it to seem heroic. Research has shown that babysitters, volunteer librarians, night-watch personnel, and security guards are among the most common of these misguided heroes, as are some volunteer firefighters.

- According to FBI statistics, in 2010, about 45.5% of arson offenses involved a structure. Another 26% of arsons targeted vehicles. The other 28.5% of intentionally set fires began outdoors, in timber, grass, or crops.

- Arsons in industrial and manufacturing settings resulted in the highest average dollar loss, at about $133,700 per fire event. In 2008, it was estimated there were 14 times more arson fires in impoverished neighborhoods compared to wealthier areas.

The Basics of Explosives

- The chemistry and physics are somewhat different from fires. An explosive is a material capable of rapid conversion from a solid or liquid state to a gas. That conversion results in energy released as heat, pressure, and sound waves.

- All explosions, except nuclear ones, are similar to fire in many ways, but explosions give off more energy than fires for a given amount of fuel, and the oxygen is mixed into the fuel during an explosion, rather than coming from the surrounding air as during a fire.

- The damaging effects of fire include the heat that melts objects, the burning that can reduce materials to ash, and smoke damage (which also carry soot deposits and disperse chemicals from burned objects). Smoke inhalation kills far more people who die in fires than the flames themselves.

- Explosions have their own set of damage mechanisms: The escaping gases from the blast pressure, called a positive pressure blast, can travel thousands of miles an hour away from the explosion site and exert hundreds of tons of pressure per square inch.

- This blast creates a partial vacuum at the explosion site that, in turn, sucks air, gases, and debris from the explosion back toward the site of detonation during the negative pressure phase of a blast. It is not as strong as the initial positive pressure blast, but it can still do a lot of damage.

- Explosions also produce fragmentation not seen in fires. The casing on a bomb can shatter and produce shrapnel that can tear apart any objects or people it hits. As the blast fragments objects in its path, those fragments can become projectiles, too. Bombers can also put nails or other pieces of metal inside the bomb casing to create additional damage.

- Typically the least damaging consequences of an explosion are its thermal effects. Sometimes there's a fireball at the moment of detonation. When high explosives are used, the thermal effects are hot and quick; with low explosives, the thermal effects are cooler but longer in duration. An explosive fireball tends to burn out quickly, unless other materials catch fire.

Investigating Fires and Explosions
- When a fire is discovered or an explosion happens, the first responders have 2 main priorities: Get everyone trapped by the fire or blast to safety, then put out the fire and/or ensure there are no more explosions. Only after those 2 things are tended to will an investigation begin.

- Collecting evidence at the scene of a fire can be far more complicated than in most other forensic investigations. Lighting and temperature control were likely taken out by the incident, the structure under investigation may be unstable, investigators may be slogging around in piles of wet materials, and hazardous fumes and residues may be present.

- Victims can be nearly completely incinerated by fire, and the highly pressurized water coming out of fire hoses can cause additional damage. Objects can be nearly obliterated by fires and blasts, and even common household and personal items may be difficult to identify. Explosions can rip objects and people apart, or throw them a considerable distance away—all complicating the investigation.

- As with any crime scene, firefighters, rescue personnel, utility workers, police officers, and even onlookers can taint a fire or explosion scene before investigators even get there. This can damage existing evidence, and may even introduce irrelevant footprints, fingerprints, fibers, DNA, or other material. But the need to rescue people and secure the scene takes priority over evidence preservation.

- Investigators collect pieces of burnt or partially burned wood, carpeting, and other materials, as well as control samples from unburned or undamaged areas for comparison if available. Samples of flammable liquids that may have been used as accelerants are collected. (Gasoline is the accelerant of choice in more than 50% of all arson fires.)

- Carpet, bedding, upholstered furniture, clothes, soil, and other absorptive materials have the most potential to retain unburned accelerant for sampling and lab analysis. Forensic labs use the same tests to figure out the nature of an accelerant as they use for identifying other chemicals, such as gas chromatography and mass spectroscopy. Investigators have many tools to detect accelerants, like chemical analyzers called hydrocarbon sniffers, as well as arson dogs.

- One clue that a fire is arson is the presence of a branching pattern called a fire trail, which does not occur in an accidental structure fire. This happens when an arsonist pours an accelerant on the floor from room to room and then lights it on the way out.

- Investigators also look for the source of ignition for a fire or whatever served as the detonator in an explosion. An igniter can be as simple as a burned match, which could possibly be linked through microscopic examination to a matchbook in a suspect's possession. A matchbook, lighter, or candle left at an arson scene might have fingerprints on it, and if a cigarette was used to start a fire, there could be DNA on the cigarette butt.

- Analysts will also look for timing devices—anything that could be used to delay ignition of a fire or an explosion so that the perpetrator can get away before the destruction starts either for his or her own safety or to avoid suspicion. These timing devices can range from simple, like a pack of matches wrapped around a burning candle, to very complex, like the cell phone bomb detonators seen in movies.

Types of Explosives

- Low explosives include the black powder and smokeless powder we talked about in our firearms discussion; both of these are commonly used in pipe bombs, where a section of metal pipe is stuffed with a low explosive, and when the bomb is detonated, the pipe fragments or sharp objects inside the pipe become shrapnel.

- Another common low explosive is ammonium nitrate and fuel oil, or ANFO. This was used in the bombing of the Oklahoma City Alfred P. Murrah Federal Building in 1995, by Timothy McVeigh, Terry Nichols, and their accomplices. The ammonium nitrate from plant fertilizer provides the oxygen source; when soaked in fuel oil, the mixture becomes highly explosive.

- High explosives include things like nitroglycerin, dynamite (which is nitroglycerin mixed with diatomaceous earth and calcium carbonate) TNT (or tri-nitro-toluene), and the military explosive called C4. Some high explosives, including nitroglycerin, are quite sensitive to heat and shock and are only used in small quantities as a primary explosive to detonate a secondary explosion.

- Secondary high explosives are more stable, easier to transport, and need a booster charge to detonate. Dynamite, TNT, and C4 are examples of secondary high explosives. Plastique, that moldable explosive sometimes seen in movies, is an example of a booster.

Where Fire Science Meets Other Forensics

- Investigators look for what is left of explosive devices, which are often homemade, as well as delivery method. Was it in a backpack left on the floor of a building, did it come through the mail, did it come in a vehicle? Investigators also need to determine the skill level necessary to make the bomb to hone in on whether their suspect is an amateur or an expert.

- In a business, investigators collect partially destroyed papers for analysis. Questioned-document examiners and forensic accountants may be able to piece together the evidence, establish a pattern of destroyed or missing documents, and establish a motive.

- Where there are injuries and fatalities, arson and explosives investigators may have to work with emergency-room personnel or

© iStockphoto/Thinkstock.

Some fires are truly accidents, such as when an appliance malfunction causes a house fire, but others are not.

forensic pathologists to collect evidence in or on the victim's body. An autopsy will also help establish whether the fire or explosion was the actual cause of death or whether the victim was murdered and then the blaze or blast executed to cover up the killing.

- Recent research suggests that setting a fire to cover up a murder is much more common than formerly thought. It was once believed that a human head would explode during a fire because so often incinerated remains would show a badly fragmented skull. Now, many previous death investigations involving fire scenes have been called into question; badly fragmented skulls are much more indicative of blunt-force trauma from bludgeoning, or shattered skulls from gunshot wounds.

- Other typical evidence may be present at fires and explosions, like glass, fibers, hair, shoe prints, or blood. But this evidence is collected differently than it would be at a nonfire scene. Any evidence needs to be kept in sealed, airtight containers because many accelerants are volatile and could evaporate. Explosives are not volatile, so that evidence does not have to be packaged in the same way.

- In suicide bombings, there are often telltale signs of who was carrying the bomb among the human remains. The bomber clearly sustains the most body fragmentation from the blast, and many body parts cannot be recovered because they were literally blown to bits.

- If any natural fuels that would have normally been present at the scene could not have reached the projected temperatures on their own, that usually points to an accelerant. When investigators see a pile of wood or rags in a structure where they would not normally be located, that is a clue to the origin of an arson fire.

- Arsonists also typically start fires on the lower floors of a large building. If the point of origin is on the 14th floor of an office building, it is less likely to be arson since it would have taken much more time for the perpetrator to get out—and think of all the witnesses or surveillance cameras they might have to pass during their exit.

- If the point of origin seems to be a space heater, or a candle left burning on a dining room table, investigators may quickly have their answer and move on, but regardless of the circumstances, point of origin determination is standard in all fire investigations. This not only helps establish the cause, which can be important for insurance purposes, but can lead to safer appliances and lives saved.

Suggested Reading

Almirall and Furton, *Analysis and Interpretation of Fire Scene Evidence.*

"Arson."

Lentini, *Scientific Protocols for Fire Investigation.*

Marshall and Oxley, *Aspects of Explosives Detection.*

Noon, *Engineering Analysis of Fires and Explosions.*

———, *Forensic Engineering Investigation.*

Stauffer, Dolan, and Newman, *Fire Debris Analysis.*

Questions to Consider

1. What are the 2 major differences between a fire and an explosion?

2. How are the damaging effects of fires different from those of explosions?

3. What are the roles and responsibilities of an arson investigator at a crime scene?

Fire Science and Explosion Forensics
Lecture 17—Transcript

Have you ever actually watched a building burn? It's a terrifying and mesmerizing thing to see. We all know what fire looks like—but what is it, really? Fire happens when oxygen combines with some fuel in the presence of heat. The dancing flames we observe are gases that are burning, as the combustion takes over one substance after another in its path. Really, everything we see is chemistry and physics in action. In this lecture, let's take a look at the forensic science used to analyze fires and explosions.

We know that some fires are truly accidents, such as when an appliance malfunction causes a house fire. A clothes dryer vent gets clogged with lint, and at some point the heat the appliance generates may cause that wad of fibers in the vent to catch fire. Explosions can be accidents, too.

If the pilot light in a gas furnace goes out, and natural gas builds up inside a closed area, something as simple as flipping on a light switch can be enough of a detonator to ignite that gas and blow up an entire building. Other times a short in an electrical system can start a fire. There are also fires that originate naturally, like those from lightning strikes.

How do investigators determine if a fire was accidental or not? Even in the examples I just mentioned, fire and explosion science need to be used to figure out the cause. Was that furnace faulty by design or manufacture? Was it somehow rigged to explode? Could the homeowner have modified or misused the furnace in some way? Or did the pilot light simply go out from a gust of wind that came in through an open doorway that was later closed, without anybody realizing the pilot light was extinguished.

Now, consider that this fire investigation will have to be carried out on a building that may be completely incinerated—just like engineers may have to reconstruct the events from a building collapse just from the rubble, or vehicle accident experts figure out the cause of a plane crash, a subway collision, or an auto accident, sometimes from not much more than a twisted heap of metal.

Unlike in the courtroom where innocent until proven guilty is the rule; since any of these incidents could be a crime scene, "suspicious until proven otherwise" is the way these cases are approached, so as not to overlook any evidence.

In their analysis of fires and explosions, investigators will look for accelerants, igniters, pieces of a bomb, or explosive residues. They'll also have to look for the point of origin in a fire; multiple origins will nearly always rule out an accident. Other evidence of a fire that was intentionally set could include signs of a breaking and entering—like toolmarks on a doorframe or glass shards from a broken window. Critical thought should also be given to points of entry and exit and their proximity to the fire—an arsonist would need to get in and out of the building safely and with time to get away.

As we've seen before, motive needs to be considered, too. The most common motives for arson are to conceal some other crime—like murder, burglary, embezzlement—in other words, to destroy evidence. Another familiar reason is the financial gain that can come from insurance fraud. Power over others can also be motive, as in intimidation, extortion, terrorism, or sabotage; other emotions like revenge, jealousy, or hatred can cause somebody to set a fire.

Still other arsons are caused by vandals who are being malicious and destructive—especially in the cases of what are called pyromaniacs, who have fire obsessions. It's estimated that half of all arson arrests involve juveniles. Occasionally, an arsonist will set a fire and then "discover" it, in order to seem heroic. Research has shown that babysitters, volunteer librarians, night-watch personnel, and security guards are among the most common of these misguided heroes, as are some volunteer firefighters.

According to U.S. FBI statistics, in 2010, about 45.5% of arson offenses involved a structure, including houses, storage facilities, and public buildings. Another 26% of arsons had cars, trucks, and other vehicles as their targets. Although probably not what most of us think about when we hear the word arson, the other 28.5% of intentionally set fires begin outdoors, like timber and grass fires, or crops.

When all of these settings are considered, arsons in industrial and manufacturing settings resulted in the highest average dollar loss, at more $133,000 per fire event. In 2008, it was estimated there were 14 times more arson fires in impoverished neighborhoods compared to wealthier areas.

Now, before we go on to talk more specifically about forensic investigations, let's talk a bit about the chemistry and physics of explosives to understand how they're different from fires. An explosive is a material capable of rapid conversion from a solid or liquid state to a gas. That conversion results in energy released as heat, pressure, and sound waves.

All explosions, except those that are nuclear in origin, are similar to fire in many ways; but there are a couple of main distinctions that can be made. First, explosions give off more energy than fires for a given amount of fuel, and, secondly, oxygen is mixed into the fuel during an explosion, but tends to come mainly from the surrounding air during a fire.

The damaging effects of fire are pretty self-evident; they include the heat that melts objects, the burning that can reduce some materials completely to ash, and smoke damage—which can carry with it soot deposits and dispersed chemicals that come from the substances and objects that are burning. You've probably heard that smoke inhalation kills far more people who die in fires than the actual flames themselves.

Explosions have their own set of damage mechanisms. The escaping gases from the blast pressure can travel thousands of miles an hour and exert hundreds of tons of pressure per square inch. There are really 2 phases of pressure waves associated with an explosion. First is what's called the positive pressure blast. It moves away from the site of the explosion and causes a wave that shatters anything in its path. The damage from the positive pressure blast decreases with distance as the wave dissipates energy and then loses power.

Because the gases from the explosion were expelled so quickly, the positive pressure wave creates a partial vacuum at the site where the explosion occurred. This vacuum, in turn, sucks air, gases, and debris from the explosion back toward the site of detonation. This second wave is called a negative pressure phase of a blast. It's not as strong as the initial positive pressure blast that moved away from the explosion, but it can still do a lot of damage.

Explosions also produce fragmentation not seen in fires. For instance, the casing on a bomb can shatter and produce shrapnel that can break up or tear apart any objects or people it hits. As the blast itself fragments objects in its way, the pieces of those materials can become projectiles that, in turn, tear up the other things they hit. Other fragmentation can be caused by the bomb's design, as when bombers put nails or other pieces of metal inside the bomb casing to create additional damage.

Typically the least damaging consequences of an explosion are its thermal effects. Sometimes there's a fireball at the moment of detonation. If what are known as high explosives are used, the thermal effects are hot and quick, but in the case of low explosives, the thermal effects are less but longer in duration. An explosive fireball tends to burn out quickly, unless there are lots of other materials that catch fire from it.

Obviously, when a fire is discovered or an explosion happens, the first responders have 2 main goals before doing anything else: Get everyone who may be trapped by the fire or blast out, whether they're inside a building, a car, or the cabin of a downed plane. The next responsibility is to put the fire out, or try to ensure there are no more explosions—in other words, make sure things are as safe as possible. Only after those 2 things are tended to, will an investigation begin regarding the cause of the incident.

When you consider collecting evidence at the scene of a fire, things can be far more complicated than in most other forensic investigations. For one thing, there might not be any light or temperature control because there's no power. Investigators might be slogging around in piles of wet materials and objects because of firefighting efforts. Personal safety might be at issue due to hazardous fumes or other residues present. And as I've seen myself, the area may not be entirely safe because of structural damage.

In 1999, during the early morning hours I was called to assist in finding a body in a terrible house fire not too far from my own home. All 2 stories of the house had caved into the basement, and the fire was so intense, investigators weren't even sure they could recognize what had been a body. When I got there, I was told that a sixth-grade girl who was babysitting died after aiding 2 of her siblings in getting out of the house safely—a 10-year-old sister, and a 13-year-old brother who had cerebral palsy. She also got the family dog out. Why she went back into that burning house at 1 o'clock in the morning is still not known. Investigators thought she went back into the house to see if, in fact, her parents had already come home and were asleep in their bedroom, since the fire had started after the children had gone to bed.

After we had searched for several hours, it was determined that the scene was too structurally unsound for us to continue going, and I was told to go home and get some sleep, while they brought in heavy equipment to remove some of the larger pieces of construction that threatened our safety, one layer at a time. We would return to the site later that day to continue our search. It was only after I got home that I received word from a family member, that the little girl who died was my niece's best friend from school. I was so busy that morning with my responsibilities, that I hadn't picked up on the family's last name and made the connection.

Her body was eventually recovered, but those are the kind of cases that make it difficult to be a lifelong Cincinnati resident, with most of my family and many of my friends still there in town. Especially since many of my victims are often visually unidentifiable at the outset, I never know when I might be looking for—or even examining—someone I turn out to actually know.

Victims can be nearly completely incinerated by fire, and the highly pressurized water coming out of fire hoses can cause additional damage. Objects can be nearly obliterated by fires and blasts, and even common household and personal items may be difficult to identify. Explosions can rip objects and people apart or throw them a considerable distance away.

As with any crime scene, firefighters, rescue personnel, utility workers, police officers, and even onlookers can taint a fire or explosion scene before investigators even get there. This can damage existing evidence, and may even introduce irrelevant footprints, fingerprints, fibers, DNA, or other material. But given the need to rescue people and secure the scene, investigators have to work with what's available to them.

What kinds of things or materials should be collected from a fire or explosion scene in an effort to find out its cause? Investigators should collect pieces of burnt or partially burned wood, carpeting, and other materials, as well as control samples from the same materials from unburned or undamaged areas for comparison, if they can find them. Samples of suspected flammable liquids that may have been used as accelerants should be collected. Gasoline is the accelerant of choice in more than 50% of all arson fires, but lighter fluid, paint thinner, kerosene, propane, and any other fuel can all be used to start or spread a fire.

There are also some materials that can prove more fruitful in a search for accelerants than others. Things like carpet, bedding, upholstered furniture, clothes, or soil—really anything that will absorb a liquid—has the potential to retain unburned accelerant for sampling and lab analysis. Forensic labs use the same type of analytical chemistry to figure out the nature of an accelerant as they use for identifying other chemicals, like drugs and poisons, such as gas chromatography and mass spectroscopy, among other high-tech methods.

At the scene, arson investigators might be clued in by what's called a fire trail. This happens when an arsonist pours an accelerant on the floor from room to room and then lights it on the way out. The branching pattern of the fire trail essentially causes all the areas to blaze up at about the same time, which doesn't happen in a typical structure fire. Investigators have different tools and partners to detect accelerants, like chemical analyzers called hydrocarbon sniffers, as well as arson dogs.

Dogs can be trained to detect small quantities of common accelerants and can find them in really tiny amounts; they can even smell the hydrocarbons after extensive burning. Arson dogs enable much quicker processing of fire scenes, and follow-up results from forensic labs show good correlations between arson dog hits on suspected accelerants and the actual presence of those hydrocarbons in the materials they test.

The only real problem is that fire itself can produce hydrocarbons as it burns, and dogs can't differentiate between those and any hydrocarbons used as accelerants. But remember, we're OK with field tests that produce false positives, but investigators can't afford false negatives that would allow evidence to be completely overlooked.

Scene investigators will also look for the source of ignition for a fire, or whatever served as the detonator in the case of an explosion. In the case of a fire, an igniter can be as simple as a burned match that could possibly be linked specifically through a microscopic examination to a matchbook in a suspect's possession. If a matchbook is left at an arson scene, it might have fingerprints on it—so might a candle or a cigarette lighter that was used as an igniter—and if a cigarette was used to start a fire, there could be DNA on the cigarette butt.

Some arsonists don't even enter the building or area they intend to burn down. You may have heard of a Molotov cocktail. That is a container made out of glass or something else breakable that has an accelerant inside of it, with a wick hanging out the top. You may have seen one of these hand-held firebombs shown on TV, like a beer bottle filled with gasoline, and a rag stuck in the top. The arsonist lights the rag and then throws the entire container into the structure or vehicle he wants to torch, maybe even through a window. It goes without saying, of course, this is not something you should try at home.

At the scene, analysts will also look for timing devices, anything that could be used to delay ignition of a fire or an explosion so that the perpetrator can get away before the destruction starts—not only for his own safety, but to avoid suspicion. These timing devices can range from simple to very complicated.

To start a fire, the arsonist can take a pack of matches, and wrap it around the base of a burning candle. When the candle burns low enough to heat the match heads, the pack of matches will light up and start the fire, or the same device can be used to light a bomb fuse. Considering how slow some candles burn, this simple timer could delay the start of the fire or the explosion for hours. A perpetrator will get far less time if they use a smoldering cigarette on a pack of matches. Again, do not try this at home!

Bombers have developed all kinds of detonation devices for their package bombs, briefcase bombs, luggage bombs, and car bombs. In many cases, a small spark is all that's needed. So a device as simple as a spring-loaded nail that hits a metal plate could be a detonator. We've seen on TV and in movies where a cell phone can be set to detonate when it rings, so that the bomber can literally phone in his damage.

Specific to explosions, investigators can search for unburned or partially burned explosive residues. As I alluded to before, there are low explosives and high explosives. Low explosives include the black powder and the smokeless powder we talked about in our firearms discussion; both of these are commonly used in what are called pipe bombs. That's when the perpetrator takes a section of metal pipe and stuffs it with a low explosive, and when the bomb is detonated, the pipe fragments become shrapnel that tears up things and people.

The Unabomber, Ted Kaczynski, used pipe bombs to maim and kill his victims. His devices started out relatively simple, and over his reign of terror they became more complex and more dangerous. Initially, he used a pipe bomb that was about 1 inch in diameter and about 9 inches long, filled with smokeless powder. Because he used wooden plugs to seal the ends, though, the ignition of the powder didn't create enough pressure buildup inside the pipe to do a tremendous amount of damage.

That was one of the reasons his initial victims suffered less physical damage than those who encountered his more sophisticated devices. When Kaczynski graduated to including nails and wooden splinters inside his pipe bombs, people suffered much greater harm. In fact, wood became part of his signature. We'll talk a lot more about the Unabomber in another lecture.

Another example of what is considered a low explosive is called ANFO, which stands for ammonium nitrate and fuel oil. This was used in the bombing of the Oklahoma City Alfred P. Murrah Federal Building in 1995, by perpetrators Timothy McVeigh, Terry Nichols, and a couple of accomplices. At the time it was carried out, the Oklahoma City bombing was the deadliest act of terrorism in American history.

Remember that I mentioned that explosions differ from fires because of their oxygen source? The Oklahoma City bombing is a good example to explain that. Ammonium nitrate is found in plant fertilizer, and it provides the oxygen source; when the fertilizer is soaked in fuel oil, the mixture becomes highly explosive.

At Oklahoma City, the perpetrators used 13 barrels of fuel oil combined with fertilizer to create over 3 tons of explosive material all packed into a rental truck, which they parked outside the federal building. The explosion was estimated to be the equivalent of a 3.0 magnitude earthquake and was heard over 50 miles away. The blast killed 168 people, and injured over 600 more. It destroyed half of the Murrah building, as well as damaging cars and over 300 other structures, some of which were blocks away.

This 1995 bombing was carried out as a revenge against the federal government for its involvement in 2 prior confrontations with citizens: First, the 1992 FBI and U.S. Marshall's siege of Randy Weaver, his family, and an associate at Ruby Ridge in Idaho; and secondly, the 1993 Branch Davidian standoff in Waco Texas, where cult leader David Koresh had his compound. The bombers at Oklahoma City spent well over a year planning this attack and clandestinely gathering some of the resources and materials they needed—but it was estimated the entire operation cost only about $5000, including the bomb materials, the rental truck, and a cheap getaway car.

Back to explosives and their residues. High explosives include things like nitroglycerin; dynamite, which is nitroglycerin mixed with diatomaceous earth and calcium carbonate, and then rolled into tubes; and TNT, which is the abbreviation for tri-nitro-toluene, and also the military explosive called C4. Those are all examples of high explosives. Some are much more sensitive to heat and shock, and so are typically very unstable and used only in small quantities; for example, a small amount of nitroglycerin may be used as what's called a primary explosive, to detonate a secondary explosion.

Secondary high explosives are more stable. They're easier to transport, and they need what's called a booster charge to detonate. Dynamite, TNT, and C4 are examples of secondary high explosives. You may have heard of plastique, which is that moldable explosive stuff we sometimes see in movies; plastique is an example of a booster, so is a blasting cap.

In addition to explosive residues, scene investigators will look for what's left of the devices themselves, which are often homemade, as well as try to figure out how the explosive was delivered. Was it in a backpack that got left on the floor of a building, did it come through the mail—that was a method Kaczynski often used—or like at Oklahoma City, did it come in a vehicle? As we saw with computer crime, investigators also have to determine the skill level necessary to make the bomb, in order to hone in on whether their suspect is an amateur or an expert.

What else should investigators look for to collect as evidence? In a business, things like burned or partially destroyed papers should be carefully collected for analysis that may prove useful in establishing motive, say if they point to evidence of insurance fraud or embezzlement. Questioned document examiners and forensic accountants may be able to piece together the evidence and the facts to see if there's any pattern regarding specifically what items were damaged, or what files may be missing, things like that.

Where there are injuries and fatalities, arson and explosives investigators may have to work with emergency room personnel or forensic pathologists in a coroner or medical examiner's office, because some of the evidence may be in or on the victim's bodies, like accelerants on clothing or shards from a pipe bomb lodged in an injured or dead person. An autopsy will also help establish whether the fire or explosion was the actual cause of death, or whether the victim was murdered and then the blaze or blast executed to cover up the killing.

Recent research suggests that setting a fire to cover up a murder is much more common than formerly thought. In the old days of arson investigation and the effect fire had on bodies, it was commonly said that a human head would explode during a fire, because so often incinerated remains at a fire scene would show a badly fragmented skull.

Some colleagues of mine conducted studies using unembalmed, donated bodies and homes that were scheduled for controlled burns to train firefighters, and they found out that skulls do not explode in fires. This research has called into question many previous death investigations involving fire scenes. Badly fragmented skulls are much more indicative of blunt force trauma from bludgeoning, or shattered skulls from gunshot wounds.

Other typical evidence we've discussed may be present at fires and explosions, like glass, fibers, hair, shoe prints, or blood. But this evidence will have to be collected differently than it would at a non-fire scene. Where arson is suspected, any evidence needs to be kept in sealed airtight containers, from recovery at the scene up to the time of analysis. That's because many accelerants are volatile and could evaporate. Our local crime lab, like many others, uses the same kind of gallon containers that house paint is sold in. Because explosives are not volatile, they don't have to be packaged in the same way at a crime scene.

Another important consideration in arson and explosion investigations is determining the precise location they emanated from. In a fire this is called the point of origin, and with an explosion the term "bomb seat" is typically used. At the scene of an explosion, the bomb seat is where the highest concentration of explosive residues will typically be found. Sometimes it can be pretty difficult to specifically locate where the bomb was detonated, because it's buried under tons of rubble. They have to pull out all that debris and sift through it to find maybe one small piece that can point to who made the bomb and how they made it.

Another complication I mentioned earlier are the positive pressure waves that throw materials away from the explosion, which are followed by the negative pressure wave that sucks things back in; you can imagine how this twofold mixing of evidence complicates the scene.

In suicide bombings there are often telltale signs of who was carrying the bomb by what's left of his or her body. In cases where the perpetrator straps on explosives or carries them in a backpack, often the only thing left at autopsy, are portions of the bomber's lower legs and feet. The other victims of suicide bombings may have missing limbs, shrapnel, and other kinds of injuries, but usually the bomber clearly sustains the most body fragmentation from the blast, and body parts that cannot be recovered because they were literally blown to bits.

In fires, the point of origin is usually where the most burning takes place. Arson investigators can interview firefighters to learn about the hotspots, and in what direction the fire traveled, and how fast it was moving. Usually, but not always, the hottest spot is the point of origin, so looking at the fire destruction and noting which areas show the most damage from heat exposure is important.

Deeper burns in a wall stud, for example, means the fire was there longer and started there earlier than other areas. Things like blistering or spalling of concrete surfaces will happen where the heat was most intense. The point of origin might also be indicated by a V-shaped pattern of burning on a wall, where the bottom of the V may point to where the fire began.

By looking at objects that are differentially melted, like metal or glass, and things like paint that's peeled or bricks that are chipped, fire investigators can figure out how high the temperature may have been in a particular area. The way things melt can even show the direction in which the fire traveled. For instance investigators especially look at light bulbs, which commonly occur all throughout a structure, and that gives them some directional fire clues. Once they figure out how hot a fire got by looking at the kind of things that melted, investigators can go on to make additional assumptions. And if any natural fuels that would have normally been present at the scene—such as papers in an office, mulch in a shed, or wood cabinets in a kitchen—could not have reached the projected temperatures on their own, that usually points to an accelerant.

When investigators see a pile of wood or rags in a house or structure where they would not normally be located, that's a clue to the origin of an arson fire.

Arsonists also typically start fires on the lower floors of a large building. If the point of origin is on the 14th floor of an office building, it's less likely to be arson since it would've taken much more time for the perpetrator to get out. And think of all the witnesses and surveillance cameras they might have to pass during their exit.

If the point of origin seems simple, something like a space heater or a candle left burning on a dining room table, investigators may quickly have their answer and move on, but regardless of the circumstances, point of origin determination is standard in all fire investigations. This not only helps establish the cause, which can be important for insurance purposes, but can lead to safer appliances and lives saved.

Blood Evidence—Stains and Spatters
Lecture 18

Bloodstain analysis is a complex and occasionally controversial part of forensic investigation. Investigators use the known physical qualities of blood and surfaces, the biological behavior of blood as it leaves the body, and the physics of weaponry to reconstruct crimes from blood evidence left at a scene. This evidence can be used to determine things like the relative locations and sizes of the perpetrator and victim and sometimes even hint at the perpetrator's state of mind.

Bloodstain Analysis Enters the Mainstream

- Analyzing bloodstain patterns goes back well into human prehistory, when our ancient ancestors tracked wounded animals in much the same way that a hunter would today. Using bloodstain interpretation in modern forensic investigations first appears in the 19th century in Europe.

- After a high-profile 1954 murder, bloodstain evidence was used in the controversial Dr. Sam Shepard case. Sheppard was accused of beating his wife to death, but a month after Sheppard's verdict, forensic scientist Dr. Paul Kirk visited the crime scene and used bloodstain patterns to help show the position of the victim and assailant, alleging that Mrs. Sheppard was beaten to death by someone left-handed. Dr. Sheppard was right-handed.

- Sheppard won a retrial in 1966 and was found not guilty in the second trial. Although this outcome was controversial, the Sheppard case was a major step in getting the legal system to accept bloodstain pattern evidence.

- The theoretical and scientific underpinnings of bloodstain pattern analysis have been argued by some to be highly variable and somewhat subjective, but that could be said for plenty of areas in forensic science.

The Basics of Blood

- Looking at a visible record of bloodshed in terms of the shapes, locations, and distribution patterns can give clues about the objects and forces that have generated the bloodstains. Examples include areas where blood has been ejected, sprayed, dripped, walked through, or smeared by the victim or perpetrator.

- This is an area of forensics where extensive photo documentation is crucial because it may be the only way to capture the evidence. For proper interpretation, bloodstain experts have to understand physics, the nature of blood and the cardiovascular system that moves it around, as well as the pathology of wounds. Clues can lead to the positions of the victim and perpetrator during an assault, as well as how many blows or shots were delivered and in what order.

- Depending on body size, the average adult has roughly 5 liters of blood, around 8% of total body weight. Blood plasma is the liquid fraction and is mostly made of water, along with some various ions, proteins, nutrients, and wastes. Red blood cells, white blood cells, and platelets—which are cell fragments—are suspended in the liquid blood plasma.

- When blood vessels are damaged, the lining of the vessel walls exposes proteins that attract blood platelets. The platelets then change their nature and stick to each other, forming a plug that can help close up a small wound. The damaged vessel walls and platelets also release chemicals that ultimately form a polymer of insoluble protein strands, called fibrin, that causes coagulation as the liquid plasma evaporates.

- Inside the body, blood movement is governed by the work of the heart acting as a pump, combined with the pressures within blood vessels. Other forces act on blood when it is outside the body, and this movement will depend, to some degree, on whether the heart is still beating or has stopped.

- Blood plasma, like other liquids, has cohesive properties that holds its molecules together and makes them flow; it also has surface tension. Outside the body, blood can separate into smaller droplets when gravitational or impact forces break its surface tension and viscosity. A drop of blood will form a sphere that minimizes its surface area. Once a drop forms, it will not fraction into smaller droplets unless it hits something or is acted on by another force.

Types of Bloodstains by Appearance
- The major types of bloodstains can be categorized based on their appearance. Some experts break bloodstains into 3 main groups: passive, spatter, and altered. Other experts prefer to focus on the speed of traveling blood and classify stains as low velocity, medium velocity, and high velocity.

- A major factor in how a stain will look is the type of surface that it hits. Blood will look and behave differently when it's on a smoothly painted wall, an upholstered piece of furniture, a leather car seat, rough concrete, carpeting, grass, and so forth.

- Passive bloodstains are the result of gravity, like when blood drips vertically, a pool of blood surrounds a bleeding victim, or large droplets of blood run down a surface. Some types of transfer stains are also considered passive, like when hands or fingers move blood from one surface to another, which is sometimes referred to as a swipe.

- Spatter stains result from the application of some other force besides gravity that affects the movement of blood. Here, investigators will see features that show directionality and distribution. This would include impact spatter from blunt-force trauma or gunshot wounds.

- Altered stains have been changed in some way, whether through natural clotting action, insect activity, or mixture with some other material, like soil. Altered stains also include blood evidence that has been modified when someone attempted to clean up a crime scene, which is called a wipe, rather than a swipe. Other stain alterations, called voids, represent an area where an object blocked the spatter of blood but was then picked up. Alteration can complicate bloodstain interpretation.

- Any circular distortion of a stain helps reveal the angle of impact on a flat surface. If there is a right angle between the blood source and the surface, there will be a nearly perfectly circular stain. The stain gets more elongated as the angle of impact decreases. So, if blood flew toward the surface at a low angle, the resulting stain will be very oblong.

- The oblong shape tells investigators about the direction the blood was traveling in, too. The more pointed end of the elongated droplet faces the direction of travel. The linear tip of the oblong stain may even be fractured because tiny blobs of blood break off from the surface of the parent stain once it hits, and they continue to travel even further.

- Surface texture is also a factor here. The harder and less porous the surface, the fewer tiny spatter droplets will result. Rough, textured surfaces show spines extending from their spatter droplets and can also show peripheral spatter that will complicate figuring out directionality.

- Investigators can figure the point of origin of a bloodstain if they have a group of related stains in a spatter pattern. Once they figure out the direction the spatter came from, they can take a half dozen or so really diagnostic elongated droplets and trace them to a point where their centerlines converge.

- From that horizontal point of origin on the flat plane where the spatter is, they use trigonometry to estimate the height above the surface where the blood drops were flying from. Sometimes on television you see this done with strings, and they call it "stringing the crime scene." These days, lasers and computerized software can do the necessary calculations.

Types of Bloodstains by Speed

- A low-velocity bloodstain pattern would be produced if a bleeding victim is still standing or walking away from an attack and some blood drips to the floor. These patterns are said to produce the greatest variety of shapes and sizes compared to medium- or high-velocity stains and are usually larger in size.

- Low-velocity drip patterns can produce some tiny droplets that fly off the edges of the drop of blood on impact. Blood experts call these satellite droplets, and they are more likely when drips of blood fall from a height or if someone steps in a pool of blood and splashes it.

For proper interpretation, blood-spatter experts have to understand physics, the nature of blood, and the pathology of wounds.

- Medium-velocity spatter occurs when the moving blood is subjected to a force in addition to gravity—for instance, in cases of bludgeoning. Medium is typically defined as greater than 5 feet per second up to about 100 feet a second. When blood hits a surface at that rate, it will be broken up into smaller droplets, producing that fine pattern known as spatter.

- High-velocity patterns are usually said to result from blood traveling at speeds of greater than about 100 feet a second; this usually only occurs in gunshot wounds or where high-speed machines are involved. High-velocity bloodstains form tiny spatter patterns that are mistlike.

How Blood Leaves the Body

- When an artery is cut, blood will exit the body under greater pressure than when it flows from a vein. This is because blood pressure is much higher in arteries, and there are characteristic bloodstain patterns associated with arterial spurts. When a major artery like the carotid or femoral is cut, the rise and fall in blood pressure with the heart rate will cause an intermittent, arching, low-velocity pattern.

- When someone is forcefully coughing up blood after an injury to the face or chest—essentially choking on their own blood—the bloodstains will show a low-velocity spatter pattern, and sometimes investigators will see air bubbles in the droplets.

- How fresh a drop of blood is—especially as it is drying on a nonabsorbent surface—can sometimes be roughly approximated from skeletonization—the way the edges of a drop dry faster than the center.

- Castoff patterns are created by blood droplets being slung off of a moving bloody object, like a blunt-force weapon. The pattern is made in the opposite direction of the blows, when the perpetrator is making a backswing to strike again. The second and subsequent blows make the pattern, so when a cast-off pattern is clear, it can give investigators an idea of the minimum number of blows that were struck.

- The clothing of the killer can be analyzed for bloodstain patterns. This could include wipes, swipes, castoff, and sometimes back spatter from a gun. Sometimes the image of the weapon can even be transferred to clothing as if it were stamped in blood. A perpetrator can leave bloody footprints and fingerprints behind at a crime scene, too.

Fake Blood for Fun

You might want to make some of your own practice blood to repeat some of the experiments in this lecture yourself. I have tried quite a few fake blood recipes with my students, and some are better than others.

This recipe will not clot, but this is my preferred concoction because it has similar properties to fresh blood but it does not use anything too sticky or hard to clean up—although it will stain because it is made with (optional) food coloring.

- 500 ml powdered milk

- 325 ml water

- 1.5 oz. red food coloring

- 25 drops green food coloring

- 5 drops of blue food coloring

Slowly add the water to the powdered milk while stirring constantly until you get the right consistency, adjusting the water–to–powdered milk ratio as necessary. The mixture will keep for about a week or so, but the consistency might change over time.

Suggested Reading

Bevel and Gardner, *Bloodstain Pattern Analysis with an Introduction to Crime Scene Reconstruction.*

Englert, Passero, and Rule, *Blood Secrets.*

James, Kish, and Sutton, *Principles of Bloodstain Pattern Analysis.*

1. What kinds of information can be gained from examining the pattern of bloodstains at a crime scene?

2. Does the specific shape of a drop of blood have any meaning?

3. How do investigators document and collect patterns of blood spatter at a crime scene?

Blood Evidence—Stains and Spatters
Lecture 18—Transcript

Analyzing bloodstain patterns goes back well into human prehistory, when our ancient ancestors tracked wounded animals in much the same way that a hunter would today. Using bloodstain interpretation in forensic investigations first appears in the 19th century, in Germany and Poland. Professor Balthazard's presentation of experimental data in Paris, in 1939, impressed the forensic medicine crowd. And after a high-profile 1954 murder, bloodstain evidence was used in the controversial Dr. Sam Sheppard case, from my state of Ohio.

Sheppard was a neurosurgeon who lived in Cleveland with his wife and 7-year-old son. The night Mrs. Sheppard was beaten to death, in 1954, Dr. Sheppard claimed he was sleeping on a downstairs couch when he heard his wife screaming. He went to see what was going on and said he saw a "bushy haired man" who had apparently bludgeoned his wife, and then began attacking Dr. Sheppard.

Sheppard said he lost consciousness, but when he awoke, felt his wife's absent pulse, went to his son's room and saw he was unharmed, he then ran downstairs to see the intruder running across the backyard. A couple of neighbors also claimed to have seen this "bushy haired man," and Dr. Sheppard's medical bag with his watch and ring in it, were found in the weeds behind the house.

During interviews Dr. Sheppard's story was said to be stilted and changing. The few signs of an attempted robbery were suspicious to investigators, as was the fact that there was no forced entry, the couple's son didn't wake up during the crime, and the family dog did not even bark.

A full 35 blows were apparently struck to kill Mrs. Sheppard before Dr. Sheppard even got up to her room, which is definitely overkill for a burglary, and there were no signs of a struggle in the bedroom. Sheppard said a single blow to his head by the same man knocked him out. Bloodstains on

Sheppard's watch and pants were also suspicious, he couldn't produce the t-shirt he had been wearing, and he was charged with the crime.

The trial became a media event that some have compared to the O. J. Simpson trial, especially when the mysterious woman who had been referred to as Miss X took the stand and admitted to having had a 2-year affair with Dr. Sheppard. In late 1954, Dr. Sheppard was found guilty.

A month after Sheppard's verdict, forensic scientist Dr. Paul Kirk visited the crime scene and used bloodstain patterns to help show the position of the victim and assailant, along with alleging that the beautiful and pregnant Mrs. Sheppard was beaten to death by someone left-handed, and Dr. Sheppard was right-handed.

After spending nearly 10 years in prison, Sheppard won a retrial, which happened in 1966. Sheppard was found not guilty in the second trial with a young F. Lee Bailey as his defense attorney. Later, Sheppard actually had the nerve to pull a short stint as a professional wrestler who called himself "The Killer." Despite all its controversy, the Sheppard case was a major step in getting the legal system to accept bloodstain pattern evidence.

What I'll be presenting here is really the theoretical scientific underpinnings of bloodstain pattern analysis, which has been disputed by some to be highly variable and somewhat subjective, in practice—but that could be said for plenty of areas in forensic science.

Physics and chemistry do support bloodstain patterns analysis; that's certain. But, like other specialties, it has been criticized, especially lately, because some experts have been accused of extrapolating beyond what can be legitimately supported by science.

Bloodstain pattern analysis is part of crime-scene investigation that—like computer forensics, engineering, vehicle accident investigation, among others—is an attempt to reconstruct a sequence of events. Looking at a visible record of bloodshed—in terms of the shapes, locations, and distribution patterns—can give clues about the objects and forces that have generated the bloodstains.

Examples include areas where blood has been ejected, sprayed, dripped, walked through, or smeared by either the victim or perpetrator. Cases involving weapons, and the evidence they leave behind, can develop a sequence of violent events.

This is an area of forensics where extensive photo documentation is crucial, because it may be the only way to capture the patterned evidence at the scene. For proper interpretation, blood spatter experts have to understand physics, the nature of blood and the cardiovascular system that moves it around, as well as the pathology of wounds.

Scene examination and photo documentation can help these experts figure out the source where a bloodstain originated, help estimate distances from that origin to the surfaces blood hit, and even the speed and direction that blood traveled. Clues can lead to the positions of the victim and perpetrator during an assault, how many blows or shots were delivered—and in what order—using clotting and drying to estimate time since bloodshed.

Let's start by understanding blood as a substance, in terms of its physical properties and how it responds to gravity. It is definitely true that blood is thicker than water. The average amount in an adult body is 4 to 6 liters of blood, depending on body size, so we can say the average adult has roughly 5 liters. Our blood is usually around 8% of our body weight. Blood plasma is the liquid fraction that's mostly made of water, but also contains various ions, proteins, nutrients, and wastes. Red and white blood cells, and platelets— which are really cell fragments, not whole cells—are suspended in the liquid blood plasma.

We also need to briefly address blood clotting here, which is scientifically called coagulation. When blood vessels are damaged, the lining of the vessel walls exposes proteins that attract blood platelets. The platelets then change their nature and stick to each other, forming a plug that can help close up a small wound.

The damaged vessel walls and platelets also both release chemicals that act in domino-type reactions that ultimately form a polymer of insoluble protein strands, called fibrin, that further bridges the wound. When blood moves outside the body, and hits a surface, the coagulation mechanism can also take place by a slightly different pathway, but the result is the same—blood solidifies to some extent—first into a gel that, outside the body, can later dry and harden as the plasma component evaporates.

Inside the body, blood movement is governed by the work of the heart acting as a pump, combined with the pressures within blood vessels. But other forces act on blood when it's outside the body. And this movement will depend, to some degree, on whether the heart is still beating as an active pump in someone who is wounded, or the heart has stopped in a victim who has died.

As I said, blood plasma is mostly made of water, and we've all seen how water behaves—for example, we're familiar with how it flows, splashes, and forms droplets when smaller amounts break off from larger amounts. Water and blood plasma, like other liquids, have cohesive properties that hold their molecules together and make them flow; they also have surface tension— you know, that property that lets a water strider insect "walk" on water. But because blood is more viscous than water, its thickness alters all these properties, but only slightly. Viscosity relates to molecular attraction within a liquid, and causes it to resist flow or resist changing form.

Outside the body, blood can separate into smaller droplets when gravitational forces or impact forces are sufficient to break its surface tension and its viscosity. In combination, surface tension and viscosity will cause a drop of blood to form a sphere that minimizes its surface area.

The size of the drop that forms relates to the maximum speed it will achieve when it travels due to the resistance of air. Physicists call this terminal velocity. Once a drop of blood breaks away from a larger amount of blood and starts to travel, it won't fraction into smaller droplets unless or until it hits something or is acted on by another force.

When blood comes into contact with something, it produces a bloodstain or blood pattern—you can call it either. There are a couple of ways that major types of stains can be categorized based on their appearance. Some experts break bloodstains into 3 main groups: passive, spatter, and altered—and the term is spatter, not splatter, there is a difference. Spatter is when droplets of something are scattered on a surface. The result can be a splatter, but the tiny residual droplets themselves are called spatter.

Other experts prefer to focus on the speed of traveling blood, which also has to do with the patterns it produces, and classify stains as low velocity, medium velocity, and high velocity. Regardless, a major factor in how a stain will look is the type of surface that it hits. Blood will look and behave differently when it's on a smoothly painted wall, an upholstered piece of furniture, a leather car seat, rough concrete, carpeting, or even grass.

Now, let's go through each type: Passive bloodstains are the result of gravity, like when blood drips vertically onto a flat surface at a 90° angle. Another example is the blood flow that happens when a pool of blood surrounds a bleeding victim or when large droplets of blood run down a surface, like a wall or an angled driveway. Some types of transfer stains are also considered passive, like footprints in blood or when hands or fingers move blood from one surface to another—which is sometimes referred to as a swipe.

Spatter stains result from the application of some other force—not just gravity alone—that affects the movement of blood. Here, investigators will see features that show directionality and distribution. This would include impact spatter from blunt force trauma, which basically means a beating where a non-sharp object was the weapon. And we're not necessarily talking about bloodstains on the victim, here, but spatter from the incident on nearby surfaces. Gunshot wounds can also cause impact spatter on any surfaces that blood exiting the body hits.

As the name implies, altered stains have been changed in some way. Whether that's through natural clotting action, insect activity, or when blood mixes with some other material, like soil. For instance, fly activity where blood is exposed can complicate interpretation, because flies can ingest blood and regurgitate it.

They can also excrete tiny amounts of digested blood that could be confused with spatter. Altered stains also include blood evidence that's been modified when somebody's tried to clean up a crime scene to hide it, as we discussed earlier. This is different than the passive stains of handprints I mentioned a moment ago, because clean-up is deliberate, so it's called a wipe, rather than a swipe.

Other stain alterations are called voids, because they represent an area where an object blocked the spatter of blood, but then was picked up. Like if a piece of evidence or a weapon got hit with spatter and was then retrieved by the perpetrator, there would be a blank spot on the floor, or wherever that object had been.

Now, let's analyze some specific bloodstain geometry. You might want to make some of your own practice blood and play around with some of the following concepts we're about to cover. In my forensic science class, I've tried quite a few "blood recipes" I've found, to show these principles, and some are definitely better than others.

Hollywood blood just has to look real—it doesn't have to have realistic properties—so a lot of the stuff you find online is after the appearance of blood, not its properties. This recipe won't clot, of course; but here's my preferred concoction that doesn't use anything too sticky or hard to clean up—although it will stain since it's made with food coloring, so be careful there.

You need about 500 milliliters—which is the same as 500 cc's—of powdered milk, and then you'll have to add slowly to that, while stirring, about 325 or so milliliters of water. Keep stirring until you get the right consistency. If it gets too thin, sprinkle in a little more powdered milk, and if it seems too thick, add a little more water. You can actually use it like this, if you just want to get the consistency of blood to play around with, but if you want the right color, add 1 1/2 ounces of red food coloring, about 25 drops of green food coloring, and about 5 drops of blue. The mess will keep for about a week or so, but the consistency might change over time.

On with our analysis. Keep in mind that all of this geometry stuff is dependent on the surface of impact, as I mentioned before—so for the sake of simplicity, we're going to assume a flat surface for our discussion. All of these pattern generalities relate to standard physics principles that govern the behavior of fluids in motion, under the influence of gravity.

First, any circular distortion of a stain helps reveal the angle of impact on a flat surface. If there's a right angle between the blood source and the surface there's a nearly perfectly circular stain—equal in width and length. So, you might try dripping a drop of your fake blood straight down onto a large sheet of cardboard and see if the spot doesn't pretty round. You can use an eyedropper, or just make a drop fall from the end of a spoon or a popsicle stick.

The next analytical principle is that the stain gets more elongated as the angle of impact decreases. So, if blood is flying toward a surface at a low angle, the resulting stain will be very oblong. If you're experimenting with me, you can put some of the fake blood into a spray bottle, but I am not claiming responsibility for the mess that will make!

Each year I have to get some cookies or something for our housekeeping guy the day we do our bloodstain lab, and we even use those huge rolls of brown paper to cover the floors. This is a real mess. Anyway, you can't drop blood easily at an angle without flinging it all over, so you could try to cheat the angle by slanting the paper you're dropping it the fake blood down on down a little bit, and it makes sense it will be oblong, rather than circular.

Now when blood flies onto a surface at an angle, the oblong shape it creates tells investigators about the direction the blood was traveling in. The more pointed end of the elongated droplet faces the direction of travel. The linear tip of the oblong stain may even be fractured. That's because tiny blobs of blood break off from the surface of the parent stain, once it hits, and they continue to travel even further, drawing out the shape of the stain and leaving some tiny droplets at its farthest extent. In a sense, the blood is kind of skidding when it hits the surface, as it meets the resistance of whatever it hits.

But, surface texture is also a factor here. The harder and less porous the surface, the less tiny spatter droplets will result. Rough, textured surfaces show what are called spines extending from their spatter droplets and can also show what's called peripheral spatter that will complicate figuring out directionality.

Another thing that investigators can figure out from blood spatter analysis is the point of origin, if they have a group of related bloodstains in a spatter pattern. Similarly to what we talked about of fires, the point of origin is the location from where the blood spatter pattern emanated—meaning its height and distance from the spatter pattern, not necessarily the origin in terms of the person or the weapon used. To do this, bloodstain analysts need to first figure out directionality, using the stuff I mentioned about the elongated tips and little cast-off drops.

Once they figure out the direction the spatter came from, they can take a half dozen or so really diagnostic elongated droplets—the ones that really show good features—and use something long, and straight, like a meter stick or yard —and place it lengthwise through the longitudinal center of each of their best oblong droplets, and then they need to trace all those droplets, one at a time, back to the point where their lines converge. I have my students literally run a pencil along the meter stick and draw a line from the center each of their best droplets to the place where all lines they draw ultimately meet. The result is a bunch of rays that all intersect at a common point that was the direction of origin.

That's the horizontal point of origin the flat plane where the spatter is, but what about height? Well, to get that, we use trigonometry principles of triangulation. Investigators—or my students—measure the length of those most diagnostic elongated blood droplets, and then use geometry of angles, they can then estimate the height above the surface where the blood drops were flying from. Sometimes on TV you see this done with strings, and they call it "stringing the crime scene." These days, lasers and computerized software can do the necessary calculations, but I'm sure stringing is still pretty impressive to a jury.

Remember I mentioned that some experts prefer to categorize bloodstains by the speed with which they are produced? Low velocity, medium velocity, or high velocity are pretty gross generalizations about traveling blood, but here's the gist of it.

A low velocity bloodstain pattern would be produced if a bleeding victim is standing still or walking away, and then some blood drips to the floor. These low velocity patterns are said to produce the greatest variety of shapes and sizes compared to medium or high velocity stains, but low velocity bloodstains are usually larger in size than either of the other categories. In low velocity patterns, gravity is the only force that has to be considered, and there really isn't any spattering.

That's not to say that low velocity drip patterns can't produce some tiny droplets that fly off the edges of the drop of blood when it hits. You've probably seen some slow motion photography of a drop of milk hitting a bowl of milk, and then that little crown of droplets rise up—blood experts call these satellite droplets. Satellites particularly happen when drips of blood fall from a height or if someone steps in a pool of blood and splashes it.

If you're experimenting, you can try dripping your fake blood from different heights. Get some cardboard and then a meter or yard stick, then make a drip from a height of about 20 centimeters, which is about 8 inches, then move to a fresh spot on the paper and drip from 35 centimeters which is about 14 inches, then use 50 centimeters, and keep increasing your distance at regular 15 centimeter or 6-inch intervals until you reach a meter or even a meter and a half. Then compare the appearance of the drips from the different heights to see if you don't see satellites on your higher drops. It's also interesting to try dripping the fake blood on different materials to see what happens— like a couple different types of cloth, a paper towel, a brick, and other types of surfaces.

Medium velocity spatter travel would happen, for instance, if a person was bludgeoned with something like a baseball bat. Medium spatter occurs when the moving blood is subjected to a force in addition to gravity. "Medium" is typically defined as greater than 5 feet a second to up to about 100 feet a second. When blood hits a surface at that rate, it will be broken up into smaller droplets, producing that fine pattern that I call spatter.

High velocity patterns are usually said to result from blood traveling at speeds of greater than about 100 feet a second; this usually only occurs in gunshot wounds or where high-speed machines are involved—like if someone gets caught in a propeller, an industrial fan, or something awful like that. The result of high velocity blood flow is tiny spatter patterns that are almost like a blood mist.

Now, here are a couple of variations on the theme of blood leaving the body. When an artery is cut, blood will exit the body under greater pressure than when it flows from a vein. This is because there's much higher blood pressure in arteries, due to the work of the heart. It's pretty dramatic, if you've ever seen it. My son once cut his ankle deep enough to hit an artery, and it's pretty sickening to see someone's blood jetting out somebody's wound in time with his heartbeat, especially when it's your own teenager!

In the emergency room, my son was snickering at me, because I was feeling almost faint. He told the ER doc that I was a forensic scientist and taught gross anatomy for a living, and there I was cowering in the corner. My reply was, "Wait until you have kids of your own." Then I looked at the ER doc and I told her, "All my patients are already dead, I don't know how you stand this." The 2 of them laughed, while my son was stitched up.

Anyway, back to forensic science and arterial blood: There are characteristic bloodstain patterns associated with arterial spurts. When a major artery like the carotid in the neck or the femoral in the thigh or groin is cut, the rise and fall in blood pressure with the heart rate will create an intermittent, arching, low velocity pattern that is pretty diagnostic.

I've seen it on a wall, and it looks like up and down waves of droplets reflecting the higher pressure when the heart is pushing blood into circulation on the up arches, and the lower pressure between heart beats on the low parts of the wave. Of course, that pattern is going to only be produced for so long before the victim loses consciousness if a major artery has been cut.

Here's another pattern: When someone is forcefully coughing up blood after an injury to the face or chest—and they're essentially literally choking on their own blood—the bloodstains will show a low velocity spatter pattern, but sometimes investigators will see air bubbles in those droplets. Even after the blood dries, the signs of bubbles that were in the drops can usually still be seen.

Also, how fresh a drop of blood is—especially as it's drying on a nonabsorbent surface—can sometimes be roughly approximated, at least in comparison to other drops, from what's called skeletonization. And you know I love anything that has a name like that! You have probably seen the skeletonization of a drop if you've ever had something like gravy or milk drip on your counter. When you just wipe over it the first time, you will easily pick up the wettest center of the drop, but the drier edges will be a circular skeleton that's left behind until you really scrub on it.

Another interesting, but awful, crime-scene phenomenon is known as a castoff pattern. These signs represent blood droplets that are being slung off of a moving bloody object, like a weapon. The pattern is actually made in the opposite direction of the intended blows of the weapon. The pattern happens when the perpetrator is making a backswing to strike again. Castoff patterns are seen many times in blunt trauma cases, like when a baseball bat, a crowbar, or even a fist is repeatedly used to bludgeon someone.

The first impact doesn't cause castoff staining from the weapon—it can't, because the weapon hasn't drawn blood yet. It's the second and subsequent blows that make the pattern. The weapon has to get blood on it before additional swings of the bat or the fist fling off blood.

Basically, the first blow breaks the skin, the second blow picks up some blood, and then when the assailant swings back to develop the force of the next hit, blood will fly off of the weapon and onto the ceiling above or the wall behind. More castoff is produced in the backswing than the forward swing in these kinds of assaults. When a castoff pattern is really clear, it looks like a series of linear drop patterns, and can give investigators an idea of the minimum number of blows that were struck.

You might ask what difference does that make in an assault, but the difference can be great. In one of my cases, I was asked to assess some pretty serious fresh skull trauma in a case that I still call Cain and Abel, because one teenage brother killed another, right in the family room of their home.

This was a really disturbing case. The skull was pretty much pulverized; there was hardly anything left of the brain at all, and the investigators were asking me if I thought that amount of damage could be done with a single blow. And I said there was no way that I could envision.

Well, besides the physical damage to the skull, I saw the crime-scene photos, too, and there was cast off in several directions around the room, including the ceiling and the walls. That kind of bloodstain pattern speaks to the horrendous nature of a crime like that.

There's no way the killer could say that he and his brother were arguing and he got so mad he hit him once in the head with a baseball bat. The bloodstain pattern analysis not only pointed to repeated blows, but also showed that the victim was probably asleep on the couch when his brother came up from behind and murdered him with a baseball bat. It was a horrific crime that I will never forget.

Also, keep in mind that the clothing of the killer can also be analyzed for bloodstain patterns. This could include wipes, swipes, castoff, and sometimes back spatter on the shooter of a gun. Sometimes the image of the weapon can even be transferred to clothing as if it were stamped in blood. And don't forget that a perpetrator can leave bloody footprints and fingerprints behind at a crime scene, too.

Let me end this lecture with a story of a lighter note from a world-renowned bloodstain pattern expert who is a personal friend of mine, Paulette Sutton. Paulette has a wonderful series of photographs that illustrate how these principles can be used to analyze non-blood cases, too. This was a case where a guy stole several large industrial-type containers of paint—from of all places, a church that was being renovated. He put the containers into the bed of his pickup truck, and then he left the scene.

What he didn't realize was that one of the drums of paint had a hole in it and was leaking. Once the church leader reported the theft, the investigators were able to literally follow the path of droplets all the way from the church to his pickup truck; the paint was like a trail of breadcrumbs.

Paulette has images of the drop pattern as the guy approached and stopped at a traffic light, turned the corner, stopped to visit his girlfriend for a while—still not realizing there was now a puddle of paint behind his truck—and then drove on to his house where his truck was ultimately parked until police knocked on the door to arrest him. Now, Paulette's from the deep South, and I love to hear her say in her great Southern accent, "Sometimes forensic science is nothing much more than stupid detection."

Bibliography

Alison, Lawrence. *Forensic Psychologist's Casebook: Psychological Profiling and Criminal Investigation*. London, England: Willan Publishing, 2005. A case-based book about profiling and forensic investigation.

Almirall, Jose R., and Kenneth G. Furton. *Analysis and Interpretation of Fire Scene Evidence*. Boca Raton, FL: CRC Press, 2004. Advanced reference for arson investigators.

"Arson." Department of Justice, Federal Bureau of Investigation, Criminal Justice Information Services Division. Accessed 14 September, 2011. http://www2.fbi.gov/ucr/cius2009/offenses/property_crime/arson.html. Statistics and information on arson in the United States with links to statistics for other crimes.

Bass, William, and Jon Jefferson. *Death's Acre: Inside the Legendary Forensic Lab the Body Farm Where the Dead Do Tell Tales*. New York: Berkley Books, 2003. A case-based approach to forensic anthropology written by one of the world's most widely known forensic anthropologists, Dr. Bill Bass.

Bevel, Tom, and Ross M. Gardner. *Bloodstain Pattern Analysis with an Introduction to Crime Scene Reconstruction*. 3rd ed. Boca Raton, FL: CRC Press, 2008. An advanced but comprehensive reference book for bloodstain analysts.

Black, Sue, G. Sunderland, L. Hackman, and X. Mallett, eds. *Disaster Victim Identification: Experience and Practice (Global Perspectives of Disaster Victim Identification)*. Boca Raton, Florida: CRC Press, Taylor & Francis Group, 2011. Covers all facets of the use of forensic science in human identification—with particular emphasis on mass disasters—using a case-based approach.

Bodziak, William J. *Footwear Impression Evidence: Detection, Recovery, and Examination.* 2nd ed. Boca Raton, FL: CRC Press, 1999. Detailed overview of footwear impression evidence, including case studies.

———. *Tire Tread and Tire Track Evidence: Recovery and Forensic Examination.* 2nd ed. Boca Raton, FL: CRC Press, 2008. Detailed overview of tire evidence.

Bowers, C. Michael, ed. *Forensic Dental Evidence: An Investigator's Handbook.* 2nd ed. Waltham, MA: Academic Press/Elsevier, 2004. Color-illustrated comprehensive look at the science of forensic odontology.

Brenner, John C. *Forensic Science: An Illustrated Dictionary.* Boca Raton, FL: CRC Press, 2003. Includes the basic terminology of forensics with images and brief explanations.

Burke, Michael P. *Forensic Medical Investigation of Motor Vehicle Incidents.* Boca Raton, FL: CRC Press, 2006. A comprehensive reference on all facets of vehicular accidents—from causes and vehicle technology to injuries, including some graphic illustrations.

Butler, John M. *Advanced Topics in Forensic DNA Typing: Methodology.* Waltham, MA: Academic Press/Elsevier, 2011. Very advanced, but good depth for those with some background in DNA and genetics.

———. *Fundamentals of Forensic DNA Typing.* Waltham, MA: Academic Press/Elsevier, 2009. A good overview of forensic DNA analysis from the scene to the lab, including cases and history.

Caddy, Brian, ed. *Forensic Examination of Glass and Paint: Analysis and Interpretation.* Boca Raton, FL: CRC Press, 2001. An advanced book—for those with a background in chemistry and materials analysis.

Carper, Kenneth L. *Forensic Engineering.* 2nd ed. Boca Raton, FL: CRC Press, 2000. An advanced book—for those with an engineering background. Covers fires, structural failures, and relationships to the legal system.

Carrier, Brian. *File System Forensic Analysis*. Upper Saddle River, NJ: Addison-Wesley Professional, an imprint of Pearson, 2005. An advanced book—for someone with a detailed knowledge of computers and operating systems.

Casey, Eoghan. *Digital Evidence and Computer Crime*. 3rd ed. Waltham, MA: Academic Press/Elsevier, 2011. A textbook that introduces the topic of computer forensics.

Cole, M. D., and B. Caddy. *The Analysis of Drugs of Abuse: An Instruction Manual*. Boca Raton, FL: CRC Press, 1994. A bit dated, but a good textbook that covers all aspects of the forensic analysis of abused drugs, including types and technologies—for those with some chemistry background.

Craig, Emily A. *Teasing Secrets from the Dead: My Investigations at America's Most Infamous Crime Scenes*. New York: Three Rivers Press/ Random House, 2005. Forensic anthropology at Waco, Texas (David Koresh cult), the Oklahoma City bombing, and September 11, 2001.

Delatte, Norbert J. *Beyond Failure: Forensic Case Studies for Civil Engineers*. Reston, VA: American Society of Civil Engineers, 2008. A completely case-based look at structural and mechanical failures, including many familiar examples from around the world.

DeNevi, Don, John H. Campbell, Stephen Band, and John E. Otto. *Into the Minds of Madmen: How the FBI's Behavioral Science Unit Revolutionized Crime Investigation*. Amherst, NY: Prometheus Books, 2003. Covers the history and development of profiling.

Douglas, John, and Mark Olshaker. *The Anatomy of Motive*. New York: Simon and Schuster, 1999. Forensic-psychology and profiling stories and history from the FBI's John Douglas.

Eckert, William G., ed. *Introduction to Forensic Sciences*. 2nd ed. Boca Raton, FL: CRC Press, 1996. Was a standard textbook for many years. Contains history and a range of chapters by experts in the field with black-and-white illustrations.

Eisen, Mitchell L., Jodi A. Quas, and Gail S. Goodman. *Memory and Suggestibility in the Forensic Interview*. Oxford, UK: Routledge, 2001. Looks at interview techniques with an emphasis on psychology.

Eliopulos, Louis N. *Death Investigator's Handbook, Vol. 1: Crime Scenes*. Boulder, CO: Paladin Press, 2006. A pretty comprehensive book that covers crime-scene analysis for many different settings where bodies could be found.

————. *Death Investigator's Handbook, Vol. 3: Scientific Investigations*. Boulder, CO: Paladin Press, 2006. Covers numerous disciplines—including odontology, anthropology, toxicology, serology, and firearms—highlighting the many ancillary forensic science analyses that intersect with the work of a death investigator.

Ellen, David. *Scientific Examination of Documents: Methods and Techniques*. 3rd ed. Boca Raton, FL: CRC Press, 2005. An advanced and comprehensive look at the analysis of questioned documents.

Englert, Rod, Kathy Passero, and Ann Rule. *Blood Secrets: Chronicles of a Crime Scene Reconstructionist*. New York: Thomas Dunne Books, 2010. A case-based book that covers a variety of investigations through the autobiographical accounts of investigator and bloodstain expert Rod Englert.

Esherick, Joan. *Criminal Psychology and Personality Profiling*. Broomall, PA: Mason Crest Publishers, 2005. Geared toward young adult readers. Covers only the basics.

Evans, Colin. *The Casebook of Forensic Detection: How Science Solved 100 of the World's Most Baffling Crimes*. New York: Berkley Trade/Penguin Books, 2007. A very basic book that does not provide in-depth coverage but is suitable for young readers and those wanting an introduction to some of these notorious crimes.

Ewing, Charles Patrick. *Minds on Trial: Great Cases in Law and Psychology*. New York: Oxford University Press, 2006. A case-based look at 20 high-profile courtroom dramas from the second half of the 20th century that involve forensic psychology.

Feder, Harold A., and Max M. Houck. *Feder's Succeeding as an Expert Witness.* 4th ed. Boca Raton, FL: CRC Press, 2008. A comprehensive overview of expert testimony in forensic science.

Fisher, Barry A. J. *Techniques of Crime Scene Investigation.* 7th ed. Boca Raton, FL: CRC Press, 2003. Information on many types of evidence as well as techniques for collecting the evidence.

Fisher, Barry A. J., William J. Tilstone, and Catherine Woytowicz. *Introduction to Criminialistics: The Foundation of Forensic Science.* New York: Academic Press/Elsevier, 2009. A general reference textbook that is illustrated with color images but is not as comprehensive as others. It is mainly focused on standard lab analyses and does not include all specialties.

Gaensslen, R. E. *Sourcebook in Forensic Serology, Immunology, and Biochemistry.* Ann Arbor, MI: University of Michigan Library, 1983. Somewhat dated, so it doesn't include the latest technology, but it gives a good and clear introduction to the basics of serology in forensic science.

Garret, Brandon. *Convicting the Innocent: Where Criminal Prosecutions Go Wrong.* Cambridge, MA: Harvard University Press, 2011. An in-depth look at why wrongful convictions happen and what can be done to prevent them in the future.

Gennard, Dorothy E. *Forensic Entomology: An Introduction.* Hoboken, NJ: Wiley, 2007. An introductory textbook on forensic entomology that is suitable for any adult reader.

George, Robert M. *Facial Geometry: Graphic Facial Analysis for Forensic Artists.* Springfield, IL: Charles C. Thomas Publisher, Ltd., 2007. An advanced reference guide for forensic artists.

Gibson, Lois. *Forensic Art Essentials: A Manual for Law Enforcement Artists.* Burlingtonm, MA: Academic Press/Elsevier, 2007. An overview of forensic artistry.

Goff, M. Lee. *A Fly for the Prosecution: How Insect Evidence Helps Solve Crimes.* Cambridge, MA: Harvard University Press, 2001. A case-based book about forensic entomology that is written by one of the best in the field.

Guiberson, Brenda Z. *Disasters: Natural and Man-Made Catastrophes through the Centuries.* New York: Henry Holt & Co., 2010. A coverage of historical disasters that is geared toward younger readers.

Gunn, Alan. *Essential Forensic Biology.* Hoboken, NJ: Wiley, 2006. A comprehensive guide to many uses of biological materials in forensics, including protists, plants, and animals.

Haglund, William D., and Marcella Harnish Sorg, eds. *Advances in Forensic Taphonomy: Method, Theory, and Archaeological Perspectives.* Boca Raton, FL: CRC Press, 2001. Case-based examination of many facets of forensic anthropology including decomposition, water environments, and mass graves.

———. *Forensic Taphonomy: The Postmortem Fate of Human Remains.* Boca Raton, FL: CRC Press, 1997. A case-based examination of decomposition and environmental influences on human remains.

Hanzlick, Randy. *Death Investigation: Systems and Procedures.* Boca Raton, FL: CRC Press, 2007. An inexpensive reference that describes the different systems of death investigation in the United States, the roles of different experts involved, and autopsy procedures.

Harrendorf, Stefan, Markku Heiskanen, and Steven Malby, eds. "International Statistics on Justice and Crime." Helsinki, Finland: European Institute for Crime Prevention and Control (HEUNI), in association with the United Nations Office on Drugs and Crime (UNODC), 2010. A summary and analysis of crime trends for countries and regions around the world—including information on whether country-to-country comparisons are reasonable—covering the areas of homicide; drug-related crime; complex crimes, including organized crime; and statistics for criminal justice systems, including trends in prison populations.

Hayes, William, and the editors of *Popular Mechanics. What Went Wrong: Investigating the Worst Man-Made and Natural Disasters.* New York: Hearst, 2011. Covers the major world disasters from the past 100 years, including natural phenomena and transportation accidents.

Heard, Brian J. *Handbook of Firearms and Ballistics: Examining and Interpreting Forensic Evidence.* 2nd ed. Hoboken, NJ: Wiley, 2008. An advanced and case-based approach to ballistics analysis.

Houck, Max M., and Jay A. Siegel. *Fundamentals of Forensic Science.* 2nd ed. Burlington, MA: Academic Press/Elsevier, 2010. A comprehensive, detailed, and illustrated textbook that covers all the major specialties and uses cases to clarify.

Hunter, William. *DNA Analysis.* Broomall, PA: Mason Crest Publishers, 2005. A good introductory overview of forensic DNA analysis that is geared toward young readers but is suitable for anyone interested in the basics.

Huss, Matthew T. *Forensic Psychology.* Hoboken, NJ: Wiley, 2008. A good general textbook about the field of forensic psychology.

Iserson, Kenneth V. *Death to Dust: What Happens to Dead Bodies?* Tucson, AZ: Galen Press, 1994. A comprehensive look at cultural and scientific aspects of death.

James, Stuart H., and Jon J. Nordby. *Forensic Science: An Introduction to Scientific and Investigative Techniques.* 3rd ed. Boca Raton, FL: CRC Press, 2009. A very detailed and comprehensive textbook with many color illustrations (some quite graphic). Chapters are written by experts in the fields.

James, Stuart H., Paul E. Kish, and T. Paulette Sutton. *Principles of Bloodstain Pattern Analysis: Theory and Practice.* Boca Raton, FL: CRC

Press, 2005. An advanced and comprehensive case-based reference for bloodstain analysts that includes connections to other forensic sciences.

Kranacher, Mary-Jo, Richard Riley, and Joseph T. Wells. *Forensic Accounting and Fraud Examination.* Hoboken, NJ: Wiley, 2010. A fairly advanced book that is geared toward those with a background in accounting who want to learn more about how fraud examinations are carried out.

Kurland, Michael. *How to Solve a Murder: The Forensic Handbook.* New York: MacMillan, 1995. Not written by an expert, but it is a fun and easy read that focuses on the types of criminal and forensic sciences used to analyze homicides using cases and black-and-white line art.

Largo, Michael. *Final Exits: The Illustrated Encyclopedia of How We Die.* New York: HarperCollins, 2006. A somewhat irreverent look at causes of death through the ages.

Lentini, John J. *Scientific Protocols for Fire Investigation.* Boca Raton, FL: CRC Press, 2006. An advanced look at the science, history, and theory of fire scene analysis.

Li, Richard. *Forensic Biology: Identification and DNA Analysis of Biological Evidence.* Boca Raton, FL: CRC Press, 2008. Covers all aspects of serology by providing information on a variety of body fluids and how they are analyzed in forensic laboratories, including a lot of detail about DNA analysis from body fluids and tissues.

Libal, Angela. *Fingerprints, Bite Marks, Ear Prints: Human Signposts.* Broomall, PA: Mason Crest Publishers, 2005. A young-adult read about several types of forensic evidence.

Loftus, Elizabeth F. *Eyewitness Testimony.* Cambridge, MA: Harvard University Press, 1996. Written by one of the world's leading experts on the fallibility of memory.

Lyle, D. P. *Forensics for Dummies*. Hoboken, NJ: Wiley Publishing, Inc., 2004. Not written by a forensic scientist, but it is a fun and easy read with limited black-and-white line art that is suitable for young readers or adults.

Maples, William R., and Michael Browning. *Dead Men Do Tell Tales: The Strange and Fascinating Cases of a Forensic Anthropologist*. New York: Broadway Books, 1995. A case-based book about the work of Dr. Bill Maples.

Marshall, Maurice, and Jimmie C. Oxley. *Aspects of Explosives Detection*. Waltham, MA: Elsevier Science, 2008. An advanced but comprehensive look at the many types of explosives and how experts attempt to detect them, including the use of dogs and high-tech advances.

Meyers, Charles. *Silent Evidence: Firearms (Forensic Ballistics) and Toolmarks*. Boone, NC: Parkway Publishers, 2004. A book that provides case-based coverage of firearms and toolmark analyses.

Molina, D. K. *Handbook of Forensic Toxicology for Medical Examiners*. Boca Raton, FL: CRC Press, 2009. A very advanced book—for those with a pharmacology or medical background.

Murray, Elizabeth. *Death: Corpses, Cadavers, and Other Grave Matters*. Minneapolis, MN: Lerner Publishers, 2010. Offers background information on the science of death and is geared toward young readers but is suitable for anyone with an interest in the topic.

―――. *Forensic Identification: Putting a Name and Face on Death*. Minneapolis, MN: Lerner Publishers, forthcoming. Touches on several topics—including fingerprints, anthropology, odontology, serology, and DNA—all geared toward identification. Suitable for young audiences but appropriate for all beginners in the topic.

Napier, Michael R. *Behavior, Truth, and Deception: Applying Profiling and Analysis to the Interview Process*. Boca Raton, FL: CRC Press, 2010. A fairly advanced but comprehensive look at the psychological interview.

Navarro, Joe. *Hunting Terrorists: A Look at the Psychopathology of Terror.* Springfield, IL: Charles C. Thomas Publishers, Ltd., 2005. A book that puts specific emphasis on the theories behind terrorism and how intelligence can be used to seek out terrorists.

Nelson, Bill, Amelia Phillips, and Christopher Steuart. *Guide to Computer Forensics and Investigations.* Boston, MA: Course Technology Books, 2009. An advanced reference that covers many aspects of computers and how investigators analyze computer crimes.

Noon, Randall K. *Engineering Analysis of Fires and Explosions.* Boca Raton, FL: CRC Press, 1995. An advanced and comprehensive look at the forensics of both fires and explosions, including case studies.

———. *Forensic Engineering Investigation.* Boca Raton, FL: CRC Press, 2000. Includes investigations of fires, explosions, vehicle accidents, and more.

———. *Introduction to Forensic Engineering.* Boca Raton, FL: CRC Press, 1992. Covers many applications of engineering in forensic science, including basic and common events such as hail damage, electrical circuitry issues, frozen pipes, and slip-and-fall accidents. Contains lots of information about vehicle accidents and includes equations and examples.

Nuland, Sherwin B. *How We Die: Reflections on Life's Final Chapter.* New York: Vintage Books/Random House, 1993. A scientific, practical, and thorough examination of death and some of its causes.

Osterburg, James W., and Richard H. Ward. *Criminal Investigation: A Method for Reconstructing the Past.* 6th ed. New Providence, NJ: Matthew Bender and Company, 2010. A textbook that is largely aimed at law enforcement and includes comprehensive coverage of how numerous types of crimes are investigated from crime scene to courtroom using both behavioral and physical sciences. Contains limited black-and-white images (some graphic).

Peterson, Julie K. *Understanding Surveillance Technologies: Spy Devices, Privacy, History, & Applications.* 2nd ed. Oxford, UK: Auerbach Publications, an imprint of Taylor & Francis, 2007. An advanced textbook for those with an interest in much greater depth on surveillance devices and related topics.

Petherick, Wayne A., Brent E. Turvey, and Claire E. Ferguson, eds. *Forensic Criminology.* Burlington, MA: Academic Press/Elsevier, 2010. A comprehensive textbook with very limited black-and-white images that is focused on criminalistics and legal issues, including historical contexts.

Prahlow, Joseph. *Forensic Pathology for Police, Death Investigators, Attorneys, and Forensic Scientists.* New York: Humana Press, 2010. An easy-to-understand overview of death investigation, autopsy, postmortem interval, human identification, and many related topics.

Rainis, Kenneth G. *Hair, Clothing, and Tire Track Evidence: Crime-Solving Science Experiments.* Berkeley Heights, NJ: Enslow Publishers, 2006. Uses experiments to teach limited aspects of forensic science and is geared toward young readers.

Ratay, Robert. *Forensic Structural Engineering Handbook.* New York: McGraw-Hill Professional, 2009. An advanced reference—for those with an engineering background.

Redsicker, David R. *The Practical Methodology of Forensic Photography.* 2nd ed. Boca Raton, FL: CRC Press, 2000. A comprehensive textbook covering information about all facets of forensic photography.

Ribowsky, Shiya. *Dead Center: Behind the Scenes at the World's Largest Medical Examiner's Office.* New York: HarperCollins, 2006. Stories from the 15-year career of a death investigator in the New York City Medical Examiner's Office, including during September 11, 2001.

Robertson, James R. *Forensic Examination of Hair.* Boca Raton, FL: CRC Press, 1999. Provides information about DNA analysis and drug testing on hair as well as general principles of forensic hair analysis.

Robinson, Edward M. *Crime Scene Photography*. 2nd ed. Burlington, MA: Academic Press/Elsevier, 2010. A textbook that covers many aspects of crime scene documentation using photography.

Rogers, Richard. *Clinical Assessment of Malingering and Deception*. 3rd ed. New York: The Guilford Press, 2008. An advanced reference for those with a strong background or interest in psychology.

Saferstein, Richard. *Criminalistics: An Introduction to Forensic Science*. 10th ed. Saddle River, NJ: Pearson Prentice Hall, 2010. A basic introductory textbook that does not include all specialties but has good explanations of the bases of chemical, microscopic, and physical analyses—including some case profiles and illustrations.

Scammell, Henry, and Douglas Ubelaker. *Bones: A Forensic Detective's Casebook*. New York: M. Evans and Co., 2000. A case-based book about some of the most noteworthy cases of the Smithsonian's Dr. Doug Ubelaker.

Seaman Kelly, Jan, and Brian S. Lindblom. *Scientific Examination of Questioned Documents*. 2nd ed. Boca Raton, FL: CRC Press, 2006. An advanced but comprehensive reference on all facets of document examination.

Senn, David R., and Paul G. Stimson. *Forensic Dentistry*. 2nd ed. Boca Raton, FL: CRC Press, 2010. A detailed overview of forensic odontology.

Shaw, Mark, Jan van Dijk, and Wolfgang Rhomberg. "Determining Trends in Global Crime and Justice: An Overview of Results from the United Nations Surveys of Crime Trends and Operations of Criminal Justice Systems." *Forum on Crime and Society* 3, nos. 1 and 2, December 2003. A good explanation of the difficulties that can be encountered when comparing different countries' crime statistics. Includes data up to the year 2000 for total crime and specific crimes, such as homicides and robbery.

Shelton, David. *Forensic Science in Court: Challenges in the Twenty-First Century*. Lanham, MD: Rowman & Littlefield, 2010. A comprehensive look at the legal issues surrounding forensic-science and expert-witness issues in court.

Siegel, Jay A., and Kathy Mirakovits. *Forensic Science: The Basics.* 2nd ed. Boca Raton, FL: CRC Press, 2010. A comprehensive and color-illustrated textbook that is suitable for beginners. Covers all major forensic specialties— except the behavioral sciences—and uses cases to clarify. The textbook used in Professor Murray's forensic science course.

Slyter, Steven A. *Forensic Signature Examination.* Springfield, IL: Charles C. Thomas Publisher, Ltd., 1996. An inexpensive textbook that covers handwriting analysis—but not all facets of document examination.

Snyder Sachs, Jessica. *Corpse: Nature, Forensics, and the Struggle to Pinpoint Time of Death.* New York: Basic Books/Perseus Publishing, 2001. Not written by a forensic scientist, but it is an interesting and inexpensive read on a variety of topics related to death and forensic investigation of the dead.

Stauffer, Eric, Julia A. Dolan, and Reta Newman. *Fire Debris Analysis.* Waltham, MA: Academic Press/Elsevier, 2007. A very advanced reference that includes the history of analyses.

Steadman, Dawnie W. *Hard Evidence: Case Studies in Forensic Anthropology.* 2nd ed. Saddle River, NJ: Prentice Hall, 2009. A case-based textbook that illustrates the uses of forensic anthropology.

Tapper, Colin. "Criminal Law Revision Committee 11th Report: Character Evidence." *The Modern Law Review* 36, no. 1 (January 1973): 56–64. Summary of Committee findings on the difficulties of including or excluding eyewitness evidence, particularly in regard to the character of the accused.

Taupin, Jane Moira, and Chesterene Cwiklik. *Scientific Protocols for Forensic Examination of Clothing.* Boca Raton, FL: CRC Press, 2010. This not only covers clothing, but due to its comprehensive nature, also includes information about serology, bloodstain patterns, DNA, soil evidence, protists, plants, and animals as related to the analysis of clothing.

Taylor, Karen T. *Forensic Art and Illustration.* Boca Raton, FL: CRC Press, 2001. A very comprehensive overview of all facets of forensic art.

Thompson, Tim, and Sue Black, eds. *Forensic Human Identification: An Introduction.* Boca Raton, FL: CRC Press, Taylor & Francis Group, 2007. A thorough discussion of all facets of human identification as used in forensic settings and mass disasters.

Tibbett, Mark, and David O. Carter. *Soil Analysis in Forensic Taphonomy: Chemical and Biological Effects of Buried Human Remains.* Boca Raton, FL: CRC Press, 2008. Includes information about decomposition and the effects of burial on the body.

Trestrail, John Harris. *Criminal Poisoning: Investigation Guide for Law Enforcement, Toxicologists, Forensic Scientists, and Attorneys.* New York: Humana Press, 2007. Covers many facets, including the history of poisons, types, and psychology of poisoners.

United Nations Office on Drugs and Crime. "United Nations Surveys on Crime Trends and the Operations of Criminal Justice Systems (CTS)." http://www.unodc.org/unodc/en/data-and-analysis/United-Nations-Surveys-on-Crime-Trends-and-the-Operations-of-Criminal-Justice-Systems.html. Provides crime statistics from around the world—both by country and by region. New surveys are completed every few years.

Walton, Richard H. *Cold Case Homicides: Practical Investigative Techniques.* Boca Raton, FL: CRC Press, 2006. A case-based textbook that covers many intersections between forensic science and the investigation of old homicide cases. A very comprehensive book with good detail that is illustrated in black and white with some color plates.

White, Tim D., and Pieter A. Folkens. *The Human Bone Manual.* Burlington, MA: Academic Press/Elsevier, 2005. A comprehensive guide to the human skeleton, including concepts at the foundation of forensic anthropology.

Why the Towers Fell: An Exclusive Investigation into the Collapse of the World Trade Center. DVD. PBS, NOVA, 2002. An overview of the structural engineering failures that caused the World Trade Center towers to fall after the terrorist attacks on September 11, 2001.

Wong, Raphael C., and Harley Y. Tse. *Drugs of Abuse: Body Fluid Testing.* New York: Humana Press, 2010. Discusses the history and uses of body fluid testing in forensic drug analyses. Contains somewhat advanced content.

Zulawski, David E., Douglas E. Wicklander, Shane G. Sturman, and L. Wayne Hoover. *Practical Aspects of Interview and Interrogation.* 2nd ed. Boca Raton, FL: CRC Press, 2001. Highlights interview and interrogation with emphasis on memory and eyewitness issues.

Internet Resources
American Academy of Forensic Sciences. Accessed March 2, 2012. http://aafs.org. Provides brief descriptions of the various specialties that have sections within the AAFS. Also includes information about careers in forensic sciences and the educational pathways to reach them.

ASTM International. Accessed March 2, 2012. http://www.astm.org. Information on soil testing and on standards and certification for engineering and other disciplines. (ASTM International is formerly known as the American Society for Testing and Materials.)

British Standards Institution. Accessed March 2, 2012. http://www.bsigroup.com. Information on standardized soil testing and for various other disciplines.

Federal Bureau of Investigation. Accessed March 2, 2012. http://www.fbi.gov and http://www.fbi.gov/about-us/cjis/ucr/ucr (Uniform Crime Reports). Shows the breadth of FBI involvement, including Most Wanted lists of criminals and terrorists, information on kidnappings, white-collar crime, crime statistics, and law enforcement in the United States.

Home Office. Accessed March 2, 2012. http://www.homeoffice.gov.uk. Covers the range of issues that the Home Office in the UK is involved in—including immigration, drug-related crime, and counterterrorism—with statistics for individual types of crimes.

Innocence Project. Accessed March 2, 2012. http://www.innocenceproject. org/understand/Eyewitness-Misidentification.php. Details the Innocence Project's goal of using DNA evidence to prove the innocence of individuals who have been wrongfully imprisoned, reasons for wrongful imprisonment, and suggested changes for the court systems to prevent more innocent people from being wrongfully convicted.

Interpol. Accessed March 2, 2012. http://www.interpol.int. Contains individual web pages for the various types of crimes and issues that Interpol deals with, including drug-related crimes, criminal organizations, pharmaceutical crimes, financial and high-tech crimes, intellectual property rights, fugitives, public safety and terrorism, human trafficking, corruption, maritime piracy, and property crimes such as the theft of art and cultural objects.

McCrone Research Institute. Accessed March 2, 2012. http://www.mcri.org/ home. Information on the independent, not-for-profit organization dedicated to teaching and research in light and electron microscopy, crystallography, and ultramicroanalysis.

Royal Canadian Mounted Police. Accessed March 2, 2012. http://www.rcmp-grc.gc.ca. Covers the gamut of issues that the RCMP are involved in, including border security, drug-related crime, firearms, missing children, and human trafficking.

Statistics Canada. "Police-Reported Crime for Selected Offences, Canada, 2009 and 2010." http://www.statcan.gc.ca/pub/85-002-x/2011001/ article/11523/tbl/tbl04-eng.htm. Statistics on crime in Canada for the years 2009 and 2010.

The National Academies Press. Accessed March 2, 2012. http://www.nap. edu/catalog.php?record_id=12589. A free download of the 350-page 2009 report by the NAS entitled "Strengthening Forensic Science in the United States: A Path Forward" (also available for purchase).

The National Archives. Accessed March 2, 2012. http://webarchive. nationalarchives.gov.uk/20110218135832/http://rds.homeoffice.gov.uk/rds. Contains links to crime statistics for England and Wales.

U.S. Geological Survey. Accessed March 2, 2012. http://www.usgs.gov. Information on soil testing as well as other environment- and Earth-related topics, such as earthquakes and water issues.